D1538809

Recounting the Seasons

POEMS, 1958–2005

RECOUNTING
THE *Seasons*

POEMS, 1958–2005

JOHN ENGELS

University of Notre Dame Press

Notre Dame, Indiana

Copyright © 2005 by John Engels
Notre Dame, Indiana 46556
www.undpress.nd.edu
All Rights Reserved

Manufactured in the United States of America

Library of Congress Cataloging in-Pulication Data

Engels, John.
Recounting the seasons : poems, 1958–2005 / John Engels.
p.   cm.
Includes bibliographical references and index.
ISBN 0-268-02770-6 (alk. paper)
I. Title.
PS3555.N42A6   2005
811'.54—dc22
2005025263

∞ *This book is printed on acid-free paper.*

This book is dedicated to the memory of
my friends and teachers

Richard Sullivan

Ernest Sandeen

John Nims

Frank O'Malley

Sunt lacrimae rerum et mentem mortalia tangunt
—Virgil

A Short History of My Voice

Tonight there's to be a wind, although
as yet nothing has occurred, no more than a slight
stirring among high clouds, the moon
rising white from behind Bean Hill,

the east a minor radiance. In my youth
such weathers deeply moved me, I considered them
connatural, allied with me to burst
all the genial balances. I recall

I slouched about disguised in voices
forever falling mute, unsure despite
the utmost passion of my urgings, my most fierce
attentions—then when I was least

ready to be heard, would blurt
abrupt, insistent, loony, vulgar, loud. I'd thought
I must be doomed forever to those
absurd fastidious perplexities

of verbs: to love, to hate, those new
unnatural confusions. Seldom
could my voices be restrained, but shouted, raved,
strangled, choked, gobbled like the trickle

of thick liquids down slow drains . . . but then
what else should I have expected? I was
vastly ignorant, and full of scorn, in short
afraid, and failed to trust both what I could

and could not say. Unremarkably
my voices took offense, and so went sour
in my mouth. One quiet hour yet until the storm
overwhelms the hill, pours down

through the pines and makes the needles hiss
against my screens. I've known
it was coming, waited for it, still
it's caught me by surprise,

and leaves me, apart from reason, knowing
the scoured night's aswarm with every voice
I've ever required myself to yearn to speak . . . at least
now that the rain has died away and a remnant gust

has taken to creaking somewhere an open door.

CONTENTS

From VIVALDI IN EARLY FALL
(UNIVERSITY OF GEORGIA PRESS, 1981)

From WALKING TO COOTEHILL

(MIDDLEBURY/UNIVERSITY PRESS OF NEW ENGLAND, 1993)

Newborn

The Naming

From BIG WATER

(LYONS & BURFORD, 1995)

Preface: Gutting Bluefish

Part I   Looking for Water

From SINKING CREEK
(LYONS BOOKS, 1998)

From HOUSE AND GARDEN
(UNIVERSITY OF NOTRE DAME PRESS, 2001)

The Guardian of the Lakes at Notre Dame

UNCOLLECTED POEMS

ACKNOWLEDGMENTS

Grateful acknowledgment is made to the following for permission to reprint *previously published material:*

The University of Pittsburgh Press:
   The Homer Mitchell Place
   Signals from the Safety Coffin
   Blood Mountain

The University of Georgia Press:
   Vivaldi in Early Fall
   Weather-Fear: New and Selected Poems, 1958–1982

Tamarack Press:
   The Seasons in Vermont

Graywolf Press:
   Cardinals in the Ice Age

Lyons & Burford:
   Big Water

Lyons Books:
   Sinking Creek

University of Notre Dame Press:
   House and Garden

Middlebury/University Press of New England:
   Walking to Cootehill: New & Selected Poems, 1958–1992

Middlebury/University Press of New England: Contemporary Poetry of New England:

"Bleeding Heart," "Raking the Leaves," "Perennials," "Moving from Williston," "Storm"

The Breath of Parted Lips: Voices from the Robert Frost Place (Fort Lee, New Jersey: CavanKerry Press, 2001):

"Poem for Your Birthday," "My Mother's Heritage," "The Dead," "Rising Stream"

Hunger Mountain:

"Memento Mori," "Family Photograph"

Notre Dame Review:

"Onlooker"

Shenandoah:

"Family Photographs," "Killing Ants," "A Short History of My Voice," "Outelot Creek in Flood," "Stove Cleaning"

In addition, the author wishes to thank the editors of the following periodicals in which have appeared many of the poems in this collection:

Academic Questions, Agni Review, Antaeus, Atlanta Review, Atlantic Salmon Journal, Black Warrior Review, Café Review, Carleton Miscellany, Chelsea, Choomia, Chowder Review, Claymore, Colorado Quarterly, Columbia, Commonweal, Crazy Horse, Critic, Georgia Review, Gray's Sporting Journal, Harper's, Hollins Critic, Hudson Review, Iowa Review, Ironwood, Jam Today, Kenyon Review, Massachusetts Review, Nation, New England Review, New Letters, New Virginia Review, The New Yorker, The New York Times, Ploughshares, Poetry, Poetry Ireland, Poetry Northwest, Prairie Schooner, Quarterly, Quarterly Review of Literature, The Reporter, Salmagundi, Seven Days, Sewanee Review, Southern Review, Texas Review, Tri-Quarterly, Review, Vermont Life, Virginia Quarterly Review, Yale Review.

I wish to express my gratitude to my editor Katie Lehman for her extraordinary care and attention to the details and form of this collection. Her help and suggestions have been, as I hope she knows, warmly appreciated.

FOREWORD

The pages that follow contain nearly half a century's work by an extraordinary American poet. Few living poets are granted a collected poems, but John Engels deserves this one because he writes poems like nobody else—language performs for him in ways it won't for other poets. The sheer range of this work is one of its distinguishing qualities—long, short, easy, difficult, philosophical, casual, despairing, joyful, silly, bawdy, heartbreaking, angry, affectionate, uplifting, abrasive, sexy, chaste, polite, and bad-mannered poems now inhabit a volume that finally allows us to take measure of this most completely human poet's achievement. Though it's a late poem, a good starting place is "The Garden in Late Summer":

> Who among us can truly say
> he outlives the thick matters
> of cold? Meantime
> the world flowers: foxglove,
> hollyhock, calendula wrenched
> sunward, cosmos by its own weight
> downsprawled, cumuli
> of marigolds, beaded lily stalks,
> curl and shrivel of peony leaves,
> lightburst of gloriosas,
> and from the beds of alyssum, pink
> and white, shastas, dahlias,
> all manners of rose. Thus
> summer arrives, bedizened, decorous,
> old, male and uncertain, riding
> conclusion, unwilling to last.

In seventeen lines counting the title, "The Garden in Late Summer" *demon-strates* creation's heartbreaking joke on human creatures: life is a feast that death will snatch away from us. The "thick matters of cold" shadow this poem from the second line on, but then its jazzy extravagance of flower names conjures up the spell of summer's prodigious ripeness. Sage student of minerals, plants, creatures, clouds, weathers, and seasons, Engels assembles a dynamic vocabu-lary to generate the surging energy of this single stanza. Notably bold diction engineers the poem's visual and aural power—*wrenched . . . downsprawled, cu-muli . . . beaded . . . shrivel . . . lightburst . . .* [and the shining treasure of the poem] *bedizened.* Finally, the poem proposes a delicious paradox by assert-ing that summer is both "male and uncertain." Amused and disturbed by the uncommon personification of summer, we're invited to wonder how this un-certain old man can be "riding conclusion" and to consider why he might be "unwilling to last." Modest in its brevity, graceful in its virtuosity, tantalizing with its riddles, the poem transports us into the crux of existence. It doesn't want to tell us or teach us—or even finally to show us: it wants to make us dance out in the garden even though (or even maybe *because*) death stands just out-side the gate.

This poem's amalgamation of morbidity and exuberance is a dominant aspect of Engelsian vision. From the beginning, Engels has written with his tongue in his cheek—"Mine is the manner of fly fishermen without fish." If you get it, you really get it—which is to say that you find this poetry simultaneously exhilarating, funny, heartbreaking, and deeply, oddly, singularly comforting. To appreciate how serious John Engels is you must first understand how hilarious he is. Both the comedy and the seriousness reside in the language—in the dic-tion and the syntax. Though Engels doesn't "do" light verse, his humor is purely poetic. Here, for example, is "Turtle Hunter":

> fingers and forearms terrified and chill,
> I grabbled blind in the murky water
> for the sawtooth edges of carapace,
>
> caught desperate hold, tussled and flung
> into the boat the raging snapper I'd trod up
> from the cobbled bottom, scabrous,
>
> spraddled and pissing, stony jaws
> agape, plastron a fringe of leeches,
> the one stone that of all

the dark-enclosing others had humped
under my foot, in the dangerous throb
of startlement thrust back.

With "grabbled" and "sawtooth edges of carapace" of the first stanza, we begin to hear a high-toned account of a lowly comic episode. Simultaneously the narrative drama descends into slapstick, while the syntax and diction lift toward the technically sublime: "raging snapper I'd trod up / from the cobbled bottom, scabrous, / spraddled and pissing, stony jaws / agape, plastron a fringe of leeches . . . " This is a very funny description of a "hunter" foolish enough to pull a snapping turtle out of the water with his bare hands—one can imagine Mark Twain devoting at least a couple of pages of prose to such an encounter between man and nature. The joke at the end (*Stepped on a rock that turned out to be a snapping turtle, ha ha!*) is really the merriment of Genesis: Since the nature of creation is such that bizarrely different creatures inhabit the same planet, a foolish man and a pissed-off snapping turtle can end up eye to eye. Like Twain, Engels plays it for laughs, but what he's really up to is transporting the reader into that almost unspeakable realm of experience, the deeper current of perception that's nearly beyond language and thought—the purest essence of life-consciousness. Understatement here conveys both bemusement and cosmic fear. These twelve lines accomplish a bio-spiritual tragicomic-linguistic penetration of the nature of existence, but "Turtle Hunter" sings to us so modestly that unless we're unusually attentive, we might not give the poet credit for its stunning achievement.

Imagine that as an adult, you become a fan of classical musical. One at a time, you buy the recordings and listen to Beethoven, Bach, Brahms, Chopin, Mozart, Vivaldi, Tchaikovsky, and Dvorak; then you find your way into opera with Puccini, Wagner, Bizet, Verdi, Rossini, and Donizetti. But somehow over the years, you don't listen to Mahler. Maybe your friends recommend him to you, but for some reason you don't give him a try, or you listen casually to Mahler's Symphony Number 9, and it just doesn't grab you. Or maybe you even listen to a few pieces from *The Song of the Earth*, and you think they're okay but nothing to get excited about. Then one day—maybe driving in your car and listening to NPR—you hear the divinely grieving fourth movement from *Symphony Number 2 in C Minor*. Suddenly you understand. In a few minutes of listening, you grasp the utterly basic and gloriously complex nature of Mahler's genius. So now you have all of Mahler out there in your future, ten huge symphonies and the song cycles—months and months worth of listening, an opportunity for pleasure you could hardly have imagined.

In the galaxy of classical music, such a scenario is unlikely, but on the planet of contemporary poetry, it's probable. John Engels is a master you may never have heard of, or you may not have given his work the moments of attention necessary to see what it has to offer you. But at this very moment, reader, you're holding a copy of *Recounting the Seasons: Poems, 1958–2005*. You've opened the covers, you've begun. Just keep turning the pages.

—David Huddle

PREFACE

Putting together *Walking to Cootehill,* my second collection of new and selected poems seemed an absurdly simple undertaking, for all I had to do was to choose among poems all lined up and exaggerating their best features, panting with eagerness to be chosen—crying *Me! Me! Me!* My aim as I understood it then was to publish a representative collection of my poems, suppressing even the minorly flawed, so that the resulting book would display my work at its blinding best. I thought I would look at the six books written over the course of thirty-five years, pick out from them the best fifty-odd poems, and arrange them in order of publication. These poems would form the first half of a collection the last half of which would consist of new, uncollected poems.

But it turned out to be neither easy nor satisfactory. I had been walking round and about my subjects from the beginning, looking at them in the changing lights of time and circumstance. The result was that some of the poems seemed orphaned, out of place, far separated from what ought to have been companion pieces. And so what in fact I did was to arrange the poems not chronologically but according to theme and motif, so that new poems came to live side by side with poems written years earlier.

In subsequent books, none of them identified as "New and Selected," I followed the same pattern of organization. There was *Big Water,* a collection of poems about water and fishing, *Sinking Creek,* about aging and the dissolution of a marriage, and finally, *House and Garden,* in which Adam and Eve speak of the Expulsion and of their lives since. In each of these books most of the work is new, intermingled with older poems provided with the company and context to which from the beginning they had looked forward.

Between the publication of *The Homer Mitchell Place* (1968) and the moment of this writing, I've gained a little objectivity. I recommend to my students that they put the first drafts of their poems into their sock drawers and come back to them some days later when infelicities that might have escaped them the first time around will have become apparent. In my case some of those earlier poems have been in my sock drawer, so to speak, for more than forty years, and some, released and blinking in the light, have come to seem not wholly what they were when I laid them down, turned away, and left them to their long sleep.

These poems are, of course, the same ones that at the time had pleased me; I hadn't tampered with it, so it must have been *I* who'd changed, so drastically that I could no longer love them as before. So with *Walking to Cootehill* and the three subsequent books, I began trying to rewrite—and what I discovered was that that old work was highly, even indignantly resistant to my efforts, the poems far more alive than at first glance they had seemed to be.

They made loud claims to their original forms, and try as I might, I have been unable to wholly ignore these in the process of revision. In fact, right or wrong, I have been reluctant to rewrite or very drastically to cut, and the revisions I've attempted have been often purely from the outside, patching and pointing, so to speak. I haven't always been able effectively to re-enter those poems, and I've been tormented by the idea that it's no more proper to attempt to improve the aspect of a product so substantially personal as a poem than it is to force plastic surgery on an ugly child. (Besides which often enough it has seemed to me that quite improperly I am rewriting someone else's work, that of a young man to whom I have not been properly introduced.)

I'm not wholly convinced, however—I have not achieved that eminence from which to manipulate my early work constitutes an injustice to the critic and literary historian. Of course any alteration results in a new poem, but there is, after all nothing sacred about the past—and poems are by definition lively creatures, proper subjects for the diagnostician, and possibly responsive to corrective surgery. At the same time I consider with great unease the examples of Yeats, Auden, Marianne Moore and others who could not stop their tinkering, not always to the improvement of the work.

What I *have* decided for *Recounting the Seasons*, for better or worse, is to keep almost all the early work with few exceptions unrevised, to arrange the books in order of publication, but to maintain the poems in their original contexts. Also this arrangement will demonstrate a stylistic unfolding, from the highly mannered work that Henry Rago once called "overwrought and overwrought" to a simpler, more direct voice.

The beginnings of this can be seen in the second part of my first book, *The Homer Mitchell Place,* in which the death of my infant son displaced abruptly and violently my notion of the poet (myself) as hero. I hope I have shed that mask, though there are discernible remnants in *Signals from the Safety Coffin.* But *Blood Mountain* has a quiet lucidity which has always pleased me, *Vivaldi in*

Early Fall, Big Water and *House and Garden,* are most thematically realized, while *Walking to Cootehill, Cardinals in the Ice Age* and *Sinking Creek* for the most part focus on places that have been particularly important to me, Wisconsin, Vermont, Ireland, Yugoslavia and Maine.

John Engels
Burlington, Vermont
April 2005

From THE HOMER MITCHELL PLACE

(UNIVERSITY OF PITTSBURGH PRESS, 1968)

To My Mother

You will understand me:
Where is the evidence of breath?
This stenciled dovecote tray?
These promised candlesticks?
Your letters are burned;
now your voice leaps in my fireplace.

It doesn't matter
that tonight the bronze boy
in his coat of crimson lake
still gestures around the dovecote
at his gold-powder girl.
My bones will break
to say again love is!

Mother, I refuse.
Love is to refuse that voice. Love is
the coppery betrayal
of the blood, more fiercely cold
than that you have died. Gold birds

freeze in the asphaltum sky,
the boy treads roses on his way.
My hands lie on the bronze
and flowered belly of your grave
and I will not come back.

—December, 1967

PART I

Cellar Springs in Winter

Angler

I am back from Bristol
and the marble sand of the New Haven River
is drying in my shoes,

and I have left behind me
for the fourth consecutive day
great browns and brooks and rainbows

lying easy in their colors to the head-on stream.
They, by local account, feed
once a week only,

if in that week has come a heavy rain
to scour the mountains downstream
to their gullets. Now I'm home

arrived hungry, without a wife,
to a house that smells of bats
and flowered carpets. Until next season

I'll rest here, while below
the eddies of my windows swirl
dark fish-shapes gaunt and savage

from such hunger as ignores
my tinseled hooks. Mine
is the manner of fly fishermen

without fish. I starve
with all my strategies, sleep here
in spite of my dream

of big fish slashing
at the fly, of dun and imago
spent to those gorgeous

appetites. This August
has seen little rain.

Salmon

This salmon, belly ripped up with my blade,
bloodies my hand. His gasping eye
defined by generation to despise
any but shape and shadow of the fly
pricks in the brain. And tender with
packed duns and spinners, beetles' zigzag
legs, a minnow's feathered bones, his gut
bursts at the barest touch of knife.

Why if his swollen belly ached with food
did he gape in that stiff-finned rush and long
slant of the feeding run, the taut and final
water humped and flung, and in the rubric of that
free rise take and turn with to the grinding
riverbed the fixed fly coursed of angler
stream and light? *O Angler, let the hunting hand*
grow sensitive as that fierce appetite!

Rainbows False-spawning

for Marvin Fuller

You call in the news,
amazed by what you've seen
in the flat of the Falls Pool
in an obliquity of sun: the scarlet spasms
of rainbows finning over marble redds
in false spawn. You saw an April-breeding fish

hungry with fall, full-colored
in the flat of the year, frenzied
over stones, fins set and flared
in a fire of gills, lateral vermilions
twisting in spring patterns. Around you
October paled in milty hazes,
and maples burned in clusters orange as roe.

But I understand nothing
but patterns of unreason, fall skies
bright and heavy as an April flood,
a child in an instant dead and out of breath,
a newborn Hereford lying in snow
in a steam of blood, October ludicrous
with color, red leaves in a bitter stream.
You call to tell me how
these fool fish spawn in all and fierce
conviction out of season,
under the naked lindens where in August
we heard a million bees roar among
the sweet twigs like a wind,
while spent flies eddied at the roots

in yellow drifts. Now it is time,
and we ache to know
what cold and color drift in the autumn runs
and flumes of our mistaken blood.

Weightless in Hell

We are weightless in Hell, we two,
mere skeletal illuminations holding to
a gold-and-ruby flesh and hue.

These vestibules of blackness
where no one was before we came,
they are the very worst, and less

in making *black* a not too unimaginable name
than in not telling which is finally best,
the gold-limbed doll or antique ruby eye

that wonders coldly where we've come from,
by which holy waters we were blessed,
away from which pale sky

(for color is but one
sad weightlessness in Hell, a slow warm sun
of no attraction towards which we lightly run.)

Sister Vincent Couldn't Pray

Sister Vincent couldn't pray
and told us so each school day.
We prayed for her. In every prayer
we never doubted our despair.

Bribed once with convent apple tart
I quicksilvered her Sacred Heart.
She wore it blazing on her gown
until in time it tarnished brown

and she grew stern and red of eye
but did not weep. I wondered why
and wonder still—she'd paid me well
to wear the brightest heart in Hell.

Grown old and somewhat stout
Sister Vincent went in doubt,
once she'd found the heart could dull.
Apples thundered in her skull

when Sister Vincent tried to pray.
She died at Lauds one holy day.
I have not prayed since I was young
but tasted apples on the tongue.

Miss Addleman Revisited

Mourners come and go. The family stands
in corners of the parlor shaking hands. I wait
among the raftered shadows of your vestibules
in line at length respectfully to view
your straightway bones, and leave in my good time.
A child makes croupy coughing in her hands,

and from the stairwell windows to the west I see
where up on Schoolhouse Hill the maples dry
in winter bud beneath an easting sky. The halls
are stacked with Crisco tins for kindergarten clays.
I step the attic stairs through nested hay
your old man laid ten years ago, and died.

Your grave is elsewhere, here was where you lived.
From Schoolhouse Hill I hear the playground bell
or merely slate scrap rattled by my feet.
Miss Addleman, I mutter at your sheets. I fear
the diverse bone distracts and teaches me
my chalky heart is monitored too well

to dare again, Miss Addleman, as in those years
you made me wait the noontime recess out
upon your creaky office cot for fear
my doctored heart might die of playing, all
the fierce attentions of the dying child
pinned down to sleep beneath your chalky shawls.

Prodigal

I hunted the fields through stubbles of late wheat.
Four pheasant's eggs lay crushed beneath my feet.
By noon the grass had rubbed my boot soles dry.
I'd thought perhaps it was not time to die.

One war I phoned my folks to hear them say
"Come home, the war is over now." But they,
grown old in hearing had put out the lights
and left the house. The phone rang half the night.

Tonight I seem to starve and suck for air.
I crush a child's bones in stepping where
I've dreamed the dead lie stretched upon
the muddy gardens and neglected lawns.

The bedroom lights still burn, the windows craze,
Doors stand open, all the chimneys blaze,
and cock-birds strut the kitchen floors and crow.
What question's like an egg-shell in the throat?

A Domesticity

In spite of table, child and wife
we drove for greens one Christmas day
and tried the stomach bitters in
some Polish tavern on the way.
The forest pine was dry and thin.
We swung the heavy brushing knife
and skittered ice-pucks on the lake
until too late. In time we came
back home to find our wives awake
we had abandoned while we played,
so danced set measure in our shame
at child asleep and supper made
and spoiled upon the table, grown
cold as wind across the ice
had played and tasted at the bone.
Grown seasonal in artifice
we lock our days. Our children dream.
If angry women wept alone
we played at cutting evergreens
in our good time. And have come home.

A Visitor

We rented here, the only house
was the village madman's, very cheap.
Being strangers, we tried
not hearing what the neighbors told:

locked up tight for fulfilling
a few town maids, he never
came around.
We used the place, and then one day

in a seethe of July dust, all
tags and tears, the town dogs
in a fury at his heels,
we found him grinning at the door

as we discovered we had often feared.
"Welcome!" he cried. It appeared
we had been from the very first
not far from his thoughts,

never wholly absent from his heart.

Fall Move

The first day renting in this house I'd found
where in the cellar neighbor kids had cooked
in a rusty skillet over paper-ash
the bones and feathers of a rooster's wings.

Then stepping carelessly from stair to stone
I felt my heel skid and saw the eyes
and bulged guts grained with cellar loam,
all but the knotting tail a long time dead.

It was the Landlord's salamander, come to feed
on spider casts and catch mosquitoes from
the fouled cisterns, growing bold and fat
from hunting the basement where he'd died at last

of tenantry about the Landlord darks.
All night the crushed tail coiled and pulsed
as if it hunted where it lay. I knew
because I'd done it he was dead, and feared

that having killed the Landlord's beast
now heaven help me I must pay
or watch the Landlord sell the house away.
I packed up skillet, charred wing bones, and all

my sleeping children from their beds
to other Landlord rooms. It was
because I had not feared his house I was surprised
before this fearing mostly what I'd owned.

Cellar Springs in Winter

In the cellar room dug out
last summer, first a moisture carried
up the walls and dried
into a blotched and estuaried

map-edged stain upon the stone.
And then there grew a small run
stirring up the gravel
of a far-back corner. It was

for weeks a sound I thought
merely blood in an ear-vein
beating when I stood to watch
the push of my white breath

onto the clay-cold air.
And now something of a welling,
a currenting, a live stream
grown and noisy in a single night

while I slept and heard
nothing. And now,
because the water surges so
in the dark and freezing room

the rooftree thunders overhead,
the pine log joists
shred in the hand,
the walls slide

and heave. I carry
all that darkness wherever I am
through the stable upstairs rooms,
hold my breath

so as to hear below the soft slip
of the mud floors falling in
and down to heavy gathering.
All day and night I listen:

the cellar springs run underneath.
Not in the memory of any here
has cellar water run
when snow was on the ground,

and ice is damming up the eaves.
This water is the gathering
from hill land that I own.
Behind the house the land I own

goes dry to flood me while I sleep.
I do not sleep. The cellar springs
run stronger every night. From beneath
both house and hill

the planet's ruptured dome
is bleeding to the cellar hole,
the one room in all this house
where breath is visible.

A Christmas Play

They act this play out in a northern cold,
four angry children fighting over parts.
One, weary at the inn-door, has become
a raucous Magus who forgets his part
and will not sing, or will not sing the words,
resenting he must give up what he is

to what he never was or will be. In the end
the Virgin has become a shepherd boy
and Joseph bellows *glorias* upstairs
sent there to be an angel, but born obstinate.
One won't play at all,
but sits and strokes the plaster ox which stands

four-square beside its empty stall and chews
a year's dry upstairs-closet dust. The night
is thickening with snow, and none believe
they take their part to any end, but are
what blood of season makes them out to be:
Virgin, Angel, King or bitter Spouse.

They fight to play whatever part they take; none fight
to play the mute Child unattended in the straw
but watch the snow dust on the window screens and taste
dusts of Eden thicker than snow.
Their voices freeze in gardens on the glass.

PART II

For Philip

Distances

It is the final grief, how color echoes on the eye
in distance and its cold perspectives.
I see a child in a red hat and jacket walking down
the lines of the severe fences

through a snowy field and spare bristle of weeds
till his brave color dances
random on the retina, and blots. The eye reflects
back traveled distances

of its cold fields, and color dies at the farthest range
of the green pine peninsulas
Ghosts walk in color where the brain most dazzles white
and strains at distances the eye refused,

fearing most that fierce geometry that angles sight
to the utter point the blood eludes.
O our children die beyond our seeing always,
in the green trees, among frozen roots,

in the fenced fields' extremest ranges always,
having outwalked color, having moved
beyond the shadows of the neighbors' farthest trees, until
the eye breaks on the fearful residues.

Poem at Daybreak: Before the Grave

Half-turning to the window lights my eye.
Snow runnels on the sulfur piles at dawn,
and from the elms' intaglio on sky
I watch the rake of shadow down the lawn

and hear the rooftree roaring in its bark
as if I had awakened it to dark
of leaf and flower or some such dispraise,
and later than its branching could be drawn

or figured for the sight again. Such brawn
of elm-bone braces in my house, and groans
its grave tune to this point of day,
the rotting spine leafs violently in praise,

the fingers flower inward on the bone.

The Grave

Perched on the barn sill, racketing at dawn
to see the red and wattled sun come up again,
the furnace cockerel cries raucous from his blood.
He sings you to your last and bare-boned name.

You cried for sequence like this fiery beast
who calls the day in when the day gives voice.
It is the born bone you took balance on to sing
the bright and fiercest measure of our time.

After the Grave

I have forgotten, it was time or not
and we had come this distance from that place.
The late streets burned with ice, the car was hot,
and season drew the white breath from my face

and froze it to the windshield, leaf and flower,
stem and pod. But we were coming near
and late—for all that proof of breath (God knew the hour)
we stopped someplace to scrape the grown glass clear.

Whether we had come or we had gone
from home or host it still remained to see.
The winter cracked and flooded on the lawn.
Our clean glass caught moon-shadows from the trees.

The clear grain of the white road turned to mud.
The roadsides leaped and hollowed. We were home.
We saw the garden greening with his blood.
This child's hands rake and ravel at our bones.

Two Children

I am beset by cellars where dark waters rot
to stink in hallways, and I have begot
by some confusion out of some fierce game
one child who died, another who did not.

I have a living child whose greenstick bones
sprout from my father's tillage and my own.
We were the soil and gave enough to die.
Now she is branch and flower of the stone.

She rackets through my rooms, her voices mock
the raucous belling of the household clocks.
The cellars flood. This living child breathes
to make my rounds, unsnapping all my locks.

In time at last the narrow body grieves
at flood of season. Twigs dam up the eaves.
The maple's dead, the mornings turn to stone.
My lot is littered with the bones of leaves.

The Homer Mitchell Place

The mountains carry snow, the season fails.
Jackstraw clapboard shivers on its nails.
The freezing air blows maple leaves and dust,
a thousand nails bleed laceries of rust,
slates crack and slide away, the gutters sprout.
I wonder do a dead man's bones come out

like these old lintels and wasp-riddled beams?
I ask in simple consequence of structure seen
in this old house, grown sturdy in its fall,
the brace and bone of it come clear of all
I took for substance, what I could not prove
from any measure of design or love.

Or is it rather that he falls away
to no articulation but decay,
however brightly leaped the brass-hinged bone,
beam and rafter, joist and lintel stone?

For Philip Stephen Engels

August 23–October 24, 1965

Swarming by your head
red plastic butterflies
danced patterns on their strings
because that night you cried

and would not sleep; and I
in my dark rooms rejoiced
to know that bright beasts moved
to the measure of your voice.

The sun came red as wings
to fix the swimming dusts
in all our rooms. My son,
your caught voice moves in us.

The house drowns in its lawns.
We watch the morning sun
thrust deep into the sky
a bright and bloody tongue

and in that roar of light
you sleep. Above your head
the blazing wings grow dull
and larval on their threads.

You were no voice at best.
I measure what I tell.
The housed and swallowed bone
grows hollow as a bell.

The breath swims in the throat,
the sun rings in the sky.
What color we remember
burns inward from the eye.

From SIGNALS FROM THE SAFETY COFFIN

(UNIVERSITY OF PITTSBURGH PRESS, 1975)

Behold, in the lout's eye,
Love.

—Roethke

PART I

Signals from the Safety Coffin

When in Wisconsin

When in Wisconsin where I once had time
the flyway swans came whistling
to the Green Bay ice, set down and stayed
not feeding, four days, maybe five, I shouted

and threw stones to see them fly.
Blue herons followed, or came first.
I shot a bittern's wing off with my gun.
For that my wife could cry.

My neighbor's wife mistook the spawning frogs
for wood ducks nesting the white pines
up on Bean Hill. I straightway
set her right. Each April on the first

rainy night I lantern-hunt for salamanders
where they hide toe-walking the bottom
mucks and muds. I shudder
at the scored skin of their sides, those deep

flesh tucks. In hand they dry. I walk
in frogspawn on my lawns. One time I hoped
the great white birds might brake
for the frog ditch and alight,

but all the addled past falls in upon itself,
splash rings close inward on the rising stone,
my gun sucks fire, the bone becomes
whole bone, light narrows back

on filament and point, the forest turns to sand
and only season, lacking source, rolls round
and round till I in my turns fall forever back
clutching my stone, my gun, my light.

When in Wisconsin where I once had time
and spring beasts crawled my marrows and my tongue,
I was not blind. The red eft clambered in my eye.

The Floods

This is celebration   the brown
yards are showing again   the floods
may be coming   everyone
worries   last year
the house was surrounded and nearly carried away
ice buried the yards until June

now I think about the river swelling
I think mud softens in the spine   the skull
buds   ribs root in the heart
the road by first spring light
is marrow brown   trees are feeding again
it's time again   it gets
awfully lonely
lonely maybe I'm
mad or

I will turn and all my dead
and the next poem will turn
and I will awaken to the nice pivots the neat
fulcrums and the rain will come down
in chalky pellets on the roof

I am relentless at celebration
it's spring and time for spring poems
I favor celebration
when there is time and light lasts and I
begin to think after a winter of slant light
deflections   wavering shadows   I begin to think

of the river thrusting into the lake and the lake
blown westerly beating upstream
houseward into the narrowing channel
and in an eddy of the mainstream
under a dog otter's oak under
a cutback in a red flare of willow roots
a lamb's corpse haired with elvers
burrowing the guts   the carrion
brain entered and leaping

with spring eels   spring salmon
lying starved in the current at the edge
of the fouled eddy   clots of wool
circling   sediments of blood
from the belly hole

the appetite is clearly
seasonal   I celebrate
this spring whatever comes to gorge
on plasms of the flooded bone
the burrowed eye

Spring Prophecy

Each year near the beginning of spring
you will think you have found something again
that once you had lost and never remembered.
And because it was small and of little worth

you will remember only the losing, but for that
you will weep. It will be the shape
of a house, a tree's death, a broken
bottle, a spring wind cushioning

your face, yellow as the smell
of camphor in sheets. It will be
no more than that. And near
the beginning of spring snow will hang on

in the pockets of timothy and water
will spread on the yellowing ice. The corn stubble
will root in orange and brown shadows
and it will seem only an hour before a warm rain.

In the river a trout will rise under a dark
overhang of cedars and something will be
given to you, you will have a vision: one day
driving to work along the river road

you will see the convergence of the road
to be no farther than the end of a hallway,
a fog boiling in the cut, no farther
than the far wall of your room, brown

as the smell of old timbers. There will be
a death somewhere, the cellar of an old house
will fill with smashed bottles, there will be
a snarl of rotting dresses, papers

spilling down a muddy stairwell. This death
will be behind you, in another town, but you
will be reminded by friends. You will think
you have found something again, but in a day's time

you will have forgotten.

Fall Inventory

The car shudders with Mozart
in the driveway
flutes and harpsichords

the timothy lawn is in fall growth
too wet and nearly too long
to cut   one hundred years ago

some lurching itinerant bay-window builder
hit it big in this dark-parlored town
and my house was his uneasy first

and practice job   he was
soon followed by an itinerant front-porch builder
whom no one hired

after my front porch had eaten up
two twelve-light windows
and a Christian door

the car doors
stand open like yellow wings
and the car sings in the driveway

flutes and harpsichords
a confident builder of off-center dormers
came next and possessed

by some sad notion
of symmetry died
after half the job

an inventory of trees
shows one burly abdominous maple
single-limbed and sparely green

and one great yellow poplar
hemmed in by utility wires   dead
from road salt or detergents

the bedroom-window white pine went
in a spring two years ago
detergented to death

while this summer the young maple
in the front yard began dying redly
just for the hell of it

and two rank poplars stick it out
bristling with widow-makers
back to the house   the cellar hole

springs up in fungoid cupolas
and when I am dead an itinerant turret maker
will find some way of bricking in

the dormer-porch-bay window with
off-plumb towers   canted battlements
and crooked embrasures   living

I cannot get the kids to close
house or car doors when they run outside
to tangle on the lawn

the lawnmower clogs and stalls
one knows where centers ought to be
when porch sills rot away and floors

have dropped four inches and the car
stands open ludicrous
with song   O Christ but everything

is added on   I sulk
in my bay window   past
the bullseye lights

from high up poplar deadfalls
whistle down

Hallowe'en

I lie in wait for the egg throwers,
the neighborhood hoodlums, hidden
in the dark yard in the hanging thicket
of willow branches, my shadow

from house light lost
in the grass, while they, invisible
in the cowfield across the street,
likewise hide and wait and mutter to themselves

against my house, and do not know
I'm listening. But here I am,
the dead yellow of the narrow leaves
whipping my face. I am crept in

upon. Behind me the old house
shudders with wind. The dark sky
darkens. I'm pasted all over
with willow leaves,

and the tendrils of my breath lengthen,
twine out and fix into the grass.
I think I can wait forever, and then,
raucous with joy, they move, they move

against me, and the egg
at the end of its high invisible arc
splatters in yellow plasms
on a window glass.

     They run
away, they've done what they came for
and I've waited for nothing again, my boundaries
broken, my house smeared. *Come back,*

you own this house, enter, the sleepers
and dreamers in their warm rooms
call back and forth between themselves
in dreams. You out there,

you imagine you are invisible,
no different from the shadows of hollows
grass and hill. I call you in
who yearly hunt me, who have

no bed or garden of your own. For you
I'll wait forever,
shaking with wind and rage!

The Mailbox

The mailbox is down again
knocked in the ditch by the snowplow.
It's the fourth time this month.
Isham, the driver, doesn't care.

He watches me as he passes.
He turns to stare out the back
window of his cab. And when
I'm home again and think to look,

there across the road the mailbox
is down, half-buried in snow.
I've never spoken to Isham.
I wrote on behalf of my mailbox,

but only once, and he never
answered. It was then
he began to watch. Weekly I prop
the mailbox up, chop an inadequate hole

in the frozen dirt, and wedge
the post with broken sticks. It stands
wavering, lopsided, the door
hanging down like a broken jaw.

The flag is jammed, and if
I'm being careless I think
there's mail, maybe a letter
from Isham: "*Dear Sir,*

I got nothing against your goddam
mailbox, I'll be more careful
in the future, sincerely,
Henry Isham." Not yet, though, nothing

but *Natural History,* bills and an occasional
sexually-oriented ad. I go to bed
fearing that Isham will pass in the night,
a huge plume of sparks bursting

from his monstrous blade,
and this time it may be
the house itself, and no letter
will ever follow.

Hawk

I find a redtail's mummy cruciform
on a wire fence, talons fisted
on a strand, the orbits stuck through
with a whittled twig,

beak agape, a snake's tail
protruding, the rest the bird gorged
stripped in the gullet to a hair
of ribs and convolutions

of vertebrae, hawk and snake
this fierce formality, bone
within dead bone.
I watch, my eyes likewise

transfixed. I stare, not seeing
as my eyes see. I see our names. I see
this bird is dead, that
is the first name.

And blind, that is the next.

Of Mortality and the Nature of True Christian Stewardship

When at night
you shall awake
to hear the rooftree
creak and shiver
and the first
cold droplets down
the cellar walls
foretell the river

*Wherein the Householder
is warned
through ominous signs
of his mortality . . .*

that shall a day hence
swell and rise
to quench your fires,
be, Householder,
not surprised
it is God warns you
that you own
wherein you live

*. . . that it is by God's
grace as Landlord that he
possess the dwelling-place
wherein he resides . . .*

not board nor bone
nor hinge, tooth, lock,
spoon, hair or pin.
God harries you
lest you give in
to false regard
for what He lends
that you may know

*. . . in a manner of speaking
by reason of the Divine Lease
which by God's
whimsy may
at any time
be broken . . .*

how time depends
from both the rooftree
and the bone.
And yet, my friend,
do not despair:
what House God's season
shall invade
is of God's holy

*. . . and yet it is of the
nature of things & no
cause for despair, instead . . .*

marrows made
while men who
pridefully repel
God's timely inroads
shall reside
amongst their properties
in Hell. Remember then
that all shall pass

. . . if man acknowledge
the Divine Landlord and
His holdings, & lie
in His Holy bed in
the Grace of full
Humility & Stewardship,
though he will certainly . . .

and you recline
beneath God's grass.
Forswear Venality and Pride—
It is God's House.
You cannot hide.

. . . die, there is no
help for it.

A Riddle, the Answer to Which Being of Such Import It May Be Spoken Aloud, Yet It Shall Improve the Householder to Great Benefit to Address Himself to Its Solution

I ask you this   *In which the Nameless*
by God's Necessity: *proclaims the Riddle*
I have no name.   *to the Householder . . .*
Who am I that you see?

I alone eat   *. . . and begs indulgence while*
though lacking appetite.   *he cites his Gluttony &*
I of all creatures drink   *Genius in one breath . . .*
though lacking thirst.

I can make fire   *. . . he speaks of the glory*
so that it will not burn.   *of his Patrimony & of*
I count my fathers back until the first.   *his undoubted piety . . .*
I pray to God.

I fear the sun   *. . . and displays a certain timidity when*
as precedent to Night.   *he confronts the Eternal*
I watch the season turn   *Cycle . . .*

by Season turned.   *. . . and he affirms*
Whatever worm   *the necessity of*
may burrow in my bones   *his Mortality . . .*
and famish me, I cannot do without.

God does not send me dreams: *. . . yet concludes*
I make my own.   *in unseemly pride.*

Poem for My Mother

Snow hurtles
and the planet freezes.
My children in bright

coats stand waiting
in the winter yard.
The yellow bus arrives,

they board and go.
Snow flies and I think of you,
my most brilliant confusion,

sunlight interrupted
by leaves, rooms defiantly
in disarray. Last night all night

wind burst on the house . . .
In the morning
the children waited

standing in litters of pine twigs
green on the salt-white snow.

The Pine

The pine poisoned
by road salt slowly
browned and died

over one long summer
the needles all summer
in steady fall to gatherings

of rusty drifts
under the windows
of the bedroom where

you slept. Owls lived
in that tree. On the calmest days
it sounded with wind,

the needles raining down.
At its foot grass roots lace
into a brutal turf

that feeds on salt.
Pine needles shower
onto your grave. Locks snap

in the plasms of my tongue.
Locks snap.

Moonwalk

What sticks with me is the pit
of the walker's shadow,
snatches of the white fantastic carapace
of Neil Armstrong in his

cautious dance and testing step,
his final graceless posturing
for balance in the moon's
feeble and uninterested hold.

His shadow tracks him;
he has been cautioned,
and routinely vigilant looks only
sunward or at the oblique

for in the whole blackness
of his shadow he will be able
to see nothing, will be in effect
blind either from shadow or from

the coronal glare about the black
total hole of his head shape,
a simple diffusion effect, nothing
more difficult, nothing

but the illusion of sunburst
spraying outward from the crater
of the black skull, an intense
halo. Hell, I've played

that game myself, I've had the dream
where I must be careful
to not look back, or the skull
will burst outward and the eyes

become brief flares like bombs
or supernovae. How about courage then,
how about it, when the brain
crumbles, clicking

as it cools, and the teeth
blackly powder, and the tongue
drains backwards down
into the belly's open pits?

Everything's in shadow.
The flickering white hero
sticks with me. The walker
climbs white as salt

from the grotesque ricketry
of his machine, the walker stares
sunward: man
is on the moon. Behind him

is flung the black cast
of the freezing shadow
where he must not look,
for all time must not look.

At sunrise the white distance
dissolves in light before him, the sky
becomes the memory
of no light. It is the first time

I have wanted to walk here
myself. I can see the black
deep of the center drawing near
and the man-shaped night remaining total.

Signals from the Safety Coffin

Outside in the night in the graveyard
the awakened corpse breathes once,
Count Karnicki's patented

glass ball rolling from his chest,
and—the safety spring released—aboveground
alarm bells ringing, the red flag waving,

a beacon flashing. And he stares, doubtless,
up the opened breathing tube
into thin moonlight, and if I listen

I can hear him no matter
how feeble his cries. I know
he is twisting his ring, his fingers

slippery with embalmer's talcum,
swollen as oak galls,
and I will not come to save him. *Why*

should I? The sky
encloses me, I am myself a ring
encircling this bone, this bone

encircling the buried blood,
unable yet to breathe
the black grains of the soil without

harm. And O how I fill my walls
sweat fat scratch at the maggoty
crotch! I think now of Count Karnicki,

moved by the piteous cries of the Polish girl
interred alive and awakened just in time
by earth and pebbles roaring on her coffin's lid.

She cried, O she cried out! Now let
the dead from all their graves cry out
and flash their lights and ring their bells,

but this one, let him wait for someone else.
He is a frightened man, bewildered by the light,
the air, the muffled thudding of the bells,

as I am not, and I have loved this place:
why make nothing of that? Here in the fields
of lights and bells and flags, the dead

clamoring to return, I turn to this: the raw
meat between the legs, the sunken
nipples, here, home in the chilling house

with wind in the needles of the pine
four years dead, cut down. You have awakened
and cry out for help. I answer that

whatever the dark volumes of the graves
from which the dead whisper up their breathing tubes
and flash their lights, in which the dead

tree speaks, the moon a soft explosion
in high mists, as I lie down to sleep
my silence is greater.

PART II

An Angler's vade mecum

An Angler's *vade mecum*

1

Remember: the simplest eddy,
course and counter-course of stream
appall the cast fly and confound
its course. The hook should swim

as dun from nymph and imago
from dun, for trout lie gaunt
with waiting and grow dull
with season. Be aware

of season, know
that trout color with the trees
and that the planet trembles
to a maple leaf for trout.

Therefore be cautious
how you walk the riverbanks.
The beast may starve
from hiding.

2

I have thought about it
often. I have thought
of the salmon as a difficult
fish. I have not forgotten

he lies concealed
in his hold. I have fished
with a hot sun flooding
the orbits of my skull

so that my shadow does not
fall upon the water
and I have raised
fierce shadows

from the rocks,
and there is considerable art
to this, but it is best
to speak flatly

of such matters:
the salmon has eluded me.
My shadow has fallen
on the stream.

3

I cast to the salmon with a rod
made of a lively cane, and nicely
fitted, the male ferrule
made to go

right home. Such tackle
promises success or pleasure
while with a rod soft
in the fibers

I should be made perhaps
too much aware of the fish
grown viciously shapely,
countering my hook

with the toothed hook
of his kype, then
the maniacal humpbacked rush
downstream. I have

a *papier* model
of a salmon. I am
pleased with it, it is
most natural, as a sportsman

and angler the exact
reproduction of natural objects
appeals very much
to me. It is

with great pleasure
that I possess this
reproduction which looks
as if it were just

out of the water. I have not
taken a salmon yet,
but perhaps in days ahead.

He is a spawning fish
and does not feed. Strong tackle
is required.

4

I enclose with this letter
a photograph of the salmon
and the proud fisherman,
me. You can see

that the salmon is better
than average for the stream.
I display him from a hawthorne
branch. You see

the harebells and cornflowers
that blossom in his gills: my ghillie
put them there. It is
a custom. And I am there

at left, attentive to my kill,
although I am unsmiling,
seriously staring at the lens,
because I hold

with ritual. My ghillie holds
my Hardy's celebrated
"Alnwick Greenheart,"
built suitable for mahseer,

salmon, trout and grayling,
and he fiddles with my reel,
a brand-new *Cascapedia*. The river
eddies to a shore of daisies

in the background right.
The rapids of the holding pool
are out of sight, but it was there
the crazy beast had tried to kill

a full-dressed *Beauly Snow* one/ought
blue-furred and tinseled, orange
and heron-herled, that quartered,
flittering, across his lie, a roar of color

to exasperate the course
of the mindless blood
I hunt. But the biggest masterpiece
done by me was when I, not

with this but with another rod
got a salmon in the Äaro River, in
Sögndal, in
Sögn. The weight

of this greater fish was
forty-three pounds, and I
was three hours landing it,
and you can bet it was a strain

on the rod, but the rod
was just as good after as when
I began. I enclose
a second photograph of my

greater fish, and the proud
fisherman, me. The rod in this picture
made from well-seasoned greenheart
was my dear friend

for more than twenty-five
years. But now
old age has claimed it.

5

When, many years ago, this rod
was built, I took it to
the Miramichi, and everyone roared
at my using such a light rod

for such a strong fish, and I recall
their amazement at my handling
of two grilse when fishing
for small trout with midge flies

on a little river. Since then
it has killed thousands of fish
and considering the size of the rod
this seems adequate performance.

And with it I can reach well out
into any river against any
downstream wind to the farthest
rising fish with no effort

and the strongest fish
has no chance of beating
me. I recall
one big and fresh-run salmon

who took the line under the canoe.
We could not get it cleared,
and this rod before I knew it bent
clear round from the tip

to the center. The tip
was a little twisted
but within an hour was back
to shape, having been cut

from a lively wood. I killed
three or four nice fish
right after that, and finished them
quickly, time being too dear

on a sporting stream to waste an hour
on a fish. This rod will kill trout
in a minute to each pound of weight,
and if with this rod I cannot

handle any fish as I please,
I know it is not the fault
of the rod, which is—I say it freely—
the most perfect instrument

I have ever held in my hands.

6

Although I have used this rod
mainly for trout on small
rivers it has been pressed into service
for tiger fish. A month ago

it landed an accidental
turtle. I am glad to say
that in spite of this
regrettable incident

its power and accuracy have been
in no way impaired. And with this rod
which was my father's
for thirty-five years before

it was mine, I took
a thirteen-pound salmon in
the Miramichi in eight
minutes. The water

was low, I walked back
onto the gravel, I reeled the fish
up onto the gravel, my friend
timed the play of this fish. A little later

when time decrees I shall pass it on
to my son. I have used it
for thirty years myself,
mostly for trout

in fishing small rivers.
It is an artist's rod, powerful
enough to kill heavy trout, and yet
it fishes so light I have often

lent it to ladies. But I think
careful copies might be made
which will be
just as good.

PART III

Exorcisms

Sestina: My Dead in the First Snow

It is taking a long time.
How long it has been we cannot remember.
The house roars like the windy spaces of a field
and windows are rattling in some downstairs room.
Something is over now and nothing will follow,
except that slowly light changes, window to window

and trees go ashen in the wind. Snow drives on the window
and watching it happen is what we have come to. Once there was time
in the yearly violences, but now we have come to follow
the slide and drift of the white leaves through our rooms
where light spins clockwise. *Remember:*
the planet spinning clockwise in its dark fields

streaked the stars out into icy rings, the fields
bloomed at night. At night our windows
closed onto the green fragrances of cut lawns, the rooms
flowered with shadows, and we in time
in the seasons of our house remembered
that something was over and that nothing followed

except we slowly changed and are followed
along our tracks in the wind-ridden fields.
O you and I are more than we remember!
Our hands melt through the frozen gardens of the windows
into the darkness of the yard where we have taken time.
Light roars in the windy spaces of our rooms,

the windows are trembling in some downstairs room.
Something is over now and nothing follows
and it is time, it is taking a long time,
and the house is cold as the windy spaces of a field
and the sun moves around the house window to window
and how long it has been like this we cannot remember,

but evening comes and the wind begins and we try to remember
how shadows blossomed in our rooms,
flowers burst into blue forests on the windows,
and we walked through the trees and were followed
and our hands on the cold glass burned away the fields
and the flowers burned away and the trees. In time

we will remember. We are followed
through all our rooms, through the spaces of the fields
the sun turns on us, window to window. It is taking a long time.

terribilis est locus iste

1

I recall that when I held the leghorn
upside down her head—
lemony beak gaping and crooning—
swiveled to fix in its balances,
craned calmly to see until

I lopped it away
on the chopping block
and she ran to flap in the cold-frame pit
in the seedling kohlrabi, frantic
and palsied, the cut neck skin pursed
on the raw stem.

It is borne in upon me now
how I would stand to watch,
how sufficiently convinced
of bird fury and din
in the wholly silent yard,

the day bright and the sun fixed
among the soft feathers of clouds,
but only my brain in its dreadful balances
squawked and screamed and lay down
in the delicate tremor. Tonight

the sky drains downwards
in red trails, the sun
like an owl's eye swells,
and it is borne in upon me
how I listen,
what I hear,
the burgeoning tumor
that measures me, the orbit
blooming. Is it
the moon in silence rising
through the colors of brass,
is it the sun or the moon?

Come back, come back!
In the petals of the great
fire, in the radiant gold
of its ash I taste
my own tongue I see
the gasping still recognizable
skull I am crowded
with flowers and leaves.

2

This is no age of faith,
rats at the holy paste
and we lying down in the ultimate tremor,

the delicate subsiding blood spray
brightening on leaves—although
it has been the simplest
dying, cleanest
of butcheries. This

is a dreadful place, it is
the House of God, the
Gate of Heaven, and dwindles
finally to the bone, so the bone

teaches that blessed is the man
if at all remembered. I am appalled
by the uproars of the blood,

and it is time now to consider
how far I must go
on the road cut out of ice,
how much will be given
if I do not ask, if God is the midden
of generation, if I
so dim of form
am issue of God.

I regard the hen's foot
drowned in its yellow broth,
clenched like an eagle's claw
her cleaned thighbones agleam
in the crumbs of dumplings.

The House of the Dead

It is night and you are dreaming and you cry
into the silence and they are all
silent around you, forever in place, and the sky's
dividing around clouds like rocks
and the straight plunge of the sky is to the far

cliff edges of the world. You are fixed
in the center, you are waist-deep in dust.
They embrace you in the running darkness, you are
daily departed from, loved, remembered, mourned
where everything is held and lost: the dead

stalled in their tracks, a foot raised in mid-stride,
the dead man met at the mailboxes, yourself raised up
to ride in giant exaltation to the windowsill,
mute sparrows circling your head. Now where do you look?

skulled ghost, your voice wavering into the silences,
crying out forever from the basin of your skull because
the beaked wind is on its way to riddle you—
and when you awaken it will be night
and the doorways filled with no one who will speak

and for a voice the wind stirring in frozen bittersweet.
You will rise and run to meet your own voice opening itself
but morning will have opened in the doorways. Always you were greedy
for spring. In summer the house elm
sprayed a sticky sputum and the stone pits

in the sidewalk filled with rain and ants drank there,
circled there and drowned. You ran to meet
the dead man at the mailboxes. O how in dreams
the dead you cannot warn affect a terrible love speech,
circling, their tongues like frozen leaves,

brittle as frozen leaves, quick as fire, prattle and squeak
and grope in the final loving touch and stand away, then stand away.
It is night, nothing but night
and you are frozen in mid-stride in the first step, the sparrows
frozen and shining about your head,

a pumpkin sun fiery on green snow. And you see
as you have always seen the sleeper in his blind warmth
who cries out reaching out to you, his voice
a leaf greening in the center of your skull.

Nothing Relents

Given less by far to love than to my dead
it is I know the soul's defilement and joyous
beyond all touch or body lightly borne   the doors

of the house thrown open to the great lawns
alive with the shadows of birds that daylong
grow into blue mists and fogs

no less than those which cover my simple dead
with so long darkness   It is that the planet
is sodden and the gardens fail smothered by rain

that the corn yellows   the squash vines
are rank and infertile roots eaten away   that
there is a burgeoning of weeds   dandelions

pigwort hairy mullein   that the apple
is black with scab, the grass
in three days ankle-high and this

after the thinnest of winters
that I scrape at green
and blue molds everywhere

and my spade breaks through
into the muddy cisterns of the earth   that we
had been eating and drinking together when the floods

came suddenly to cover us   that this
is true it is true that the river broke the graveyard dikes
and burst in rapids on the headstones peeling back

the flowery turfs and the dead
arisen from their graves walked upright
on the thick flood downstream to subside

into a delta and drift heap of bones
that we have not found them yet who walked
on water   not all of them   that some

hide from us still   nothing relents
and what if the world is a horrible fit
a knot or spasm in the sky's entrails?   for Christ

that the child died is beyond belief
beyond all suffering that he was named and I
that morning in the kitchen reached

a book down careful of noise but he slept beyond
all reach and sometimes that comes upon me to such rage
as now I am torn by the alarums of my voice

to cry out into the dazzle of Thy
high noon O God such anger
festers in the tree the flood the stone such

bile and storm surge in the root and beasts
in the foul walls race the planet bursting swelled
with ripeness fat with fatness open to the light and I

like a blind grub twisting in light
mandibles wide in spasm the cold
talus falling back and in the chasm squirming   once

thinking I too would die   old
unfellowed and alone   the sky a black heave
over the house   thunder

withholding itself and crows in dense flight   I
liar vessel of fury vengeance-seeker destroyer
swore then and now to lie among all name-proud

wrathful men in the dusts and stinking shades
in the midst of this fall of things
stable in rage for that he was named and slept for all that

but discomposed   for ghosts
still commonly walk and are seen   white things
fearful of light while this beast *here*

is nourished and has excrements
the flood falls back into itself
the lawns dry and darken with birds

it suits our dead to rest beyond all reach
what feeds therefore among us   hides
in the muds   digs like a legged worm

into the belly of the planet   inhabits us
foul comb and hive seething
with famished larvae   the airs

of our dead resonant and beneath
the garden soils a breathable
air   what feeds on us   our scalps crawl

The Bed

My bedposts turned from maple
workbench boards from the margarine factory
yellow with corn oil oozed

from the unsealed dovetails
and mortises trickled and pooled
all through the hot summer nights of the hot

room and all over the house new beds
sprang up in rows and furrows like a school grove
a whale's rib cage yellow in the moon

on the yellow beach with the waves
growling   in Virginia the ghost crabs
scuttled in pale drifts   before the night was out

I'd been nibbled to my ribs.

The Frog

We'll all end up   I tamed the leopard frog
up in Wisconsin when I was eight   I flayed it
I recall the ceremony of its awful crawl

tongue forking out with pain   loose-legged
to the water the raw meat stuck with sand   eyes
pushed in and the wildly gulping throat   but

then the strong dive into the patch
of pickerelweed and the pearly muscles flashed
and the crawl of the gut coil showed

through the belly wall   I crawl
in the stinking clots of yesterday's food
in the sour juices of the house I lie

awake on sandy sheets and flies bite

The Fish Dream

It came true that in Bikini when
sudden as the mirror of a wing light came
the wind changed and hot dust

mucked our crannies up we locked ourselves below
turned off the air so greeny stack gas
fills the passageways   topside

the flight deck blooms like Ol'
Virginny with a thousand fountains
while six times a day below in salty

showers we hosed our planted selves
and held our breaths   I'd lie
like a stain in my sodden bunk

and it made for dreams the umber-
scaled and yellow-spotted fish
with six-inch needle teeth

creeps out on fins like weed
stems over the red-hot deck and
gorged our heads while

we from the steaming
humus of our eyes
stare on   afraid to wake

The Garden

I dream it yet by god that I'll
sprout in the rank mucus of that passage yet
ploughed and harrowed by its poison teeth

and seeded in every bloody furrow while
topside in wind and light
the garden of the flight deck washes

clean   surely nothing will survive me   nothing
I have feared   nothing
will grow there   salt

water floods the catwalks and the only
sea is green this is
true it is all true

as god's sweet gleaming garden overlay
the planet's foul belly hole and the rank
dirt burned to grow it is all true

that then as now beneath the scoured acreage
in the acid juices of the bellied
beast the seed of the first and

Eden fire burns and grows in the sour
armpit stink and wrinkle
wart grease scab knot sore

and scar we feel the first thrust
of the blazing root
I grow

I grow

The Bedroom

Clean rain on the final lilac   bats
in the chimney and the starling's nest
white streaks down the window glass

I dress myself   wifeside the smallest
son's a lumping in the covers   grins
to see me go   I am

leaving to write this down   notes
on a dream unaccountably remembered in which
I stare into the round mirror of a fish's mouth

and smear my face with black paint to the very
edges of my eyes then roundly so stare back
that the blood survives and shines back

my whole life I've known   in natural terror
in whole joy   and so it was last night
dreaming I'd come to my house

and the door opened wide upon
round rooms swirling
with fire clean scoured out

with flames the furniture
white ashes on the floors   now
in the chilly morning room that stinks

of starling nests his mother
sleeps and he and I burning to have me go
we stare into each other series

on series and last night's fires
feed on us and the sun
explodes

The Survivor

Unborn I rose in the memory
performed there puzzled for balance
on the spine's beam flailed and spun and

fell back into the burning bed
breathed I thought
forever in trust   now

you all of you O wait with me
in the ravenous planet for the tombs
to crack and O if the tombs crack look

out onto a yellow sand step out
with me onto ashes among leaves   my own
graves are lost to me I

have myself walked on yellow sand
but on that very day I'll seize with you upon so
beloved again a yellow of sea sand that I can say

death has its fires too
and stick my tongue out to the
chalky rain   its taste

From the Source

My dears my creatures I was
back in the clamor of the thin light
coiled like a question mark

in the original stance and stared
out from the slow blooming about the fire's
seed   I was

frail arc of jaw and palate bone
outburst of iris lobes wrenched
diaphanous skull faint

shades of bone jerked
towards awakening but in sleep yet
sucked on my glassy hands on

amethysts of flesh clear pinks
and reds white threads of vein
and sprout of the green brain down-

wards. I was spin
of ear whorl in on the roar
of the blazing oozes, basal

dusts and greening
vapors of the oceans' beds   my dears my
creatures come together now

in the bright salt breath   you
are the fishes of the seas that fill
the basin of my skull O crab-

footed dancers who feed on me tooth
rayed scale and fin   the spiral tusk breaks
the membrane of the sea and the heart spouts

From
BLOOD MOUNTAIN

(UNIVERSITY OF PITTSBURGH PRESS, 1977)

It is how I try to tell you
There are no imbalances: we stand
At whatever center most
employs us.

Damselfly, Trout, Heron

The damselfly folds its wings
over its body when at rest. Captured,
it should not be killed
in cyanide, but allowed to die
slowly: then the colors,
especially the reds and blues,
will last. In the hand
it crushes easily into a rosy
slime. Its powers of flight
are weak. The trout
feeds on the living damselfly.
The trout leaps from the water,
and if there is sun you see
the briefest shiver of gold,
and then the river again.
When the trout dies
it turns its white belly
to the mirror of the sky.
The heron fishes for the trout
in the gravelly shallows on the far
side of the stream. The heron
is the exact blue of the shadows
the sun makes of trees on water.
When you hold the heron most clearly
in your eye, you are least certain
it is there. When the blue heron dies,
it lies beyond reach
on the far side of the river.

A May Snowstorm

We are awakened this morning by
snow buntings in the lilac bush
and the glassy cold that made us
lie close all winter; and outside
there is a brilliance of snow light.
Love, this snow is a short answer:
by now we should know that winter
lies always just at the tremulous rim
of the sky ready to spill over
at a mere sneeze, a morning's breath,
as if an inch under the last
white thread of root, or in
the road's nearest hollow, the snow
waits. Blinded by this brightness

we bar the doors, pull curtains,
chain the light out, because we know
that darkness in this disarray of season
becomes us both whose hearts take
awful joy in new grass tufted
with new snow. It ought to remind us
how between one breath and the warm next
the great silence lengthens,
the blood is hindered, and somehow
we do not always resume and awake,
dreaming of snow. This dream in which a mirror,
dusted with new snow, as if struck

and resonating, suddenly
vibrates on the wall,
and the image we are seeing
never wholly subsides. And we
awaken at the last instant
of the last tremor, and outside
something is receding: the freight
from Montreal, a milk truck—
we never know. And in falling

back to sleep we recede
down bright planes of icy glass,
and never by any dawn arrive before
the whole house shivers in the night,
and our faces unfocus into a million
brilliant shards of light. By this
I remind you that with each
breath we are less than ever: now

the days are shrouded in brown spring
sunlight, and I remain shak'n
by wars, the angers not much
diminished: only now
I talk to chairs and pictures,
gesture at stoves and flowerpots from
the vicious asymmetries of breath
and season, my bitterest conviction
and most customary blessing. Love,
I would have lengthened our lives
till the trees spring green again forever,
and the flight of snow geese is high

in the floury blue mornings.
But our bodies walk on their bones
and are busy and clearly
outlive all evidence of breath.
And now the snow flies
after the first warm days. The lie
is bought back, there are between us now
so many awakenings, watery clouds, floods,
turnings of trees, yard soils heaved
by frosts and moles, trout

risen to flies, bodies risen
and laid down again, and snow
laid down as if the resuming breaths
of all of us who sleep in fear of season
freeze in the inclement glass.
May clouds shine in the brown river,
clouds shine, and the paling sun
burns itself out into a ball of gray
crusts that powder at a glance.

And walking now in *diesem wetter,*
in the murderous light of this whole
enkindling sky, I think of you
whose presence has never been
so great a joy as your departure
a darkness. And I shall be
eternally dejected with it.

A Dream with Furtwängler in It

In this dream the clearing
is somewhere beyond the river Xingu.
It is in the dry part of the forest.
I am standing hidden in a grove
of crecopia and wax palm. Behind me,

just beyond the trees, a nameless
muddy river squirms and coils,
ensnarled in its turns. There are birds
everywhere: sun bittern in the shallows,
bell birds, scythe bills scattering
in the trees. I am looking

into the clearing: a large white table
stands in its middle, and upon the table
is food broadcast largesse: huge pitchers
of lagers, pilseners, bocks, platters
of *sauerbraten, hasenpfeffer,* pyramids
of *springerles, lebkuchen,* piles

of *wurst,* heaps of *spritz.* People
are seated at the table, feasting.
I move cautiously from the trees,
preparing myself: there is a great
screeching of green and yellow parrots,
and the people see me, leap up
from the table, stare, smile. I am approached

by a fat man with white mustache
and *lederhosen.* His mouth is full
of *gemengde kloese,* crumbs
of *vekbroekle* pepper his lips.
He raises his stein, he toasts me
in a language I do not fully understand,
I am embraced, led to the table, welcomed

by these people. I wish to make them
understand my pleasure, and just
as I begin to speak, I see someone
move in the trees, step into the clearing,
scattering the flock of white arucuana,
and I realize that I have become
someone else, a young and beautiful woman
in the crowd. I see you standing there

just at the edge of the forest, the white
chickens like a cloud around your feet.
Your face is pale as a young moselle. In that instant
I love you. I think you have been lost,
that you may be hungry, and so I heap a plate
with *kraut* and *sulz* and *gaenseklein,*
and fill a mug with beer, and step forward,
and when you stop and hold out your arms,
I think it is for me, and I am faint
with love. I think you see how my hair
is gold as *schaum torte mit schlag,* my eyes
more brown than *anis kuchen.* And you

are tall and gaunt and your hair
grows in a white froth of curls
around your ears. You are dressed
entirely in black, and you hold a white baton
in your left hand, and as I drop the food
and move into your arms, you raise them,
bring them down, and behind me the music
begins: *Die Walkure,* the complete
Die Zauberflöte, Das Lied
von der Erde—I am embarrassed, I do not know

what to do, I had not expected
this. Your eyes are closed, you do not know
that I am here at all, and then, without warning,
the music stops: you have noticed me, dropped
the baton, you move to me, take me in

your arms, bring your face
to mine: you kiss me, and I begin
to fall back, and then, in the middle
of the kiss I look up into your face and you
have become a single cold blue eye—I can see
nothing else: the trees have vanished, the sound
of the river is gone, the clearing is empty,
and it is precisely as if the whole staring open sky
has come down upon me, and I reel back, I am
forced down onto the beery mud of the clearing:
and belly to belly, eye to eye
we writhe on the cold skin of the world.

West Topsham

1

In prologue let me plainly say
I shall not ever come to that discretion where
I do not rage to think I grow decrepit,
bursten-bellied, bald and toothless,
thick of hearing, tremulous of leg, dry
and rough-barked as a hemlock slab, the soft rot
setting in and all my wheezy dreams the tunneling
of beetles in a raspy dark. For now
I am fleshed at smaller sports, and grow
in time into the mineral thick fell of earth:
Vermont hairy with violets, roses, lilies and like
minions and darlings of the spring, meantime
working wonders, rousing astonishments. And
being a humble man, I at the same time acknowledge
my miscreate, the nightshades, cabbages and fleaworts
of my plot, though always I try to turn my back and scorn
upon the inkhorn term and speak as is most commonly
received with smile and wink and approbative nod,
not overfine nor at the same time reckless
of the phrase, nor ever ugly, turdy, tut-mouthed,
but always joyous at the goosey brain,
the woolpack of the solid cloud, a crowd, a heap,
a troop, a plume of trees, grass, gulls and rabbits,
in the end, no doubt, a vulgar prattle: but the planet
swells and bulges and protrudes beyond my eyes' aversions,
and tottery, fuddled, always I give up, I am not understood,
or wrongly, out of some general assumption of my innocence.

2

This much I wish to say, my nonesuch nosegay
native sweet, in someway plainer, this is my letter to you,
and out of most severe purpose: the bee,
the honey-stalk, the whole keep of the house
endanger me: the perspectives of the clapboard, the steep
falls of the lawn, the razory apices of ridges,
and the abdominous curves of the meadow into the far
trees. There are ponds below the house, and water runs.
The road crosses the water, and the road
diminishes to the reach of the next farm, and the farm
beyond that, and two miles bearing right or left
somewhere runs Highway 25. I have found my way
with difficulty, I am confused, half way I have suffered
a failure of vital powers, a swoon, have been
smirked at by the natives, and misdirected. Fitting,
for I always dream of the painless redemption, the return
from fiasco and tumultuous journey to the transcendentally
serene lawns of a transcendentally white house
with columns of oak trees and iron deer and the
affectionate greeting of One who has these many years
waited in full patience without complaint
for me to come in bleeding, dusty and deliquescent
from the fields, the blade in my thigh, or blinded,
the victim of fire or ravenous birds, the lovely blood
on my cheek like tears, one-limbed, a bullet
in my heart, my hands, my head cut off and the dark
pulses of my blood diminishing. Yet never a reproach
for my criminal self-negligence, my careless japeries
and clumsy flounderings: instead, my brow is wiped, my
wounds attended to, blood let, leeches applied: I heal,
I grow strong, I can set forth again renewed, valiant,
sturdy, full of high spirits, lively, gay, spruce

in looks, a reveler, a merry prankster, dimpled
in the cheeks from smiling, perfect pilgrim, fit
for the chemistry of the Resurrection. Yet
I am of wild and changeful moods. I am perhaps worthy
of being stoned, sometimes. I lie hid and lurk in wait
for the giggling girleries and leap out and shout
and scatter them like chickens from the boot to the safe
and flying four winds. I am easy and fluent
in the telling of lies and let it be said that I roar
and sing scurrilous songs in base places, and shall no doubt
for this little vain merriment find a sorrowful reckoning
in the end. Still, my noises please me, and what
this wretched poet overmuch desires, he easily believes.
It is his conventional cowardice; it makes him
immortally glad. But then he always grows morose
(that is in his favor), he repents, lances his soul, thinks
of the willows and the columned porch and the wind
melliloquent about the chimneys, and you
from where he sits now at the far end
of this small porch of a Federal farmhouse
in this very and summery Vermont.

I look down the pitches of the lawn:
fireflies make small explosions in the grass,
and I think that to walk down that slant of lawn
to the black waters of the brook at the dark join
of the cleft would be like dying and that if I die
I will never pardon time. I think my words
will echo only in my own mind forever, to what purpose
I do not know. I see a firefly trapped inside the screen.
I have no name for this. I know it clearly
as I know the dead cry of the starlings

in the eaves, the smell of after rain, the warm
air holding in hollows of the roads. For this
there is no name. The holding mind is likewise
without name. That is the final thought,
it is the disorder, the reason
for all this. The clouds
begin to reach up Blood Mountain,
and I am sitting on a farmhouse porch,
and there are trees, and it is late, and I am dreaming.
I dream I stare down into a fouled well and see
the white leg bones of a deer and the water's surface
matte with loose hair, the green stink welling
and bellying from the fertile sump up and flowing
outwards in a fountaining current of vines and melons
and leaves and the knot grass lawns blossoming with gilliflowers,
shoulder-high, cloud-high, the sun finally smothering
in grass, the whole bright field of the sky finally smothering
in grass, and then in the entire silence of this
growth the grasses thickening, darkening, becoming clouds,
reaching up from the ridges. And all night
there is rain. I dream that when I awaken
it is a shining milky day, four roosters
are crowing in your yard and geese
dabble in the green soft muds of the ditches.
This is the literal surface, and for all
the extravagance of what has gone before I now repent,
and make an image: all of Vermont each night
blazes with fireflies, the comet is a faint
green phosphorescence to the North, the catalpas
blossom and each noon the sunlight hardens and the sky
is a clear ground and I can look from my open doorways
into dry and fiery yards. You see, I draw back always,

I cannot be understood, *O I wud slepe all the swete*
darkemans, nor ever speke! It was as if I had forgotten
to see the steep lawns suddenly erupt in tiny lights,
it was if my fingers burned green and blazed with crushed
fireflies; and as usual no deer appeared. The strict edges
of the meadows held nothing. When I drive home
my car lights sweep the road before me. I override
the long shadows of pebbles and grasses, and the sky
grows long clouds. I drive into the soft explosions
of lightning far to the West at the end of the confusing road
where I will sleep and awaken and sleep. My hands in the dashboard
lights are glowing softly green. This whole journey
is before me. I know I am touched with the phosphors
of self-love. The light knows it is light. A great
red moon rides wedged in a crevice of clouds, and I come up
the widening road as if it is the driveway to your house.

Falling on Blood Mountain

But you slip in the wet talus
of the lower trail, and bruise
the heel of your palm,
and even if it does not show,
the rock you stopped yourself against
is itself deeply
broken, the shock of your fall
unfolding into the root
of Blood Mountain, and then
deeper; someone on the other
side of the earth awakens
and wonders why and falls
back. Meanwhile, the blood
darkly congeals in the pulsing
root of your hand.

Waiting for Kohoutek

That night was clear
and slowing the car at the top of Depot Hill
and staring to the south, the sky
still lemony over the Adirondacks,
I waited for Kohoutek. Between me

and the mountain Miles's fields
were rimed. There was nothing
in the sky. Holding
my arm out, looking
for a patchy brightness small

enough to cover with my fingertip,
I found nothing, though Venus
elegantly burned over the southern ridges,
and the wind burst on the windows,
and I stayed in the shuddering car

watching for the comet only
a little longer. Whatever
the promises had been, nothing
ever came of them. Orion
flickered in the lower sky

and next morning I found
in the freezing center of the road
a Holstein bull calf, newly born,
lying with his legs neatly tucked
like something from a crèche,

shiny as china, at that angle
of the cold sun, from that
distance, but close up matted
with barn dirt and shivering, three
starry drops of blood strung in a row

on a foreleg. He must have fallen
from Mile's pickup. Some mornings
near dawn the old man drives
a load of calves for slaughtering
and lost this one from his truck,

not noticing because he drove East,
blind into the sun, and the sun
at the top of Depot Hill rises
mornings as I always imagined
the comet would rise, in horns

of light and at the enormous arc
of the rising center the tangled
curls of its incandescent poll. Now,
watching for the comet over Miles's icy fields,
eyes frozen bright as china, I can feel

the fat blood dwindle. Nothing happens,
only out there in the cold fall
of its farthest swing, smaller than
a fingertip, a lion's roar of light,
maned and billowing beyond all brightness flies

out again beyond the farthest I
will ever see. In all the space around Polaris
swing the Bull, the Lion, and the Hunter hangs
steady in the lower sky. On these
cold nights I stay inside, containing

my own spaces, and the wind
that pours down Depot Hill from Miles's fields
bears and rings on the loose lights
of my windows, as the comet might with fire
have rung my eyes.

Vertigo on Blood Mountain

At the top of Blood Mountain I stare into
the flight of invisible ranges to the East,
into the red sun. I can't live
in a place like this for long. It is
too high, and I always feel that I am
falling off, that if I don't lie down
and belly into the stone, my fingers
in crevices, my cheek crushing saxifrage
and lupines, I will sail slowly down
spread out flat like a great kite,
sideslip to a crash landing in
the pines below. I'll be dead,
I'll be dead, and if I would mourn
for you, think how for myself and what
galas of dismal ceremony for
my poor pierced belly and
attendant bones.

Early Morning Poem

Mightily detained and allured,
I have listened to music all night,
Bix and Tram to expel austerity,
Bechet to inform the manner,
Wild Bill Davison, then Messiaen,
Haydn for grace and comeliness,
a little Chopin for
the continuity, two hours
of Bruckner, and Schumann
for the last of the wine. By two,
everything thinning and thickening,
ragged space at the edges
of things, the sofa billowing four
inches off the floor, the air
a little milky, I stand
at the door staring across
the lawns at whole distance,
the raucous, bristling landscapes
to the north, boulders, maple
forests, streams flooding.
I imagine I move out
accompanied, the circling Bear apace,
the Hunter flourishing
his bow. Dogs bark
around me all night long,
and then at dawn the sun

squirms from a black
seed onto the highest comb
of the farthest peak, and all
this time I have been coming
closer, wondering how to announce
myself, afraid I will choke
on a clot of voice, close
my eyes, pitch forward. But by noon
I shall nearly have arrived,
and at the last instant, my hand
on your door, I will find myself

precisely back where I was
at this near center: sofa, table,
a lamp, the fireplace. It is late
beyond late, the poem after five days
still does not work, the cat is scratching
to get in, there are mice
in the cornflakes. Tonight
music has been something
of an answer: the dense
speechless collisions, the mind
delicately bellowing on its fixed
centers. I think it is

by no means certain that the centers
change, being only discovered
and rediscovered. At one of them
we are afraid—of ice, of silence,
of rivers at night,
of drowning; at another I know
there is nothing final about grief
any more than about longing. I ask
at this center what there is
to see? I try not
to see. Instead I turn back
to the room, and hear strings
everywhere, horns
sonorous in the corners,
the tympani like something bearing
on the doors. And there is no voice
to trouble us.

Bad Weather on Blood Mountain

It is cold on the top of Blood Mountain, almost
the verge of snow, and you are bored because
your friends have gone down before you
and your fire is almost out, and so you try
imagining that you are not on Blood Mountain,
but on Everest, the Climber torn from his holds
and swept by the terrible snow plumes of the Summit.
You imagine your mask carried away and your eyes
frozen instantly into a million perfectly hexagonal
lenses of ice and you stare at your million hands
and one by one the fingers crack in little bloody
hairlines at the knuckles, and break away. You find it
strange that there are no visions. You feel yourself
being slowly buried by the wind, the snow is up
to your thighs, your breasts, and soon you are breathing
snow and asking yourself when you will grow angry, hungry,
frightened, want love? You realize that after this
for all time whenever you lie down, Mount Everest
will heave beneath you, roaring with ice and stone,
its snows exploding from the raw peak. And then, thank God,
you notice that here on Blood Mountain the weather
improves a little, the rocky sky softens and begins
to drift to the east, showing gold and yellow where
the clouds crack and break away. The wind is turning,
Blood Brook is beginning to clear. It is a great relief,
and you are happy because you know that in a few hours
you can see again over a northern forest of beech and maple,
leaves mostly shed, the colors of rock and lichen. You tell yourself

this is a hard climate, but not relentless. You hesitate
on the steep hard spine of the trail, wanting to go neither up
nor down, and then the rain stops entirely, and directly
before you, thrust up through a sudden towering of white clouds,
the sun appears, and it is trailing a great wind plume of
gold and yellow fires, and still you cannot decide.

The Fire

That night you dream of smoke,
and by almost dawn—awakening,
your eyes still closed—you're furious,
feel like revenge, like screaming
at someone who knows you are fully ready
to kill him, and who shrinks from your rage
into the dream.
And suddenly you are awake,
and the room is layered with smoke
and you cannot breathe, and you know
the rage in your dream was terror, and you rise
shouting at everyone to go,
get out, your wife hauling at doors,
the kids, the dog frantic on the stairs.
But they run out into the calm yards,
and you are left alone, there
in the unnatural heat of the stairwell.
You close your eyes, and unerringly blind,
make your way down into the cellar hole
under the house. And you find,
when you open your eyes again, it is like
facing the one thing still alive
besides yourself, to see the fire
heaving behind the sills. And at
the precise moment that you confront it
it explodes upward into the space between
the walls. You realize then that this fire
has been waiting for you for a long time,
through years of your sleeping
and waking and sleeping again.

Now you choke in the deepening
smoke, and here in the swampy cellar room
you face the fire at last, appalled,
and it joyously capers and dances and flies
into the tender darknesses between your walls.
And you are afraid to come closer. You think:
"It is all going to burn now!" and *"Why not?"*
After all, it has always been like this,
the dull nucleus of fire locked
into the basement beams of whatever house
you have lived in, working its slow way out.
But this is the first time you have surely met.
You stand with a too-short garden hose,
ankle-deep in cellar mud, and wet
the timbers down. The fire dies,
it faces you and flares, subsides,
reaches for the floor joists
and the hemlock lath. The light bulb dims,
the useless water splatters on hot stone
and steams, the fire blossoms, and you shout
into the darkness and the crazy flames:
"Go out go out go out go out!"

Toutes les lumières

The trees touch overhead
and stars are locked
in the angles of branches. City lights

are in the far distance. Overhead,
a lamp snows light
onto the street. There is

a moon. You stand
in the white circle
of its light. You wear

a white lace gown,
and you are gesturing toward me.
Your shadow falls

behind you, away from me,
and to your right, a red house
bulks, all its windows

lighted. Plants grow
in the windows, and the light
is torn by leaves.

The edge of the circle
in which you stand
is set with burning lamps.

There are blue shadows
between your fingers, at
your throat, but your face

is pale as the moon
and you are smiling.
But I stand

in the shadows at this end
of the street, and do not
move, because behind you,

at the far end, I can see
a woman, her back turned,
her shadow toward me. She

is standing in a circle
of white light, she wears
a white gown, and she is

holding out her hand to
someone I cannot see.

At the Top of Blood Mountain

In December when I come on its coldest
first day to the leafless peak of Blood Mountain
and find it furry with clouds, what
will I do? Will I smell on my fingers
the smoke of the fire I built this morning
with red maple chunks and cedar splits?
I will watch the water of Blood Brook begin
and break on the pebbles and descend.
I will feel the black mold at the trail's edge
and find it warm almost to fire with the slow rot
of dropped leaves. I will think
that beasts hide in the stones,
and it will be hard for me to breathe,
resting there at the end of the path,
staring out into the raw and smoky mists
between me and the next peak. I will suspect
I might feel better if I drank from Blood Brook,
if I slept for a time in the warm
trailside soil. Instead, I find myself
a hemlock to lean against, breathless. I hear
the faint cries of the climbers who will never
arrive. Then, as the day hardens
and the sun begins to organize the sky, red yet
as a maple fire and burning
with the same slow difficulty, I will
give way to my illness: I will feel cold
from the wood I thought burning, and begin
to think how from this hemlock where I stand,
at the always and unbalancing center of
this rooted hemlock, I am in some regard of time
forced to the descent of my difficult breath.
Staring straight up the trunk into the perfect
spiral climb of the branches to their terrible
conclusion high over the mountain
and my head, I think crazily of descent,
of a whelk's shell, God's-eye, spin of maple seed
and the hemlock's green leaf-needles "that will
outlast the winter"—I will stand unbalancing

into the right of time at the eyed
and rooted center of Blood Mountain
in the precise middle of all this green
and stony, winged, embracing, clawed
and calling out of which
surrounds me, and fall
into the one fixed center
of heretofore not present
always and beloved you.

The Intruder

Each time I come by chance
into the place where someone lives,
I find the bedclothes disarranged,
the mark of her head fresh in the warm pillow,
the smell of cooking just beginning to fade.
I never doubt she will return at any minute,
surprised to find the door still open,
pile her groceries on the kitchen table,
pull off her gloves, walk through the rooms
unhurried, clearly confident that she is being
foolish, that no one is truly hiding
in the place where she lives. She is not
intent: I hear her empty an ashtray, snap
a light switch, brush at a curtain. And each time
this is the moment I would like to step out
into the room where she is, and smile at her,
knowing she will think it no more
than a stupid error of inattention
that brings me here. Each time
I imagine she smiles back at me,
takes my arm, escorts me to the couch,
offers me tea and cookies. But I cannot
reassure myself that this is the way
it happens. My particular fear
is that before I can smile or say a word
she will scream, grow pale, fall back from me,
her hands before her face, scramble
undignifiedly about the room for something
to kill me with, her face ugly with rage;
or turn on me coldly and demand
an explanation, tell me I have no right
to be here. This last
is the greater fear: what do I know
that I can say plainly? Why
am I here? I know that I have come into this place
from a place I cannot remember, where I must
have risen from my bed, washed, put on
my clothes, eaten my breakfast, walked out

into the street, glanced at myself
in shop windows, avoided children
and dogs, thought about flowers, the weather,
walked purposefully without stumbling on curbstones,
and arrived. I can remember none of this.
I do not know if it has happened
in just this way. I hear her moving toward
the room where I am standing. In a moment
she will turn the knob, open the door, see me.
I will be neither hiding nor waiting.
I will smile at her. Perhaps I will tell her
I bear a name as well
as this unexpected presence.
I will tell her
that this time I cannot leave.

Photograph Taken When You Are Not Looking

As if in a photograph—taken
when you are not aware, by one
who contrives to stay

out of your sight, peering at you
from thickets of tall grass, leaping
from behind trees to focus, snap

the shutter, vanish into the shadows
of hydrangea—you are caught
with your face beautifully inclined,

your hands busy with food, a flower,
anything at all, your hair
untidy. If you knew you would turn

and say to the bare street,
the bare fields, speaking firmly
in a clear voice, knowing

you will be heard: "I *do not wish
to be seen!*" And as you speak
you will notice that from the depths

of a rose trellis, from behind
the lattice of an old porch is coming
a soft *click* and *click* and *click,*

in one latent image your hand
rising, your mouth just beginning
to open, in another your eyes

staring directly into the lens,
which is in that instant bright
as a rose with the sun, as blinding.

And there is nothing you can do
but turn and walk away and even then
this is what the last photograph

will show: the street empty before you
and the light gone bad.

Morning on Blood Mountain

Owls dived at my eyes.
I still breathe the air
their wings moved.
At dawn on the bare
mountain the day is not
beautiful. Clouds in thin
ribbons blacken half
the sky. A yellow skin
of sunlight covers
half the trail. I have not seen
a sky like this before.
I don't know what I mean
to say *you are beautiful.*
I am blind.
I know you by touching
your face. You are blind.
My fingers cover
where your eyes might be.
Your hair is bright
to my hand. Try not to see.
What is there to see?
I turn to go
down. I am
a contriver.
You know.

Portrait

Let me describe you
to yourself: let me
tell you how you are
seen: let me begin
with your hands, they are
small and pale and smooth
and I imagine them filled
with a light soil, a yellow
sandy loam, the grains
sifting between your fingers.
Your hair is more difficult:

I think of it as I might imagine
apple leaves brushing
my face. Your arms
gather timothy in August:
you hold the sweet grass to you
with your arms. Your feet
are for walking on mosses,

leaf molds, beds of partridge berry,
your legs for being brushed
by wild chicory and daisies,
and with your tongue you may
have tasted jewel weed. Now

I become guarded—I think
of the wind shattering itself
on pines, the folding of hills,
everywhere the relentless
currenting, risings of water,
coursing of small streams
through the tunnels of alder
and cedar. I imagine

your shoulders in my hands:
I have held the warm porcelains
of moon cowry from the Eniwetok
reefs. I imagine your breasts,
your belly, and I think
how the full rain washes dust
from an October day, I am forced
to a consideration of meadows,

a swirling of pools, the clear
nakedness of snowfields. I cannot
satisfy my single purpose here:
I go to your eyes, shadow upon
shadow upon shadow, in your eyes
a road in moonlight plunging steeply

between pines. Your face
is an open shade. I see
pitches of white sunlight on the floors
of hemlock woods. Your smile
is motionless at the center
of your smile, your ears

are covered by your hair:
you hear the sounds of twigs,
seedpods, apples falling. My hand
is on your cheek, your throat,

the warm hollow of your back. Now
I am at the beginning, you summon
a life so deep within me
I have come to believe the least
sequence of flesh occurs
as my most fragile artifice. Therefore
I move to touch you, and I find
your body light upon its bones.

Searching for You

In early spring, the mountain is
flooded. Water sheets on the rocks,
and the higher meadows become lakes,
and it is no use to search for anything.
But in summer I watch in the sandy
light woods near the edge
of the forest. Later, I look
along the forest roads; in the warm
days of autumn, I begin to watch closely
the scrubby slopes, the exposed soil
among mosses. Then, toward winter,
I search among the trunks of pines,
firs and spruces, sometimes in oak woods,
sometimes in the groves of sweet chestnuts
or under larches, never where maple
and hornbeam grow. Not rarely,
in the high grasses that grow
in limestone soils, I think
I have found signs.
But I have always
been mistaken.

Prince Mahasattva on Blood Mountain

Where the pine forest grows to
the very edge of the precipice on Blood
Mountain I see Prince Mahasattva remove
his crimson robe and hang it on the branch
of a tree not yet come into leaf. I do not
know what kind of a tree it is. I see him
leap from the precipice: his sash
trails behind him like a delicate
twisted flame. Below, in the valley,
a starving tigress with her seven cubs
is waiting. About the head and body
of Prince Mahasattva are flowers like birds or
birds like flowers. The tigress
is watching the body of Prince Mahasattva
in flight: his body arches
like a bent bow, his eyes close,
and he reaches out with his hands
for the waiting beast, or he is
praying, or both.

A Dream Book

1

The first dream
is always of God: it is
said to be a sure sign
of death. You may never
frustrate this design.
The second
is of blood flowering
in the corner of your right
eye: *it means:* mediocrity
in love and fortune. There
are other and lesser dreams.
They all imply your dissolution.

2

The dream of being blind
has no significance, and should
on every occasion be ignored.
It is the only dream
of its kind. Never allow it
to confuse or afflict you.

3

To dream on the same night
of butchers, of bright buttons,
of letting birds out of a cage
is a dream warning. *It warns*
that a step imprudently taken
may embitter the remainder
of your life.

4

To dream of bones
is of such clear and ordinary
significance,
we will waste no time upon it here.

5

For a married woman to dream
her arms have grown lusty
denotes: that she will have
many sons, few of whom
will survive her. If she dreams
she is driving a chariot
drawn by falcons, salmon, and pigs
it means: that her husband will arrive
at public honors, will grow rich,
will make friends, will love
this woman.

6

To dream of fish is rather
unfavorable, especially
to lovers, since it is
indicative of death
to the sick, and loss of love
to the young. It is forewarning
of that of which
at present
you know nothing.

7

To dream of the dead
is a certain sign
that you will be
unable to give warning
of danger, except
to your enemies.

8

To dream of rivers
of red mud is the same
as dreaming of the dead.

9

No one yet has come to understand
what it means to dream
of yellow flowers.

10

But should you at one
and the same time dream
all these things:
red birds flashing
like gold buttons, butchers
stone-blind and lying
in the strong arms of married
women, dead boys floating
face down in the red streams
nibbled by fishes, rivers rising
over their jonquilly banks, the trees
drowning, growing silvery
as forests of bone: *then:*

prepare yourself for some
great and important change in your
condition, prospects and circumstances.
Whether it be for the better
or worse, time alone
can tell. But the change
will be as great and sudden
as it is unexpected.

Southern Journal

1

The first thing I notice:
everything whistles with birds.
The first morning
I am looking in my mirror,
and a quail calls
outside the window. I run
to the window, but he
is gone. It is the first
time in my life. During
this one day
I do not know
the names of trees.

2

Juncos come to the feeder
and a tanager blurs
like a hummingbird at the suet.
The second night I have a dream:
I wake up shouting at a dun-colored fox
which runs away, looking over
a winged shoulder at me.
Apart from this
in the dream are no birds.
Everywhere I sense water.

3

The third night I am traveling.
It is raining. Trees
shatter into leaf. I see
myself in the watery planes
of the window glass,
and ahead on the highway
a red light flickers on and off
like a cardinal at the dark
heart of a pine.

4

Whenever I taste rain, I look
for my face: in puddles,
hallway mirrors, the bowls
of spoons. The planet
is shining with water,
and I have a dream
that in one grove the pines
become a forest of herons,
beaks straight up, their feet
fast in the earth. The needles
bloom into feathers,
and the trees shudder and flap
and take flight, trailing
long white roots like herons' legs.
They rise and cry out far
above me, flocking south.
I am left to choke
in a rust-colored dust,
and nothing is left to make shadows.
This is on the fourth day.

5

The next morning when the sun comes out
I cross two rivers in pink spate.
I see jonquils blooming white
from an orange soil. I think
snow may be falling
in Vermont. Wherever
I am is a difficult
climate, perhaps
relentless, and breathing
is hard. I try
to tell you that what I mean
by "the nature of yearning" is
"the horror of longing," or
"blindness." Until now
I have lied about this.

6

The third dream is that
I want to grow wings and a curved
yellow beak, cast a monstrous
shadow, darken
entire mountains, watch houses
empty and people point
up at me, crying out. My
feathers will shine in the sun,
green as new leaves, and at
my first sight of the sea,
I will flare up, screaming. I dream
it is the last and hunting pattern
I possess.

7

At this point the heart
somewhat diminishes, grows
more regular, falls back into
orderly plasms of recollection:
I am walking alone
for quail, in Indiana, sighting
along the corn rows for the feeding   .
coveys. The November corn rustles
like feathers, and the sun
is brown over the cold fields.
Sometimes snow is falling,
sometimes the wind is like snow.
I have always lived in places like this,
where, despite the cold, the ice
on the fields, the birds are there,
black vigorous specks far
at the ends of the rows,
and I run to flush them,

battering at the dried stalks,
startled at the flare.
It takes time for me to breathe again.
In such a manner
I am using up time
at an incredible rate.
It is how I measure longing.

8

In one bus station I see a fat
red-headed porter who is blind,
who never had eyes. His head
is like a huge pale kidney,
and he stands over the fountain,
his thumb on the button,
listening to the curve
of the water. He is clearly
amazed. He whistles
a bobwhite call over and over,
and then he kisses the water.
He never drinks. I am reading
my book, and I hear a quail
calling, and I look up
and he is there, being astonished,
brushing the water with his lips,
whistling to it like a bird.

9

Whatever I do I leave
you, wherever I am the rivers
swell and the trees drop leaves
like feathers of a sort
I have not seen before. I do not
expect to breathe only for myself.
I am easily astonished, this
is a new land, that
tangles me. I look into the dry
convergences of this place
and where on my lawns the snow
grows like a flowering of salt,
the quail come to whistle
like water like water like water!

Letter

My dear friend: notwithstanding
long silence, my thoughts
have been with you. Doubtless
all has been well with you,
or I would have known. As for me,
there is little to tell. I have
nothing but praise for the weather:
much sun, a little rain, and the garden

a full and green exuberance.
I have been able to see Blood Mountain
for over a week. The streams
are low and run clear,
and the first hatch of yellow mayfly
due tomorrow. Last night
a luna moth came to the lantern,
and at noon two hummingbirds
perched for an instant in the wild apple.
I suppose what I mean is that everywhere
I look, something is moving, a fact

which occupies my mind, not precisely
the oil and wine of consolation. If I
for example play Schumann's Third Symphony
through the open window, its molecules
instantly disperse, the horns thinning
in the hayfield, the trumpets dying
in the pines. Motion is always away from me:
beyond the pines, high up on the side
of the mountain it is still. But inside
the house is engorged

with music which beats back
on itself, wall to wall, the doors shuddering
with sound, the windows trembling. This music
overspreads the ceilings like shadows,
and glances like sunlight from the tabletops.
This is how things move in the dark house

of the skull, all the pines and birds
and mornings of the world straining
at masonries, overflowing cornices, only
a little, finally, leaking to the hillsides,
the rest moving toward the darkness that is
everywhere, the quiet, the melancholy
annihilations.

Things move: I close
my eyes for an instant and shadows
leap on the walls. I feel
a weight of cloud race in

from the west, from across the lake,
and the wind rises, sharply. The willows
hiss in the far comer of the yard. I sit
with the memory of light behind
my eyes, the recollection
of fair weather. There is
a difference of climates, and it
is growing late, and before long
night will have fallen like an austere
and bitter accident. But I do not wish to close
before I tell you how the shadows
of the high clouds are like
dark lake beds, on the eastern ridges
of the mountain. Here,
where I live, where the river
on its last run to the lake cuts through
the stone ledges of the ancient beach,
the skeletons of whales have been found.

Let me tell you a dream: I am walking
through the thin sea of the hayfield,
and then I climb, and near the top
of the mountain, in the dark mud
of a drying lake, I see without
astonishment a slow surging

of flukes, and then the gleam
of a vast white belly, and the sun
breaks through, and before me
in an open meadow the last spout of the whale
rises like a great stone tree. This dream

overspreads the walls, and it
is growing late. There are fireflies
in the grass. In the thin blue vase
on the table, the second bud of the white iris
has begun to open. The morning's blossom
crumples softly on itself,
and what I can see: the white flower,
the brown wood of the ceiling darkening
around the nails, night flooding in
upon Blood Mountain I let
enter me for contrivance. In the end
this place is as strangely good
as I am, in practice, strangely
not. I seem to bring night on myself
as some kind of desperate maneuver,
causing the moon to rise, and the Pleiades,

allowing darkness to overspread the lawns
and fill the stream beds. I walk out into the yard
and stand beside the well. At the bottom
the water shines like oil. The water
swallows pebbles and dirt clumps,
the sunlight in the yard pours down
into the well, and the water
swallows it. Soon
the yard will be dark. If I
put my ear to the grass and listen
for water running the deep channels,
the grass will roar in my ear,
and there will be the sound
of something with jaws
feeding an inch below the white

fabric of the roots. I will be able to hear
nothing else. The music is caught
in the trees high up on the side
of the mountain, and the slow
bubbles of my breath rise
to the surface of the atmosphere
and burst, silently. This is why
I must close. Assuredly, it is not
to turn from you, but
a thing I offer, as I tell you how
the sun is low and the first breeze
of a hot day moves down from the pines,
warm with the smell of resin. We will,
no doubt, not hear from one another.

From

VIVALDI
IN EARLY FALL

(UNIVERSITY OF GEORGIA PRESS, 1981)

*"Swetenesse of this paradise hath
ye ravysshed; it semeth ye slepten
apart from al diseses, so kyndeley
is your herte therein ygrounded."*

—Thomas Usk, *The Testament of Love*

PART I

The Garden

The Garden

A river bank outside a walled garden. Later
the interior of the garden. Later still
a rose-plot, surrounded by
a hedge, inside
the larger garden. Its single garnishment,
a great sun, powerfully
shines. Unhappily

this garden is empty, though
from time to time a bird sings
and there is a shower of warm rain.
But to the north, far to the north,
it is beginning, snow falls
and hardens, and all the white beasts
begin to wander south. And it is then, just then,

that from nowhere, at the very center
of the garden, there appears
someone for the single purpose
of noticing the slight
shortening of days, the bare
chilling of the air in the first
lights of morning: Love,
Beauty, Bravery take shape

in his smile, though for the moment
he gives way to the first
prophetic fancy, dreams
of a scarlet sun the size of a rosebud,
unfolding and unfolding
from its locked center.

And when in time the first snow blows
over the walls, he makes it out to be
no more than a cloud of petals
from some blooming tree. Such then
the scene, and such the character,
who finally sleeps, and is crushed
by the great ice driving over him,
his bones, the whole time,
warm in the pious dream, the body
of the earth hollowing beneath him;
and the garden, of course, no garden at all,
as if it had never been,
and all time spilled for nothing.

Dreaming of the Natural History Museum at Notre Dame

Today I wake up and recall
of the entire dream only
the ceremonial ochres
on the skull of the Miami brave,
the pickled bull snake in its jar, its pallid
coils, the gold pendulum, big
as my head, that swung forever around the red
X of center, proving the planet and therefore
Indiana truly turned.

But most of all the coldly legible
spiral of stone, the great
whorl of the six-foot fossil nautiloid,
balancing against the north museum wall, ready
to topple at my least
step. And that is all—
coil of snake, round hollow bone, circling
of plumb bob, and the stone shell,
taller than the child it might have crushed,
spinning in upon the perfect
and resolute center,

everything in memorable stance, everything
at dead center, the old dusts
in plain array. Today
I awaken and look
into the red bullseye that my son
has painted on the bathroom mirror. I see
myself, which is to say
whatever there is to say of dream,

of language, of necessity—
the waking eye dead center and each waking day
the same slow, enormous ceremony of retrieval;
however the need maintains, however
the elusive, agile shapes may grow
from the casual shelter of my bones, I know

the recollection of matter
is the suicide of angels,
the last giving-over of the dead.

Mudtrapped

for John Reiss

One time I waded far out in a lily slough
on the Clyde's back waters, and my boots
caught in powerful suctions of black ooze,

and I sank, until the water, at my chin,
stopped rising on me; something held me up.
I drank warm air, and well I might have stayed

forever there, deep-rooted in the bottom mucks
like some enormous lily; but my friends came,
I was rooted out, dragged in.

I think if it's true the black night sometimes
swallows us like that, the planet softens, liquefies,
tries to draw us in to where we drown,

it is the grace and rule of counterpoise applies,
or so Desire requires us to believe,
fearing as we do Love's natural buoyancies

are no true balance to the pulling-down.

Bog Plants

Thirty years later the night is the purple flush
the pitcher plant's throat.
Sitting alone, "which is the beginning of error,"
I think of the flower itself, the snake-mottled
belly of leaf that bulged from the loam near the hose;
and the clawed pads of the fly trap that never mistook
my probing stems for the brunt
of the entering beetle. And the sundews I moved
from the Berrien bogs to grow
in the house's north shade,
in late June, in those days when the skies
over South Bend were burning, burning, and if
there ever was rain it came down as a power of light.

I think of the light: as my eye today
unfocuses, suffers no clarity, then
it blurred and recoiled from the sun on the white
east side of the house, the house giving back
such dazes of light, so blinding, I turned
to stare into the shades of the ell, the damp
corner of bog plants, the other blindness
coming over me: and consequent
nightmare—

my body at rest in the white, cool soils of the bed,
my head foursquare on the pillow, the sheets
so neat at my chin that merely to stir
was to trouble the whole
house, its bordering acres,

I dreamed I was thorax of wasp,
the impervious chitins of beetle, carapace, husk,
a blurring, corrodible heart,
the bone sour in the belly's
vigorous juices. And there
was the slow, large, convulsive gulp of the dark.

Joyce Vogler in 1948

That beautiful pale girl with yellow hair
than whom I shall not other love, nor half so much,
stood with me waiting for the Portage Bus,
hands in her pockets, collar up against the wind,

and grinned at me, and laughed. But I
was worried, it was late, the bus
was late, or I may
have missed it altogether, and

my mother would be waiting up,
and I would not see this girl again forever;
and that has been
the terrible, slow truth of it, not wish, not love

recalling me to that night when the wind,
sweet with catalpa blossom, swelling
and softening, drifting her yellow hair
across my face, broke sternly on us. Now,

in the monstrous wake of passage, I give up
to no less love than did not understand before
in the flesh intent on its own timely bearing.
The night hums crazily with wind and trees,

and birds fly, as if it were full day.
I see her laugh at me. I look away,
I crane to see the whole black empty length
of Portage Avenue—and there, at the end,

is the late, the final bus,
ablaze with yellow light,
just turning out from the billowing night
at the far end of the street; for always

me worried me, though always
I was home in time.

Saying the Names

My name: *John. Norbert,*
my father's; my grandfather's, *William,*
David, my brother. *Margaret, Patricia,*
Julie, Euphrasia,
of the women of the family. Uncles,
James, and *Bill,* and *Vincent.*
Laura, Leon, grandparents. My mother,
Eleanor; Arlene, my wife, my

children, *Jessica, David, John,*
Laura and *Matthew;* the dead son,
Philip—all the names
said for the simple saying,
the plain acknowledgment,
always as if my ear were pressed
to the hearts of my people,
my breath warm on their breasts.

And outside, the nameless formulations
waiting for names:
the sun rising, the lakes,
the still fields filling up with snow,
my whole days filling
with the dull syllables of pulse,
the watch in my breast pocket
louder, more regular, than my heart.

Always, more than anything,
I wish to say the names:
even with my dead before me,
I say the names
into the bright, breathable air,
all the names of our uncommon time
beating in my tongue,
myself beyond
that possibility,

myself awakening
in the middle of the night, my breath
regathering, the uncommon breath;
and the last loud syllable
of what I take to be
the one great general name I never hear
just dying in the room, just
whistling backward
to the utterance.

Great Grandmother

I remember my great grandmother
wanting to die, but old and awake
in her bed in the Nicolet Home

for the Aged.
I did not know her, having come
with my father to stand at the foot of her bed

this one time only. Still,
I wished she were not blind,
and could see the blue Fox River

from her window. The room
smelled of sulfides from the mills,
and the red zinnias we had brought her.

*"Hello, Norb, I'm
old, I want to die!"* She
called me by my father's name. I

cannot recall telling her
my name. I know
I did not want to die,

having as yet
no sense of power
in such a thing.

Revisiting the Grave

for Julie and Dave

The day my mother died, I must
have looked out over the green swell
of Lake Michigan sheeting
high on the beaches,
at the last turn of the surf
pine cones rolled over and over,
the river rolled back
at the breakers, clouds
foaming in. I must have faced

into the long shudder of wind,
trusting my eyes to the sting
of the sand.
But next day:
utter calm.
I might have believed
the planet had stopped in its turns;
and except that my hand touched the wind-

sanded boles of the pines,
I might not have believed
I had witnessed those risings
of water, the drive
of the sand from the lee
shore. And today
it is calm, and except that my hand
touches this grass, I might not
have believed
enough to endure these powerful
weathers of memory, moving
my hands on the swell
of the green turf, palms

dazzling at the dark
gathers of soil; and my eyes—
for all their staring to windward, for all
that brunt of dust
they bore, suffering no abrasion,
offering no visible evidence.

Naming the Animals

Since spring I've seen two deer,
one lashed to a fender. The other fed
in a clearing on the back slope
of Bean Hill, his big rack still
in velvet. The shot buck bled,

its tongue frozen
to the rusty hood.
But the other, in its simpler stance,
felt merely the delicate itch
of antler skin.

And three does, mildly alert,
cocked ears toward where I watched from
in the hemlocks. I saw, of course,
five deer; but I count only
what by plain necessity of death

or feeding is oblivious to me,
does not watch back.

At Night on the Lake in the Eye of the Hunter

That night, drifting far out
in the center of the lake,
I watched the stars; later
I shone my torch down into the eelgrass
of the perch beds, and saw the fish
stunned into thrills and tremblings of fins.

I shone the torch onto my wet hands,
onto the wet sky-reflecting floorboards
of the boat, then onto the sky itself,
the beam widening, thinning into the white
fabrics of mist. That night

I thought I rode the center of all
the widening brightnesses,
that everything was around me, out
to the mountainous far rimstones
of the circling earth.

Later, by starlight seeing
over the blue surface of the lake
trout feeding on mayflies,
seeing the cross and recross
of rise rings, the slow
opening of ripples
from the tiny bright insucks at center,

I came to think how it might have been
my boat hung there in a net
of light, a cold, translatable fire;
however it may have been,
it was then my light began its long
reach, even now, long afterward, still

rising, widening into the body of the sky,
into the last huge widenesses of the last
meetings of light beyond which
I remember this or not, beyond which
even then fearing my life
I wished to burn.

Bullhead

for Bill Dunlop

Sprawled belly-down on the damp
planks, the breath
squeezed in my chest,
I drift the bait
into the pale moon-shadow of the dock

waiting for the blunt
emergence of bullhead,
his slow surge at the worm, glint
of the small, mucusoid eye,
sluggish black spasm of flesh.

I haul him out,
but he does not die at once:
ugly among fish, poisonous dorsal spine erect,
he endures, he swims in the air
for hours, scrabbles and grunts
in the bucket. I have fished
for more than a hundred nights
hearing that gross croak
from the bucket,
and do not forget, am granted the memory:

in that peculiar sleeplessness
which loves those things which resemble
other things, night
after watery night I have tried
to breathe the inappropriate air,
have wanted to call out into the blackness

beyond the dumb, immediate blackness
that I am about to die and cannot die,
but making so dull a voice of the dull
connatural agony, I writhe to it,
grunting aloud, the hook
of the breath snagged
in my gullet, the tongue
in my mouth like a worm.

Muskrat

When the sky
opens itself to the dank reedy smell
that is the lake at this hour,
and the moon rises in that parting of the clouds
for fully a minute,

I glance out at the water
through the cluster of pale evening duns on the screen,
through the moon-lighted dazzle of their wings,
and see the fiery V-shape bearing out
into the shatter of light on the lake,
a slow comet of small flesh,
whiskery with grasses.

A small light of stars
behind the clouds,
room light behind me:
the time comes for me
to try to detach my hand's shadow
and reach out—and therefore,
in this night without true fire,
everything cold, night deepening, the lake deepening,
the deepening clarity of flight
in the wing of the imago,

I raise my arm and the room light flings
the long, articulated shadows
of thumb and finger out
onto the lake, out there,
where, through the cold, adoptive fires
of the cold stone of the fireless moon,
the muskrat swims. It is enough, this time,

to frighten him, to make him dive,
to make me imagine him frantically, smoothly
webfooting down through the rank
blacknesses of the lake, his fur trailing light,
his wake starry with bubbles, his body
light with the last, terrified
breath-taking. He dives

into the thickening muds of the lake.
And what remains, what I am left to see,
is the floating scatter of cattails,
and how the black field of the lake
has closed on his small, inexplicable fire.

The Crows

When it was spring in Wisconsin,
and the roosting crows
screamed every morning from the birches
across the lake, alarmed
at the first predatory light,

I used to push out from shore
on the little waterlogged raft,
awash to my ankles
and find it possible to believe myself
standing on the still water, over
the dangerous place
where the sand bottom dropped away
into the muds of the spring hole.

When it was spring in Wisconsin, and morning,
the nights never far away, and the stars
always preparing to burn in the rising field of the lake,
when it was spring and what I stood on
did not fully bear me up,
and if I could drown or fly or hurl myself
into the left and right of the powerful distances,

I had not sufficiently fathomed
how to believe, intent
always on the instance of morning, the voice
of the crow, the small
shiver of air in the delicate drum
of my bones, the rising
beaked sun. I would stand

on the lake in the jaws of the opening light,
a deepening beneath me, a greater
overhead, the gesture
of my reaching out to either side
a movement of so little extension I might,
but do not remember, have shouted
in anger aloud and heard
in reply my own voice fly at me, back

from the trees of the far shore, the words
jumbled and raucous, prolonged
into warning, back
like the bright alarm
of the sun-greeting voice of the crow.

The Geese

Stepping out on the back porch
in the early evenings of November,
I hear the hissing, the dumb
unfriendly voices of geese.

But in the mornings, in the cold
decorum of light, its lovely
obligations, I walk
in the crackling garden, scuffing
my boots in the frozen
green hillocks of goose droppings,

shiver and watch the Toulouse geese
parading their coop roof, the goose yard
shining with spread wings. Then
night comes and the moon dims
in the blue web of cloud, and the birches
at the yard's far edge sway
like the white necks of geese;
and each time I feel night as a bird

and myself caught in the warm angle
between wing and body of a bird,
sharing the convulsion of desire it is
to beat down on the stony planet,
and rise, and fly.

Partridge

Eyes frosting over, its shattered beak
polished with new blood,
at my feet lay the partridge
which only an instant before had flushed
from the beech grove and hurtled
whirring low over the winter yard
to come up short against
the brick wall of the house.
I picked it up,

the wings disjointed into a soft sprawl
over my wrists, and felt
through the loose throat-skin the crop
bulging and grainy
with mast. My fingers
grew warm on the barred
breast. It was because
my hands were cold I did it,
though, it is true,
for a moment as I stood there
holding the dead bird,
my fingers warm in the soft down,

it seemed never
to have been otherwise,
that from the beginning
I had found myself
likewise frequent in my yards,

and somehow at my feet
the diffident aspect of a body
abruptly impoverished
and mute, which, living,
I could not find palpable.

The Mothwing, Ice at Dawn

1

Nearly spring, though snow
still blurs the world: no edge
to anything, air brightening
with snow, green cloud

of the willow through
the snow; and at dawn
the plain immanence
of fire, grey

blade of the lake, white stones
of the lake bed, shadows
of birds, of stones, of trees;
the icy breach which is the sky.

2

On the spray of apple twigs,
the chrysalis, pricked
from the elegant, strict sleep,
stirs; and I see,

by the first spasm
of morning light, from the frayed
cocoon the moth emerge,
softly to clamber the red

curtain: great
rosy-grey *crecopia,* uncrumpling
its eyed wings' owlstare
into the room

where I have myself begun to feel
something of what the blood's light
carries of this dumb desire
to fly.

3

I leave her there, cold pulse
of insect blood, walk down
to the shore, step out
onto the puddle meadows

of spring ice. I walk out
beyond the point, the air
pitchy with hemlocks, ice
heaving and widening to either side.

I walk into the clear,
thunderous field of the open lake,
I see the moon
thin in the red underbelly

of the sky; from shore,
a small outcry of dry leaves,
a flicker of blue light
among the pines,

some shiver of wing
instinct in the solitude.

4

Often, at dawn, in the spring,
I walk far out on the ice; sometimes,
following the long shadows
that I make, I raise my arms,

make wings of shadows; at other times
I reach trembling out
over the veined ice,
the light deepening, bright dust

upon my arms, ice hoarding air,
clear dust of light, clear
rosy dust of light, the moon
at such times fragile

in the sky, the sun
just brightening, and overhead
the sky ready to flash
with dawn, everything

on the cold verge of fire, everything cast
of the presences.

5

I come out
onto the barrens of spring ice,
beneath which the lake
is swelling: it is

the current
of the wing. I come out
onto the dangerous spring ice,
and look back

to the far shore, from which
I watch myself look back
upon this figure far out on the ice,
which spreads his arms, lies down

on the watery snow, makes snow-wings, wing-marks,
stares into the sky through the lessening snow,
and sees the bright field of the air
parting before him; and the dream

is that he is about to climb
the white, uncoiling feather of his breath;
the dream is of how
in the full light of the sky in full

view of everything, he takes
wing-shape, shape of a huge
trembling moth, feels the wing
throb in his shoulder, sees the sky

brighten in the great, faceted domes
of his eyes, a million suns
rising to meet in the splendor
of one shining, the air

filled with the soft
threshing of wings, the blue
ice of the light swelling,
and warming overhead,

everything shaken
into its separate dusts,
the body at last
bearing the wind which is promised,

though not that it will fly—old
intolerable exaltation
before things, great eye

of the Mothwing, green
opening stone of the earth!

The Cold in Middle Latitudes

1

the first of April, I stand
a little before sunrise
on the porch step, and observe
to the north a sudden
discontinuity of sky. I look

in that first light
at the houses of North Williston.
The morning
withholds itself, there is much in it
of refusal. I note
how it is that the world in early spring
exhales the odor
of damp cellars,

which in fact I have always known,
and of which I have spoken,
nor is this the last of it

2

April, which is to say,
by my measure, some small
equivocal truth about how
everything takes place
at the wrong time.
The black

locusts seem dead, the maples
have come half-alive, and wait.
In my yard, in all the yards
of North Williston, the spring muds
steam—and for the moment

(though I permit it
only for the moment)
something like the sun
takes place. For the moment
all the doors stand open,
this house airing,
readying itself,
by evening

the spring frogs chirping
and roaring from the ditches,
and one which has been hiding all winter
singing out from the cellar

3

a sullen, invisible cold
breathes from the floorboards.
Warm rain begins
at the exact instant that, in the west,

the sky clears, greens, flares overhead,
that everything becomes
as if I were to breathe at the green
fluent heart of the sea,

and looking up into the vast mirror of the under-
surface, be permitted to look back upon
myself; which would be to fail
in these imaginings

4

Perhaps I am in
the wrong place:
over North Williston
in the earliest of skies

the sun dwindles into the knot
and smother of its heart.
And my heart,
as it carries itself in me,

as I have known it to undertake to do
sings out in the seasonal
startlement from hiding, willing
and unwilling to become

nothing, but always unequal
to the one or other of it

5

as it turns out,
as I expected that it would,
the sky in this place is no more
than merely about

to deepen, to become snow
which will fall and deepen,
and I have in all this weather-lock not
come to understand how it can be

the body warms
to its own and slight
sea-bearing,
the body, as I

have knowledge of it, wishing
always to rise and to beat down
upon a green and upward-
beating shore; and this,

though I see by the blue
shine of the ice that rises
slowly in the east, though I see
by that true and signatory light,

I have
not fully deserved
this knowledge, have
not used it well

Artesian

1

When, as now,
because the pump has shorted out,
the well is dry,
I am unwilling to believe it,

and a dozen times a day reach out,
twist on the tap, expecting
bright fullnesses of water
to swell up in the pipe,

rush over my hands; instead,
am each time newly startled
by the quick back-hiss of the air
through valves, check valves

and pressure tank, the unfamiliar,
frightening soft suck
and inbreath of the long,
down-draining pipe.

2

Always, to my conviction,
it is there, bellowing
hundreds of feet
beneath the house,

the river, which has never
to this day gone dry, not even
in the hottest summer, never
in the greatest drought,

though when I lie awake
and listen for it, I
hear nothing, only
from somewhere deep

in the deepest parts
of the cellars of whatever
house I have lived in, slow
trickling of seepage

into the sumps, at times the slow
trickle and thump
of earblood: all powers of gathering
to which the heart gives rise.

3

I have not before considered,
but do not,
the downstream rising
of the river. I see

an open, marshy corner
of low meadowland, a cold
upwelling though
schists and serpentines, blue

glacial clays and muds, a rust
of water among thickets
of cattail; in the bright
shades of marsh

marigolds, tricklings
through cress and duckweed, falls
of willow, cedar, alder
hells, first

pooling, minnow-
flash, bright
riffling of
streambed, sunlit

caddis flight, first
lucid narrows of
the true
channel (Upstream, vague

issuance, the
inconsiderable
source)

4

I fail, as always, to remember
that what the source does not
give up to me, it shall
exact again—therefore and again

I walk down
into the still passage
of the house, stand
at the sink, and turn

the taps wide open: rush
of house air down the dry
well pipe—my very
breath drawn down

the breath of everything
I have ever known to be alive
drawn down
out of the dry silences

into what I have taken to be
the inaudible convulsions of water
deep under
the house, the river

gathered there and howling
through glassy arches
of rock, black flumes
and conduits, and hugely

roostertailing, its voice
the voice I have listened for
my whole and sleepless
life, its light

(if this river were to be light)
what I would all day
and every day
awaken to, see by.

After Thirteen Years

" . . . looked back from the high hill on the place I used to live"
—Ma Rainey

As always, it is snowing.
The roof flowers with new ice.
In the house the closets succeed themselves
one on the diminishing other
to the tiny locked heart
at center. The names

rise up in me
in little, gathering densities.
It is snowing and the sun is rising
into the dead center of the sky;
and everything is white,
under the snow the rocks, dirt, tree roots:
everything is white.
This late at night

the body yearns
for exactitude in things,
feels the silence
in the creature, waits
to want to sleep.
And at this moment
I begin to hear
the small wings of your heart
beating away;
at this moment
I am thinking of you,
of how softly the snow falls,
what it builds to.
In a little while

the sun will tear free
from the white cloud of the earth,
the pines on the hill will stand out
against the whiteness of the hill,
and morning will surge in, and I will see
ice, pines, the derangement of Vermont
into mountains. I will see
the fields of the snow
stretching to beyond the farthest
imaginable north.
I will hear the doors fly open, and the house
will fill with cold. Ice
will be roaring from the roof.
And I will think how, on such a day,
I held you, only an hour born,
your eyes bruised from the first
blunt stun of the light,
small blood
exulting into smaller voice;

and felt most powerfully
the impersonal separation of bloods,
took you to be, as yet unnamed,
proof of the "short day
and the long shadow,"
perhaps no more
than the bitter duty of seed,
of kinship, perhaps

gift beyond gift, the body
being what it is, weak
on the side which does not
lean upon the world.
As for the rest, you died.

If you had lived you would have come to see
how, wishing to die, the body swells and grows;
have come to be startled
by all the accidents of celebration,
even perhaps have come into the voice
which cannot be startled into celebration;
have come to believe,
that at whatever distance we care to imagine
there is only the pale light without shadows
the snow gives off at night,

only the recollection of your voice,
always as distance, always as a tiny cry
from the deep center of the house,

without much conviction to it
in the way of pain.
I dream
I am alone, and awaken,

frightened, hearing myself
trying to say one last thing
into the air of Vermont,
whispering to whatever

at that instant might seem to require
recognition, but lacking
a usable breath
to discharge what I, even at that moment,
will consider a duty. There is

a mystery here, something like a memory,
something of the voice's continuities,
that it carries long ways,
but weakly, so that hearing it
is like a memory
of the beauty of a body
recognized and welcomed.
I have been free of it,

but now again come to the recognition: snow
outside, light bursting
from the tips of icicles, cardinals
in scatters of red shadow on the snow:
on such days when I sleep
I hear you, touch you, am touched back,
you come to me rising from where you have been,

walking to me over the snow;
and if I turn
to the touch on my shoulder,
there is no one; thus
the cold center continues to achieve itself,
the world is used up.
I have not understood

how it is my mind
exults into this elaborate,
clamorous voice,
or how it is this voice
has opened itself to me,
or how what has seemed to me
the small, clear distant voice
of all the crying out of all time
I continue to hear
from the locked heart of the house
as if I were myself
among the gathering celebrative dead,
my blood upon the root.
I do not understand

how I have continued to believe
the named thing breathes,
to name what it is I see,
having named you: Philip, fifth-born,

since the naming I know I have seen you
walking across the field towards the fence,
towards the long reach of pines
into the white field,
wide-legged on snowshoes, the orange bulge of your pack
the brightest thing north of me;
and it is not from this place
you seem to have left—you are walking away
at precisely that middle distance
at which I begin not to see
you will surely return, hours later,
smelling of wood smoke, your shoes soaked, a glove lost,

forgetting to close the door behind you,
the ugly pale cold of the fields
flooding in from behind you.
And I begin not to see

what might have been your eye
encountering the young light
of the fields, your foot
on fresh snow. You are named,
you are recognized: slow course of seed
beneath the snow, vigorous
green sprouting
from the severed parts: all my children,
there is today
a soft down-spinning of snow, this
is for you, I speak to you
into the dead center of the snowing sky:

may another, warmer season yet contain
the voices you have not heard,
the shapes on which you hands
will never rest. For now
there is the slow, cold turn about the center.
Look back from the white field
on the place you used to live.

The Electric Fence Game

1

I walk
through the stupid milling
of cattle, come
to the shining wire and reach out,

not daring to hesitate, trusting
to catch hold in the dead time
between pulses, grasp
and ungrasp in perfect

dumb coincidence the wire,
and find it neutral
in my hand: a game
in which the free hand freely

dances, so long as it
keeps time

2

After the first
and risky taking-hold, everything
is safe enough. I stand
and look out over the calm pastures,

scarcely aware
of how on each side
of the instant of my fist
the blunt stun of power licks out

3

But even if I have been wrong
and have caught hold and found
the wire humming and alive,
it is the moment I understand

how all along
I have desired my heart to leap
and leap in the irregular
dark spasm and keep on,

have desired
to give up to the cold
pulse of the wire the lesser
power of my hand

to open itself or not, to splay
out fingers, free itself
of what in love or
other synchronous play

it has chanced freely
to close upon and hold.

In Panama

darker than all the other times
put together squared,
I stared up at the pale belly
of a stuffed shark
that hung over my head and circled
in the damp light of Panama
like a big and predatory
ceiling fan.

And there was the voice
of some woman at the bar, saying
it had hung there in the exact
same place since the day
her father shot it from the deck
of the fishing boat *Juarez*
in the year of
1931. Later,

with a great far cry of darkness in between,
I saw a man in a checkered hat
stand, brace himself
in a yellow circle of street light,
a voice balloon of huge moths
in a slow swirl above his head,
and knock the brains out
of a dog's skull with
a fragile-looking stick. *Brief
infrigidation of the spirit, black
night:* then
awakened on my way to somewhere

in a car which was not
my car and packed
with a great many people
whom I did not know and a cheerful,
horny mongrel which would not
give up trying to hump my knee,
and at last, on the far side of dark interval,
came to, swimming in the deep water
outside the shark net
at Fort Amador. There are some few

concluding figures, all
significant of lapse, dismemberment
or forfeiture: removing from a large,
struggling hermit crab
its legs; embracing
a horribly receptive
toilet bowl; finding I had lost
one shoe and was leaving
bloody footprints on a white rug:

all of it a pristine
radiance of discontinuity,
most hindering
to concoction.

For it has not escaped me
how there is something willful
about all this sweaty effort
at retrieval, this immoderate concern

for whatever locks itself
into some spasm or frenzy
of the brain by custom given over to
dismal conjuration
of the least moth
of the soul, and in the end

I neither sing nor sigh
but am made morose,
permit to rise
these recollections of
the body's most crude
natural heats,

merely recount here
how it happens, and to
me, and all the time.

Shark

I step into this memory
as if I have come into being a foot from myself,
the road diminishing behind me, and ahead
Marseilles; and I am walking
back from somewhere in late afternoon,

the sea blue as a flax field to my left,
and a hill strangled with vetch
to my right, orange soils
underfoot, and over it all
this same sky, everything

calm, very blue, hot,
the earth soaking up shadows, so that
it is all I can do to keep my own
walking before me into Marseilles
to stretch out at last over the foul

iridescent scums of the harbor,
over the great turnings and scatters of baitfish,
wheelings of fire, the sun
in billions flung back; and then
beneath it all, something

much larger, a slow
closing in from the sea, not mine
but a cloud's shadow, had the sky
not been as I think of it clear;
and the green milky stare of that eye looking up

through all the insane skitter and dash
of the schoolfish into the calm
bright power of the day
where I, having myself
only that moment arrived,

look down through my shadow
into the harbor of Marseilles,
look back; and I breathe
in no hurry at all.

The Harbor

My shadow swims before me
over the dry, fiery soils
until at last it cools itself

on the stone wharves, stretches
over the sea which has crept inshore
to become the harbor,

as its edges golden
with long drifts of pollen, thickening
into wracks and stoneworts,

into the slow mass
of the stone itself,
the land rising behind me

as if the sea had stolidly
heaved itself up
into the long swells of foothills,

mountains, into the whole
cresting ridge of the continent
which breaks to the North, bears

down on me, slowly
ebbs, at my feet
becomes the harbor, swells

and subsides
like breathing.

The Disconnections

When suddenly he took, whom I had sought
in my endless trolling back and forth
off Cape Bianca (froth
of bonito boiling
at sardines on the quarter, brake
and plunge of pelicans, off the bow
the huge cloud shadow
of the manta, the stony sea
shattering on the Santa Helena reefs,
and then the black fin
trailing the rigged *balao*, the cobalt bill
thrusting up from the wake, the line

unclipping from the right
outrigger, running loose)
I waited and struck
into the living shock and weight
of sea and sailfish; and at
the hookbite the sheer silver of him
leaped and leaped, the great fin
for an instant billowing
with purple light; and then

he broke away, the line end writhing
far astern, the big rod
springing back; whereupon
I reeled in and sat
stunned, to imagine his stunned
and panicked seaward flight,
the snapped line snaking
at his flank; and remembered

what in fact had been too brief
in the true light of the afternoon
to have truly recollected
with much in the way of faith, except
for the usual conviction
out of evidence: my hands
loosening on the rod, my heart

giving a little, salt crystals
grainy on my lips, my wondering
how it might have been, this time
to have brought him flaring and wallowing
in iridescences of spray boatside,
wide-gilled and azure, shimmering,
gaffed him in and lashed him down
astern, swathed him in damp sacking
against the sun. And even earlier,

heading out to sea, sighting
along the thread of current
to the oyster wharf diminishing
astern I saw the black girl

standing on a heap
of shells, waving, though not
to me, crumpling
a red hibiscus blossom
in her hand, until

the headland rose
between us; and felt again
the irrupt quickening, my body
urgent to cherish its express
knowledge of loss: girl

with flower, white
and distant flowering of the sea,
the great fish shining
in mid-air, all of it
risen or fallen
to improbable form,

though none of it
in any true or final nature
of the evidence (except perhaps
for the salt which on my tongue remains
a taste I cannot subdue, seem never
to have forgotten).
Days later

and ashore again I take
to cover, and at night
fall into something like sleep
on something like an incandescent sand,
prepared against the dry inclemencies
of loss, worry
the disconnections
in the considerable excess
of my way, consider

what has torn loose from me or breaks away
and then goes on as if
we had never touched and for
the moment caught
and held: I dream
of the bloodshock in the beautiful
pelagic bodies against mine, as if—
at least in the saltless dream as if—
each were required to be taken
as some shining, vigorous extrusion
of the sea. Here,

in the close dream
which the body bears,
out of the whole repertoire
of memory, I sense the slow

movement which conceals itself (headland
rising, the fish
suspended in its leap) and find
that what is small and far way
exhausts my sight (over the sea
which scarcely moves
and even as I say it
becomes more still,
an inclusion of gulls
hovers). And what
of all the congenerate shapes
a body makes most clearly moves
is the shadow of the girl sweeping
the white stone of the wharf from one
side to the other, power
of the circling light by which
I have come to yearn
for all that is pastless
and disjunct (slow

clasp of the strangler fig
shaping itself to the warm bole
of the palm; huge
flowering corpus of the sea
shaping itself
to the bone's
mandrel). Here,

in the dream where all my people are,
stunned valencies loosed
to the toils of the assimilation,
I stand among the white waves
of the stone which root
in the vacuoles of the graves
and bloom with oleander
and hibiscus. Here I breathe

the salt air of the slow season,
which of what might be
exhausts only the part,
and call on myself again to dream
on this ten-thousandth night without
amendment, to make of it all again
the generosity beyond the need,
extend without correction

the vision: how it might be
that in the end we come together, red
flower, fish and girl, volume
of our being here embraced,
and all that stood between us
in the dazzling, translucid sea-light,
union of particles
beyond all series, never
so light as then, the earth
closed on itself and
centered, gravid
with bodies, trembling
to give birth.

Port Cities

1

On midwatch, seeing by night vision
in the red light of the bridge,
the carrier steaming through the darkness
at dead center on my scope,
the slow sweep trailing the green
fading fluorescence of headlands
behind it. And there is nothing

I can see by staring out
into that unreceptive and un-
tongued night *out there,* those
crashes of head-on water
at the bows, crestings
astern, only the slight
hiss and phosphorescences of wake;
but mostly darknesses
of sea and sky, though there

on the scope is the bright
proof of France, say, or
Gibraltar, the soft landshadow
curling itself around the green dazzle
at the heart of the compass rose.

2

I feel the earth rising
beneath the sea, the sea itself
rising, the ship giving itself
upward, and the sky bearing down
onto the chill, red-lighted bridge.

I make it out as best I can:
I watched then from the red light of the bridge
out into the darkness, willing
by a greater outright substance of desire
than I have ever known
for light to come.
To remember this
is to undertake as I have done
this measure,
this fixed distance from the center
around which the green
translucencies of after-image
persist, but wider
than reality, so that the true
bearing lies always
at their centers.
And it is after all

not so far behind me as I feared
when I thought to fear it,
seeing how today, in Vermont,
sitting outside my house
in broad daylight in the green shade
of the big California poplar,
watching Ray Fontaine plow up
his meadow, yellow
bursts of dandelions, blue
windstreaks of the cornflowers, white
foam of Queen Anne's Lace
borne down by the plow blade
into blue earth,

it so readily persists, nothing
in it of the landbound spill
of yellow light over the hay meadow,
the wavering of dry heat
along the road,
or the circle of shadow under
the silvery shaking poplar leaves,

but given to rise to twenty-five years
and six thousand miles later and away
by no clear power of the sea (though once
this was the sea) *and everything*
wrong for it: the planet dry
and steady beneath me, the air
heavy with the smell of turned
soil and cows and tractor fumes
this silvery light, myself even
wrong for it, and yet
having it stir there, that hitch
at heart, that joy
in those cities in the washed mornings
rising before me from the bellies of the green seas,
at true bearing
in the eye of the alidade,
and still, and powerfully sleeping.

3

In those mornings came the headlands,
then Lisbon, Barcelona, Marseilles,
first pale light on the hilltops, the tops
of trees, tall
buildings, some slight
heave to the deck, perhaps, the screws

idling, the turquoise upheaval of the wake
impossibly straight
to far out from where in the night
we had begun our slow
run in towards the lights of those cities
burning deep beneath the horizon, but ready
to rise like stars as we rode in
upon them; and the green harbors
curling away to each side
of the cutwater, like the soft
turning of sod.

4

After the necessary darknesses,
in the joyous instant of the recognition,
when the sun has at last risen
beyond the last possibility of light
truly suited to the eye,

when I am alone, the long
radiant streets narrowing away from me
in all directions, the currents
of the night roaring
far overhead,
in the long power of the long reflectionless day,

even here in Vermont, far from the sea,
I try imagining at the round heart of the earth
which bears the great cities,
a green like meadow grass, like the shadows
beneath the pines; or that I am walking
down streets where, in the first of the morning,
having just arrived from the sea,
I am alone, the only one for hours
to take a breath or to watch
the bright sweep of the sky. At night
by the red light I imagine,
I try remembering the names of the trees
and flowers of those cities. At night
I wonder why it should be

we double in this manner on ourselves,
arrive from seaward, believing in the land
we have never seen before,
wishing for all the cities of the world
to rise before us like stars,
for the earth from which they rise
to lighten itself, become
one huge translucency, to free
the huge coil of its single root
to that recollection of light
which is our burden.

Poem on My Birthday

"Do you feel, in your heart, that life has turned out as once you expected it?"
—R. P. Warren

1

On those nights when I cannot sleep,
when my wife cries out beside me,
unsettled in sleep,
and I look from the bedroom window, and see
the pale upward-shedding of light
which precedes the moon,

often I permit myself
something in nature of dream,
in which, trying to call out a woman's name,
I whisper merely *you! you!*

And often then my wife,
who is beautiful in sleep,
will stir, open her eyes, turn
towards me so that for a moment I
can imagine her awake, though because

this is in the order of dream,
and because in the dreams which I permit myself,
I permit no voice beyond my own,
she never speaks. *You!*

I cry, and
turn my head on the pillow, change
the dream, see
in the cleft of the orange curtains

the moon rise into a cloud,
which act I choose to take
as a sign, having
no other understanding.

2

The moon trembles and hesitates
in the low clouds near the peak.
As usual the light
is arriving with difficulty.
Still, I wait, and patiently;
beside me my wife—
most resembling what most
I have understood myself
to wish to love—

is herself dreaming of light,
though a greater urgency of it,
as in the whole shimmering upwards

of a day, the bright
shrub of the sun
shimmering upwards
from the sea

3

On those nights when I cannot sleep,
the moon slowly discloses itself to me;
and waiting for the full grace of its light,
I must trust my eye to see
over the dark belly of what

I have taken to be the world,
never ceasing to believe
that with the moon risen
the whole round light of the sky
will suddenly become
what suddenly I know myself
to have always believed in
as the sky

4

Do I feel in my heart
that life has turned out
as once I expected it?
May I speak
into the sky? Is the sky
any less or more
silent than the cold air
of these rooms of this
old house which surrounds
this bed in which I am
awake in which
some people must
have died? and if

I speak into the general silences
as I have spoken and it
has been permitted; and if
I may ask what it is that is spoken
by the river among the boulders
at its edges, expecting
neither myself nor the river nor anyone
to answer, why then

may I not without awkwardness
address myself
to the bright stone
of the moon? And do,
for that is the need
as I have taken it to be:

Moon, I see you there,
just risen, just
free of the mountain,
just free of the unsettled
stone of the peak,
to which you have lent
some little light.

5

The moon, having risen,
is about to set.
How cool the moonlight, how decorously it drifts
in the high feathery ridges
of the pines, how it snows
down onto the fields
and the yards!
By moonlight

came here for the first time
to this place and have not left.
By moonlight once
walked clear down Ripton Mountain
out to find
my wife, who had
not left, though
wanted to; by moonlight faced

then as now into my own most
unbecoming neither
warm nor generous
desire. Truth is, O Moon,
I was not up to snuff: ask who I was

I did not offer back, indeed,
drew back from all
the humble and particular
conjunctions: empty
potencies of light, pale shapes
the body makes, though everything

hinges on it! *Moonset:* watch
the shadow draw back
on itself. O silences

I take to be reprisal!

6

White run of the yard
down to the garden,
pale stubble of trees, the sky
scarcely lighter than
the trees, Orion grazing
the horizon, starlings grazing on
so far as I can tell plain ice:
I see the first moon of the new year rise

from out of the pines, swell
coldly into the sky
trailing the torn roots
of its fires; snow dusts
on the cedars and the pines.
In the deepest winter, this far in the year,

what I wish for most is that
the white trees of the spring
might shortly root
in what I find it possible to think of,
even in this season, as
these passionate, these
reasonable soils.

7

In the Beginning, and not
for the first time, the moon
rose and fell, and that was all; except,
it is true, there was the first night

of the first dream, in which
each heard the other call out
to the other. Then, in the morning,
in the full light of the fresh sun,

in all the gorgeous outcry of that light,
neither could recall, both
having kept between them
careless watch. And that

was all, and near
enough the truth
to set it acting.

8

Speak to the Moon: O Moon,
I am grateful my wife sleeps
so that I, openly and without embarrassment,
may speak to you in this other voice,
knowing I cannot be heard
nor persuaded from retrieval. I do

not often now nor much
swell with the old abundancies, the room
is always all but cold enough; sweat
ices over, and the breath between us
whitely blooms. Moon,

I have never made my peace
with distances.

9

I endure the lateness in which the moon
is only just beginning its decline,
in which the snow is just beginning
to display shadows:

so distant before me
that it becomes one darkness
with that beneath the pines
is that last reach of the shape I make
when I stop light.

10

I walk my trail backwards through
the snow all night, circling
back, doubling on myself: and wing-marks
everywhere. When morning comes,

light breaks through the bright
veils of the curtains. I think of this
as I lie here in bed
a whole night sleepless, amazed
that in so cold and bone-lit a regime,
the weather-fear upon me, I
still consent to be led
in the struggle with
the Angel; may, in fact,
be lost; though not, in fact,
so deeply
I will not survive.

11

Beyond height, not
overhead, but simply
out there, light

springs up, the earth swims
in great encircling currents of light.
Until now,
except for the moon circling
and circling this cold
notion of center, it has been
nearly the blackest night ever
to blind me; for the first time
I think it possible
this is a dream I have not made myself.

PART II

Earth Tremor, the Sky at Night

Earth Tremor, the Sky at Night

for Alfa-Betty Olsen

In the smoky light-mix of the sky
above Los Angeles,
over the frond-bursts
of the canyon palms
the night is ready: fog moves in

and I look up to see
what I think are stars,
swollen bodies of saffron light
exceedingly too near,
as it turns out, as always in fact

no more than some bright diffusion
of the literal, this time
streetlights on the far rim of the canyon
seen through fog; not far away
the seabed dives beneath

the raw edge of the continent,
the house shivers, my reflection
doubles in the window,
and I look out, steady myself to see,
and the weather lifts and thins

so that everything out there reveals itself
in all the common logic of display,
that static magnitude of true light
such as the true stars at true
distance dwindle to, such

as the companion body dwindles to
once its weathers clear.

The Fragonard, the Pietà, the Starry Sky

1

I am happiest here on the street,
walking with this woman, my hand on her arm,
the sun bright with forsythia,
the great subterranean waves of the granite
breaking in the park;

but in the galleries, less happy,
less happy in the private light
where she abandons me to stand
on the far side of the room
to see the child Virgin in the early practice
of her art, threading a needle,
the rosy candle suffuse in her fingers,
her face white, shadowless, intent.

2

I am amazed at the brilliance
of the Northern palette,
the alizarins, madders, lakes,
bright in the folds of the saints' robes,
ceruleans clear as shallows
over a white ground.
But not far on,

among the jewels, white stocks,
blacks and umbers of the merchants,
I feel a slow darkening, a roiling
of greens and blues, shadows
taking place.
And before long
I cannot look anywhere

without wanting to bolt
from the bored, black-stockinged whores
on their sallow bed, the rose nipples
of the Polynesian girl, her basket
of scarlet berries,
the convulsed cypress that strains
to the star, the lion ravenous
in the midst of a cold, viridian foliage.
When it is time for me to leave

she walks with me halfway to the doors,
turns back, and I look after her:
small and bright in a blue shirt, climbing
the long stairs,
back to the company of saints.

3

I go out
into the shining street
and stand for a moment at the fountain,
the spray beading on the light hairs of my hands.

And I do not know what to make
of all this joyous, watery display,
seeing I am alone again.
So that when I walk back home
that city becomes the spinning-out
of the shadow from whose foot I grow,
and which persists.

4

I awaken, not knowing I have slept,
and the sun, which all night
was locked in the stone of New York City,
breaks loose, becomes fire,
grows so intense a heart that to look into it
is to go blind in a white dazzle. Then,

little by little,
the sun wearies of this burning and permits
the city to rise and cover it.
And at nightfall I witness this descent of fire,
and the rising of the streets to meet it,

and I feel myself again
at the root of the contorted tree,
at the boundary between the light storm
and the static rock.
And in the night, when it finally comes,
I see how the sun allows the shadow,
and contains it,

and cry out, therefore, impatient
for the star that is hope,
the sunset radiance that is
the body's eagerness.

5

Later, at this achromatic business,
I tell myself it must be that her face
answers to all the names in the world,
that I do not know
how the body should be written,
in what flush or ruddiness,
or how to make the hand
translucent with fire.

I try remembering in which gallery
two cupids, spirits of departed lovers,
embrace in a shattered sarcophagus,
bereft companions fluttering tearfully about,
while the smiling Genius of Love
light the scene with a nuptial torch.
I take it to be

the law of measure that applies,
love's progress, as in the panels of the Fragonard:
on the white fields of the walls
a melee of doves and flowers,
the voices of the youthful lovers,
so fair, so fresh, so likely to endure,
abounding to their pink destruction.

But the one time that my hand
moved to her breast, she turned from me;
and I interrupt myself to consider that,
to break the great quotidian joy of Fragonard,
then to imagine her alone before
the paintings, fixed

by the severities of the *pietà,*
astonished at the blue callosities,
the wounds, the blue body
of the Christ
which nothing of moth and worm
shall have to heritage; above all

desiring to be
of that sheer power of love and grief
as Mary, the Magdalen, the John
who shudder with tears, the black holes
of their mouth raised to the dead Face,
their eyes, hands, arms to one another,
bellowing, lovely, loud with grief
forever into the intractable
white field of the sky *come back!*

Van Gogh Prophesies the Weathers of His Death

One morning I will awaken
from the dream of which I did not see the end
to the visible logic of this sky
clouded and threshing with great stars,
and find myself unable to close my eyes,
staring, helpless, into the slow,
opening heart of the sun. And then
as the terrible light widens
and comes finally to bloom
in the fiery shades of the cypresses,
it will seem to me the young trees are moving,
as if to a light wind.

Or it may be
that one night, alone
in the spaces of the house my body makes,
the last partition of the heart attained, and all
the clocks gone out,
I call out, and am not heard,
and wait for a little, and then call out again,
in no despair, thinking I see the moon
move in the radiant clouds which are
the cypresses. And for a time, at least,
at least for the measure of this time,

I do not die, I am not
entirely unhappy, thinking
into the enormous roar and uprush of the light,
the dream of light that has possessed the work,
how nothing has troubled

the beauty of the world, not
the bare eye of the night
nor the eye's first gathering,
not the first rising of the breath,
nor the last,
not even the dream without color

on which my eyes will close,
for which I have this long time
prepared myself, whispering
into my dry teeth, moved
to the strangeness: how
after all the turbulent fluidities of fire
I have seen the sky to be,

it should have been
the one thing most like light, the way
the slim branches of the young trees,
themselves nothing like light,
with the wind among them turned and brightened.

Mahler Waiting

I wait at noon in the summer house
at Maiernigg, the distant
voices of children unbearable,
the scraping together of oak leaves, a dog
which has been barking
for hours. That is all. I am

exhausted. *Dear wife, I have not been*
alone! The afternoon
is exhausted: piano salesmen
bawling over the fences, Wagner
struggling with his coat; Burckhardt,
who assured me that one morning
his eyes would stay shut, and then
he would forever be blind; Schoenberg,
riddler; Pfitzner, your particular
fool; and Wolf, who is dead

in that dead silence that follows
the stroke on the muffled
drum; finally, the child
who is dead, and whose name
I will not speak *(how night descends*
to smother even the holiest
of days!) When I consider how
once I believed in the blue
flower, the indeterminate
desire; how I wished
that every man might know

by what intent I spoke
to him; how I imagined
that in the end I should have waited out
this air, cold with the coppery smell
of zinnias—dear wife, when I am dead
I will call back to you
now the danger is past! Now

I spend a quiet afternoon.
I am almost well again. I eat
with appetite. I mean to be
in perfect health. But the silence
of this afternoon is an
intolerable thing, when I
consider how by any measure *(breath,*
eyeblink, heartbeat) I hurtle in
the vast, stellar agitations, by my small
weight the very planet
perfected in orbit. And I

imagine what might be its sudden
catastrophic lurch at my least
miscalculation, shift of weight: the clashing
of boulders, trees battering one
another, floods, tornadoes, the fires
bellowing outward
from the deep heart of the world!
I want to cry out
Mozart! Mozart! as if it were

already the end. Soon enough
I will hear the footsteps
of the servant who brings me tea,
her stertorous
breathing. This place
is high on the hillside,
over the house. I look down

through oak-leaves
at the roof. Sometimes it seems to me
I am falling: for all my vigilance
I am never clear how it begins,

I never know
if I have stumbled, been pushed, leaped.
There is not much more
to say: it begins with falling,

the calling-out in mid-air, the cool
choice of stance: flight, or the posture
that will drive the thighbones up
into the heart. In this vision
I am waiting for the bright explosion
which never comes. Well, dear wife, however
Death and Genius arrogate my hand,
it is time.

I watch my fingers smoothing
the white cloth, the table
is perfectly laid, everything in high
order: the knives
gleaming, the hard,
cold bellies of spoons, everything
fixed in utter place.

For Mozart, from the Beginning

for T. Alan Broughton

So magnified with new light
as to have become estranged
from the simple work, the song
continues itself. And since

from the blue radiance of the beginning
it rose into these minor volumes of the light
the greater we dream of
must from the beginning have contained;

and since the implacable light of the new sun
shone down upon the earth in which everything
was true, since then—
in the line of those few

who, seeing clearly by this light
have been somehow informed to choose
to love us and we have perhaps
loved back—there has been this one

to whom we might, with something
like the ease of instinct, speaking with something
like joy and in the fullness
of praise, have found it possible

to have cried aloud, but did not, that he
is indeed and always loved, who,
against all amulet and recipe, against
the cold gratuities of the subjectless,

seized in the real and made to flash forth
the mute transparencies
of matter, continued
the Creation, his heart so new,

boundless and unaltered, so
inhabited by beatitude,
as to have occasioned us to rise
from the region of dissemblance toward one

another; and this despite
the effronteries of the disparate
body, sad goiter
of the other, because

his heart, and precisely by power
of the disaccord, from the first
instant of the first
spasm of light, prime turbulence, chord

of the Beginning, intent
on the immaculate bond of the ensemble, free
to cherish the light, beat, measured itself
and never otherwise gave voice

to the gorgeous numbers
of the increate sensation,
the disinterested poetry
of the source.

Vivaldi in Early Fall

O this is what it is to be
Vivaldi, in September, in my
seventy-fourth year, the pines
just beginning to sing
on the hillside, the rivers
coloring with the first rains
(which are, as usual, precisely
on time). And there is also

this young girl, who, each year,
I bring into my mind,
making it to be that if she knew
by what measure I considered her,
she would turn and look at me and smile,
thinking, "It is the priest again,
the one with red hair, who is said
to make music, and who—as every year—
has gone a little sweetly crazy,
and I think he may love how I am today
in my blue dress." And she
is right. In September I am moved
to the melancholy theme: I like to make the cello
sing with the pines, be on the verge
of the thunderously sad. And, as always,
at this time I would like to make the melody

go on forever, but cannot, being cursed
to disdain my narrow lusts
and sorrows. I have never said
that with me an innocent angel
is alone at work: it may be

I exercise the murderous grace.
But in September, the face of God
passes through my walls to show me
how the motion of song sleeps
at the center of the world, as indeed,
among the Angels, innocent of time. I hear

at this time every year the voice that loves me
crying out *return, return!* and I do, I round
on the beginning in full belief:
and the girl is gone, never having breathed
as I breathe, in the weary
exactitude of matter. The song
stops at the certain moment
of its growth. It is the truth of me, not any lie
that I imagine, and I
can do nothing with it. Still,

it is autumn, and over the whole world
the air resumes its liveliness; and I,
Vivaldi, possessed of love and confidence
in measure wonderful to me, I seek
to magnify the text: *viola, bassoon, cello,*
it is as if the trees have broken into song,
and the song roots, blossoms, thrusts
deep toward the still center, overspreads
the sky like a million breathing leaves.

From

THE SEASONS
IN VERMONT

(TAMARACK PRESS, 1982)

In March

In March I begin to think
of the difficult accumulation of days,
the difficult orders
of their accumulation,

and of the gorgeous, ambiguous trashes
of the world, none of them ever more
than the simple work itself, or less;

and of such as myself, more attentive than most,
perhaps, but never more than is owing, or so
I try to think, aware always

how this day, *this one,* moves out
from itself into the moving next
and next instant of resolution, the white

spin of the sun beginning its pitch down
to the next day, next and next
of the fiery awakenings, the helpless resurrections.

Morning Poem

In eleven years I shall be older than my mother
when she died. I shall have lived
out what at the time I did not think

could be more than a short draw of the breath,
having seen her body so sprawl with cold
as to be matter for terror,

the light that morning when I awoke
not knowing she was dead, uncentered
and spilling over the sharp lip of the mountain

as if it had arisen at once from the whole
cold circumference of the horizon,
the smoke from the damped morning fire

drifting down along the rusty channel of flashing
between roof and gable, the lawns gently steaming
in the first days of March, and shortly the wind rising,

the world becoming raucous with wind, though for the moment
it was still, only the lovely voices of the white pines on the hill,
a bright muddle of clouds *(however unreasonably*

I wish to cry out this one last time
against the sky that day, that dumb, that stolid light).

Garden

In May arrives a thin, delicate atmosphere
of willows, and much that contrives
to convince the voice

of itself, in early June
a briefness of warm rains,
in July a dimness among the flower stems.

In August spring open the orange bells
of the squash blossoms,
and on the far side of the garden

one pallid tendril of cucumber vine
wavers up from the yellow chop of mustard bloom
like the last gesture of something going under,

which is how, against all understanding,
I choose to understand it.

Autumn Poem

"One cannot ask loneliness how or where it starts."
—Priest Jakuren

Under the pines the first rusty needles
scatter about the sand like the tracks
of large and fragile birds. Already
the star moss carpeting the birch grove
has drawn back into itself, begun the withering
into its tiny straw: how have we learned

to live in this place in which the flaming outward
is the flaming back? From deep in the woods
we smell the souring of oak leaves,
from deeper yet the rankness of hickory.
We give way to the changes: everything turns
from the minor hues, ourselves as well,

bearers of an unseasonable color
which blooms inward upon a nakedness of limb
from which there is no turning. In autumn
night comes with a silky darkness
deeper than that in the lily's throat.
It is the lightlessness that in the youth of autumn
displays itself as light
in the trees and grasses.
And though we cannot often ask loneliness
how or where it starts,
how else shall we understand
and celebrate these changes?
In this season we may ask.

The Colors of October

Woodbine, precisely pulp
of nectarine; the open, milty pod of milkweed; peach
and melon of the young birches
of the fence line; aqua and salmon, the lake
seen through the fringes of sumac
and alder; bittersweet like little
orange clusters of roe; vermilion
of shadbush, dull lime

of the poplar leaf, the willow
faintly dusted with silver, powdery bronze
of the beeches—and against all this
the pines, faintly rust,
green deepening of shadows underneath
the pines; the hill
slowly baring itself, glint
of schist, light caught
in the flecks of mica, the road
paling with frost, the russet ears
of the ripe Sudan grass grainy

with rime, long thread of the fog
along the river, the hill writhing
with fog, huge
scarlet display of the sun, by each vein, leaf, branch
of maple magnified, from the icy heart of each tree
hurled back upon its own heart swelling with that light
as if a greater tree had somehow in the near sky
taken root and its radiant canopy and crown,
in an instant fully risen,
were to blaze overhead, as if it were the sun.

Shaggymanes

Late October is suddenly bright
with the caps of shaggymanes
poking up everywhere through the Armory lawn
where for twenty years we have come
to harvest them,
so many clumped under the rusty belly of the Sherman
where the grass is never cut
that we leave hundreds
to the slow, black liquefaction,

in a few hours each gone soft, each
a slimy subsidence of spores,
the whole body of the thing self-digested,
given over to, collapsed into
the rich dissolution,
into what must resemble, and closely,
the prime and nameless residues,

the first amorphous spawns from which the buried thing
grows out from deeper than where it might be seen,
distending the tender soils,
becoming the esculent body
by which we name and understand the season.

Pilgrimage

In October, on the night of the first killing frost,
I come to the river through the cornfield
above Chapman's Cove. Ahead and out of sight
the Cove's resident bittern croaks,
and what must be the last flight of mallard
flares. I come this year as every year

to leave my footprints in the frost
between the rows of stubble, to watch mists
creep on the water, to startle the night-feeding crows,
to watch the ground fog pour in soft falls
over the lip of the bank to establish

that everywhere at last
has arrived the ineradicable mark of the season.
I walk from my house on the night of the first killing frost
toward the warm river, and through a fog of birches
see the surge of the big current. I love
the sudden commotions of this season
by which I have accustomed myself

to wish to see whatever is rhythmic in event.
The maples of the Winooski begin to drop their leaves,
and the far thread of the current goes crimson,
the pools and eddies churning and frothing
with color. I come as every year I come
to sit on the big rock below the rapids,

wishing to see the plain truth of maples in autumn,
but wholly incapable, finding instead
how exhaustible are the names of color,
as usual finding that the maples of the Winooski
on the far side of the river seem

an impossible clarity of color, a dream
of trees. Later, I step into the warm water
and begin to wade, the river deepening, rising
on my upstream hip, the great down bearing of water
beginning to make itself dangerously felt, and then,
and just in time, past midstream

diminishing, so that I find myself at last safe
in the pale, minnowy shallows, and reach out
and pull myself up by the grey roots of the maples,
seeing at the top of the bank columns of rooted cloud,
in the top layers the orange moon shining through.

And then I turn back, and look out
over the whole dangerous power of the river
which has translated itself into a current of fog,
and I cannot see the far bank,
and I imagine myself standing where I am
until it is dark, afraid to cross back,

staring into the dimming cumuli of trees,
standing where I am until dark, when from the fog
will rise the orange moon, and the trees will shine forth again
as if it were full day, in the last seasonal burst
of the last color for which, on this night
of a killing frost, my breath
visible before me, I cannot
and do not wish to find a name.

Damp Rot

Water sheets on the old stone of the cellar walls,
trickles out over the floor into little deltas of mud,
worse every year, so that now I can see daylight
at the footings, and upstairs the floors sometimes
tremble and the clothes go damp in the closets. And sometimes
I think the whole place is about to come down, and have begun

to dream at night of moving, unaccountably sad
to think of leaving this house which has possessed me now
for eighteen years, in which one of us has died
and two been born, for all its elegance of detail most everything
not right in it, or long gone bad, nothing
ever done which should have been, one hundred years
and more of water rancid in the cellars, moldings
never finished or else mitered crookedly, all

the small and growing energies of dirt and rot
wherever we care to look, whenever we do.
But I dream also of the pine grove of my planting,
which I know I love and which is the green truth
of this place: ten years ago, in one day,
I dug fourteen small trees, wrapped the roots
in burlap, dragged them down from the top ridge
of the hill, spaced them carefully, watered
them each day for one whole season. Now

they are twenty feet high, thick roots
already at the cellar wall, vigorous and loud
even in little winds (only the hemlock
mournful and reluctant to do much
in the way of increasing itself). But it is clear
that if I do not freely leave this place,
it will leave me—though, as Ray Reynolds says,
digging at a powdery floor joist with his knife,
there may be more here than I think, better
than a two-by-six at least; and his blade slides
two inches in and stops at what he calls
the heartwood, meaning, as I take it, at the wood
which has not yet given way.

Anniversary: A November Poem

How dark it is up here, how cold, the ash and maple turning,
the scarlet clusters of the high bush cranberries
hauling the twigs down, tiny raisins of the fox grapes,
and the brown flower stalks of the monumental rhubarbs
six feet high—not that where I might wish to live

it would be always balmy, flooded
with sun, the hills purely green and the rivers
giving off blue light—only that in such a place nothing
would seem ever to have been utterly given up as,
here in Vermont, in this year in early November,
here beside the grey, thick currents of the Winooski,
a more than ordinarily dank sun brightening the soft scrim
of the fog which veils the willows and alders and surges
with orange light, seeming to have arisen

from the grass or from the red twigs
of the swamp osier, much seems to have been given up,
enough to make me wish to weep that I could have been
so stupidly ignorant of the possibilities of loss
to which, every morning of my life I have,
thinking it or not, dangerously awakened (though only once
to actually touch it, to see with my own hands

the empty body, the blue bruise of the baby's body
wherever its own small weight had borne it down,
wherever the earth through the comforter
had touched on it)—though why

this should come back to me, continue
to come back, I do not know, having thought,
even proclaimed to those, myself
among them, weary of it, that *it*
is finished! that everything
has after all been said, that it is after all common
practice, one tiny stillness among the terrible

many, even measured it
against the Polish fields blooming with bodies,
the sweet grey breath of Auschwitz, the children
of my time squalling and ready, folded
in their fathers' useless arms, taking the rock,
the club, the bullet in their mouths, and found

it wanting; in the balance thought
I had disentangled the cold grief at such clarities
of injustice from the general rage I am accustomed to feel
at all turns of the flesh, or—
in the greater period of the lesser vengeance—
of the world: as in the instance of the brilliant
shadow of November sweeping over me here in Vermont
and blazing crazily among the trees on the hillside behind
the house, a light arisen from the flesh
of the ice-bearing earth, and apart from what I
by birth and reason have undertaken
to understand as light; or

in the waking to such light as this morning
after a killing frost to a golden haze of alder and willow,
the yellow fog swelling up from the river, a bead of frost
burning at the edges of the pane, I have awakened,
thinking in the face of such light *how*

could I not have known? even
in the dark as I lay in my bed
about to sleep, and the child's cry
came and when it came was nothing, nothing, only
the ordinary voice in its unexceptionable lament from some
darkness of this old and powerfully retentive house.

Woodstove

The house fills with the sweet smoke
of apple wood, and I know I should sleep.

But I know that if I do,
fire will rise and roar in the red-hot, dangerous flues,

which notion I fear
as I fear what lies at the heart of this place

and works its slow way out, something
materially hid, from which,

at the opening edges of the lawn,
the snow rises.

The Cold in This Place

In April I come to the cellar holes—
gray snow rotting away in the north corners,
ground water trickling in and freezing
into a thin glaze on the free stone, the rubble
of the woods all around, pale tendrils
of pine root prying the walls—

and cannot think why they should have settled here
in the hills around Lincoln, onto the farms
dead before ever they cleared them, in the dark
pockets of these hills, no roads
to anywhere, even at the heart of summer the earth
dense and ringing as iron, the forest

forever creeping into the little fields, and then,
as they knew it would, the cold rising
and flowering on their windows, each winter seeming
never to have been before, beyond cold even,
as if the fires had never burned outward, nor water
come together into rivers, become lakes, the warm sea

blooming with weeds and grasses and lilies, nor the blood
risen to morning as ice on the cellar walls
rose with the deepening season, each morning at dawn
the sun shattered into
rosy flakes of cloud, and the fields
pink and salmon between them and the bitter
mountains. Nights they must have awakened and slept

and awakened to the pulse of their windy chimneys
and in the mornings, as if they had heard their names called
and there were no choice in it, must have walked
down through the layered cold into their houses,
as if they were to enter the sea—the air, as if it were the cold sea
closing over their heads—and they

might swim up through it, holding their breath,
staring into the clouds of their own breath
trailing up, trapped and gathered
in the teeth and hollows of the green underside
of ice, though, as they well knew,
no more than the green ceilings of their own rooms,

the sweet potatoes, grape ivies, geraniums
no more than themselves, after all, all named and calm
and rooted hard in their small dry soils, their backs
hard against the sky white beyond the windows,
and the stoves ready for fire and the wood
ready to be burned. And what they made of it they called

the weather-fear—that cold in themselves
which demonstrated itself without reference, all that was cold
outside themselves, that knowledge of ice
and the general shadow of ice
rising—which I myself have felt,
sensing some torrent of generation at work

in the icy spaces of the world, so that should it be
I have on occasion called my own name into some particular
and bitter morning of this place, awakening
myself, causing myself to rise and walk down
into the cold house, it has never been
that I have expected myself to answer with anything

like the warm truth, hearing my name, being unsure
of who has called or might have named me,
coldly entertaining the thought
of what might to my warmth and profit be retrieved
from that which is hostage to memory,
and dream of ice and the shadow of ice rising

everywhere, and all
the generations caught there, the frozen
beads of our breaths spirally expanding
upward, the sun shining down
through the miles and miles
of green atmospheres of ice, spreading

and thinning, absorbed
into the greater light
which in the end the ice becomes
and which from the cold beginnings
has spent itself outward to this place.

From

WEATHER-FEAR

(UNIVERSITY OF GEORGIA PRESS, 1983)

The rain of matter upon sense
Destroys me momently . . .

—Yvor Winters

The Word "... *Love?*" Spoken to the Fifth Floor

The word "... *love?*" spoken
as if it were a question drifts in,
and I rush to the window, and look down, and see
a woman talking with a man. And two hours later
they are still there, though now
drenched in the shadow of the building,

no more than voices rising from five stories down,
nothing distorted in them, only
the one word the first time it was said,
perhaps said the one time only,
as is common. I look across
to where the treetops interrupt the sky,

and smell, even at this height,
mimosa; and turning from the window
think at first I have been given this word
as if in some vulgar set-up (as if,
balanced on a door which I open
onto a party of strangers who have

for no reason I have understood invited me,
a bucket trembles and water thrills)—
But then the word comes to me
as it might have risen in the first
warm exhalation of the world

into the continuing and particular clouds,
bird-bearing trees, the pink light of Atlanta
growing in the sky, the sky shattered
into the spaces between leaves,
day nearly gone, thunder rising, the first rush of the rain
against the screen, the voices of strangers rising

into the evening sky,
myself listening, ready to answer,
foolishly to shout down into the fragrant silences,
but holding back, listening, in the end
trying again to make out the word,
its minor and polite interrogation.

In the Palais Royale Ballroom in 1948

Just at the end of the first set I step out
in my white tux, my white shoes
onto the sequined dais at center,
into a golden spot, another focused overhead

onto the spinning, mirrored ball,
spills and whirls of gold light everywhere,
like stars, like comets hurtling across
the blue cloth ceiling of the Palais Royale Ballroom

in South Bend. And I wait,
Kenton and the boys riffing quietly behind me,
Milt Bernhart disconsolate among the trombones,
June Christie waiting, even June, for this

is mine to do alone, and everyone
knows it; and everyone
is waiting. And then
I see out there beyond the light

the dancers begin to take notice, to turn,
to gather themselves into a circle around me,
arms linked, swaying, others, little
eager knots of them, hurrying to get back,

the word having spread, even
unto the streets. And they gather around me and wait,
knowing what is to come, the air growing dense
with the fragrances of gardenias, carnations,

the light that is like stars and comets
careening over the ceiling of the Palais Royale Ballroom.
They wait, and suddenly I raise to my lips
the red-gold Olds trombone,

and hit high G so clean, so sweet, so un-
endurably sustained, that the girls
I am remembering myself to have loved beyond desire
go faint with desire,

and the song is "Summertime," and I am alone with it,
and play it out, drive through
to the last sweet resolution of the last phrase.
And then, my solo finished, the great band

riding it out behind me, the song diminishing
forever into the sky beyond the starry sky
which was the ceiling of the Palais Royale Ballroom in 1948,
my lips still numb from the embouchure, I think of it

as if in fact it might have been,
as if those dancers to whom too late and far too late
I have thought to offer this as a memory
might truly have gathered themselves around

and have remembered such a thing: the song
in its starry, high, unlikely register,
the surging of their bodies to that song:
that fragrance of light again.

Invitation to the Class of '52

The letter lugubriously reads:
"To My Fellow Classmates, Class of '52:
We should all have enough years
for ten of these five-year reunions,
so in addition to the one that's coming up
we should have five of them left, and this one,
I suppose is just as important
as the last one, and probably
more important than the next."—

And it includes
a list of my classmates
of the Class of '52,
some thirty of them *"Deceased,"*
what the Class Secretary calls
"final and indiscriminate deaths."
Thus does life open itself
to the general continuities:
thus do I see

the name of *Bud Butler,* who died in Korea
in that first winter, listed
as if it had happened yesterday,
the only one of all of them
I seem to have known, in the sense
that I remember his face, and not
one other. And the day
is a perfect one for opening
such mail, having begun

with my awakening to the sound
of what I took to be the Montreal freight,

and then becoming aware that it did not
diminish as it ought to the North,
but continued to hold
until I realized it was the wind, and looked out
to see the pines on the hill bent east
and the yard in a thin, rivering dust of snow
blowing and eddying in little knee-high clouds
as if the flesh of the world
were being worried away . . .
Wallace Butler, dead in the Korean snow,

nor did I know him well, however it may seem,
speaking here as if I had loved him and have thought
of little else these years except his death,
and inconsolable at his and all those deaths,
those lists of men I may have known or may never have known,
in the event do not remember, not one,

only their names, their bodies falling back
into what I have dulled myself into speaking of
as "darkness," into the lightlessness
I have called "being blind." I ask
what is the name? and at once
it comes to me, it is sustained,
and I am grieved and struck at that,
Butler, Brezas, Klein, McKenna, all the rest
whom in that place I encountered and was changed

forever by and cannot be unchanged,
knowing that once I knew them and that something
has intervened, myself dismembered
beyond recall.

I am dizzy with the weathers of this place;
this morning in the deep middle of April,
the world outside a fluency of snow,
I find myself caught
in lively recollection of the dead, whose names I keep,
their passionate soils,
the atmospheres they breathe.
If there were any thought of their answering,
I would say: *what do you remember? But the wind*

flies in the face of my purpose—perfectly inflectionless
monotone about the house, holding the trees
bent sharply down, blowing the slight breath I am breathing
back on itself as if all the force of love and rage and loneliness
expended all these years had borne itself
upward into the physical torrent of this April wind
and circled the earth and circled and descended
at this moment to meet me
who has given and sustained it, blood

of battle in open field, my own breath met
and resumed, all the names spoken
in all these years resumed,
quite, as in its remote wisdom, the letter
advises us, the final
and indiscriminate survivors,
that there are only so many reunions
possible, and this is one of them.

Interlachen

1

We stand in the high loft of the barn
and look down into the pen where the last bull,
kept because "there's always been a bull
around the place," is dying, waiting it out,
down on his side on the concrete
still wet from the morning's hosing-down.
He dozes in a corner of the stall,
and though I call and pelt him with an apple core
he doesn't look up or notice me. Outside

the hired men are pumping out
the liquid manure pits, and the air is rich,
"Could sprout leaves on a fence post,"
the farmer tells us, "grow apples on a line pole!"
We walk back from the barn, and at the house
two hundred yards down the road find that the wind
is our way and the barn smell has pooled
in the cellar and blows up through the ducts
when the furnace cuts in. But it's October,
and not too warm for a fire, and so

I bring three logs in from the bottom
of last year's pile, already white
with the first scales of oyster mushrooms,
the last fruiting body of the year
which will go on until deep winter freezing

and unfreezing and between frosts
growing—going on like that
until spring as if nothing in the world
were cold enough to stop it. The barn smell
deepens: I taste it when I breathe.

2

The milk truck is rumbling down Fay's Lane,
and the whole house shakes. Little drifts of dust
shake down from the plaster ceilings
and the window bottles are set to rattling.
I go out, cross the back field, wade the ditch
and start up the hill. I don't love
the silences of such mornings as this
which has begun with my looking at something
not wholly alive. I climb through the sand
of the old Champlain Sea, the Winooski Delta,
watching as always for bones, stems of sea lilies,
brachiopods, this morning finding nothing, kicking
into the clear strata of the ancient sea beds and come at last
to the high clearing at the crown of Bean Hill
where it's cold, even in the sun.
There's a great trampling of the tall grasses

where deer have bedded overnight, a stand
of seedling hemlock browsed almost to death
during the times of the deepest snows.
And except for this small evidence of breath
it's dead calm. I look down on house and barn,
on one rutted length of the frost-heaved road.
The clearing spills from my feet down to the road,
to the huge ribbed roof of the barn, in carpets

of wild marjoram, bee flowers, one blue smudge
of wild asters at the far side, a purple tangle
of cow vetch, small foams and sprays
of pearly everlasting, that definite flower.
The cows are in the feeding alleys, haze gathers
in the pastures, even the air goes milky,
and fog laps at the clearing. But when, as now,

I am most attentive, when I have suppressed
to its least possibility my breath
and think I am about at last to hear
whatever it is that at the heart of such stillness
cannot be still, from utter windlessness
wind stirs in the tops of the big pines. It is
the renewable voice of this place. A breath arises
and everything which all night has not moved, moves.
The wind forks, roots, rejoins,

currents and eddies, the pines tremble and blur
to a green cloud overhead, the wind rises
even more, the air flashes, the tall grasses
of the clearing all at once bend sharply, are beaten flat,
and the light rises and begins to sing as if it were
a wind, the pines the whole time threshing away
with a sound like surf, the white chop
of the ground fog pounding at the hill. After a time

I walk back down, wade the field through knee-deep
shallows of fog, all around me a hatching of light,
thin atmospheres of something like ice or salt
catching a late sun, as if clouds
of small golden fish were swirling on the common
heartbeat of the school. Otherwise
nothing declares itself.

3

I hear what I take to be the bull
moaning from his stall, though the barn
is too far off for that. I think of him
down by his own weight on the wet concrete,
forelegs twisted under, flies rising and settling
on his muzzle. He's dying, he's the last
of his kind ever to die on that farm. All night

the chained dogs barked in absolute
maniacal meter and didn't stop
until dawn. Some in the woods ranged free
chasing deer, belling in long chords,
but at sunrise quieted. Around here
this time of year it darkens early.
Then at four am the barn breaks into light
throbs and hums with the turning

of the big silage augers, vacuum pumps, blowers.
The dog dances out to meet me, bearing
a calf's foot from the barn dump, severed
at the dewclaw, muddy, ragged with hair,
splays and frazzles of tendon showing. He flops
at my feet and begins to gnaw away,
works at the delicate transparent horn
of the hoof, then hides it, finally, behind the lawn chair

on the front porch where in the morning
I find it. My kids come home from having watched
a calving and tell me the culling
of the bull calves has begun,
and all over the neighborhood for days
the feet keep turning up, get dragged behind the lilacs
by the dogs, to be raked out next spring, stumbled
over on the lawns, snagged
with a handful of weeds. By five

the cows are out of the milking parlors,
and the bucket loader is skimming
a green slick into the pits.

4

The heavy voice of the bull lows from the barn.
At the door I hear the soft, imploring scratch
of the dog's nails, and clearly now
over the roar of the barn machineries the bull's
long bellows, over and over, then silence.
Inside again I close the door, light up
the first wood fire of the year, and outside

the weathers gather. This morning
is cold enough for a month from now. The air,
thick with barn smell, is already heavy
with the thought of snow. I glance from the window
and see that down the road
they're worrying the sling
under the enormous dead weight
of the bull. They hoist him onto
the rendering company's truck,
and later that day the farmer tells me

"No more, that was the last one, hated
to see him go, hated it, we done those cows
for years now with a syringe, though, don't
seem proper, I know, but that's

the way of it. That bull
was named *Paul* after my old man, the thing
he most reminded me of, always wanting
but penned up tight, though never
so tight he couldn't know
what was right out there just
the other side of the wall, so to speak.
It killed 'em both. It'd kill us too."

5

It's October and I'm a child
standing at Interlachen in Indiana
at the priests' farm, and there before me
in hock-deep mud to keep from getting the move
on the novices, the Holstein bull
churns at the green oozes, rounds on himself, hauls loose
one big mucky foot at a time, load of head and horns
borne low, eyes whitely sideways, and charges,
slowly charges the fence, taking what seem minutes
to get there, then bucks and hooks at the four-by-eights
until they groan and give a little . . . and I back off,
afraid, seeing how it is with him, how urgently

he hates me, how for him there is nothing
to hold him back, nothing at all
between us—though in the end
he gives it up, turns back from the fence,
stands lashing his tail at the flies
on his spattered flanks, nuzzles the green mud
as if he's grazing. This was in

one given fall back then, and I have no way
of saying which it was, or when, lacking
even then the names for things. I knew
that spring was the lemony shoot of sourgrass
in the barnside earth, then redbud, dogwood, the air
stained with scent and color for yards around,
then cherry blossoms, then apples, peaches, in the pasture
the white deadly buttons of the amanita.
But at Interlachen I stood shivering

and he watched me, eyes rolled to the whites,
clot of tail hairs, wet nostrils pearly
with slime flaring at my smell, slight
sideways hook of the splintered
horns, forehead matted with flies, flies
at the eye-corners, cloistering the ears, under his tail, buzzing

in the soft maxillae, long drizzle
of hairs at the cock-end, heavy balls
swung nearly to the dew-claws, flanks green
with manure, green cud foam
at the jaw corners, and above all
the low groaning which I took even then

for the recognition. We stood at Interlachen
the fence between us, each watching the other,
and stood thus each fall and spring for six years,
come on one another for a day. He must be
long dead. But once I looked down
from a plane and saw the twin lakes, the barns,
even the empty square of the bull's pen
and the blooming orchards. But then

clouds intervened, but even from that height
it was clear to me where I'd stood
and from around that mud patch Indiana spread
as far as I could imagine, myself
fixed there, the slow emergence, the disclosed
obligation of retrieval, recognition of all
at which I'd looked and which perhaps
looked back at me. Always, whatever the season,

I come musing or dreaming to the green muds
of Interlachen and to the eye
of the watching bull, a small revelation
of place in the night of the inconscient.

6

Not quite awake, I'm fearful of awakening,
the sheets at my neck, and outside
something like a heavy rain, and at the fading
edges of the dream nothing
I can put a name to. I'm aware
that all night downstairs books
have flown about the rooms, the rugs
rumpled, tables slid across the floors,
and dust devils whirled around
the kitchen, and all of this dreaming

is less to be feared
than on any morning after the dream
having to rise to walk downstairs
into the orderly rooms below
where everything has the whole night
not smoothly reposed. I think I hear

over the power of rain
the voices of bulls, at first
long and mournful, then raging,
and I feel their eyes upon me, set straight
at mine, and I turn on them and meet them blank
with fear and the moment I do they ease around
and disappear but then in an instant
I hear them behind me coming

full tilt, and then feel the horn
catch in the thick muscle of my thigh
and I crumple beneath the rank weight
and bristle of them, taste
my own blood drip back
into my face, die
to the sound of their bellowing
into the stupid fires of the sky.

7

Nightly this is the dream: rain
and the great moaning of bulls,
and I look up into the arrogant straight-on animal stare
of the sky, the snow hissing
about my feet, the trees
writhing on the hill. But I
am not cold. I do not wish
in this dream for the world

to end. I do not wish
for more or less light.
I do not wish for this place
to be purified of the breath
I am breathing. It is a fearful
isolation, but it is in
the clear grammar of possibility.
Then at last the day regathers and the world roars out
with the rich, inextricable mix
of all the breathing of all the breaths
of the bull-voiced night and the pines
groan and my scarf whips up
over my face and into the ragged edges of this dream
a loud confusion of sun, apples, snow, blood
begins to crawl. And I awaken
to the orange curtains transparent
with sunlight, and grosbeaks
in the lilac bush outside the window.
By this dream I am made watchful. In it the name

none of us has ever clearly heard,
which we lose each night together with the dream,
is spoken, which, if we knew and could speak it,
would call those we have loved who have died
back to us, would turn them back
with God behind them holding out His hands,
abandoned to the terrible first consequence

of loneliness, the silence between us
once for all affirmed. And in whatever might constitute
the pardon there would come down
in a fragile rain the whole matter of all
we have ever loved, the whole fiery blade of space,
ten billions of suns suddenly blossoming
small and cool as snowdrops
on the opening graves of Vermont, and Vermont
shimmering with the blue, delicate membrane
of the fallen sky; and above us all the empty radiance,
the mantle of the forsaken voice calling *come back come back*
as if that were our name, as if calling out the name
we had all of us forgotten, had until that very instant
not remembered as proper to our hearts.
But everywhere outside there is merely

the dense quiet of October rain,
and a cool rising of pines on the hill.
What will come of it? I look back
through the thick drift of time
and it seems all to have been gathering
and regathering to this:
the world a fragrance of snow and apples,
the voices of the bulls, the bulls dying
or raging, trapped and struggling
in the green muds, myself
in the fearful instant of wondering

why his hooves had not rotted clean away
when he stood there in his pen on raw stumps of bone,
perhaps the whole time rooted in that rich soup
of blood, water, manure and earth,
the great body seeming as if arrested
seconds after an unimaginable explosion, the eye stunned
and white at center, and from the center
everything flung out in a huge projectile matter,

suddenly stopped or moving so slowly
as to seem no longer to move, or to have come
about and begun to storm back
on the center, everything about to readhere,
become the original, rich conglomerate,
the body of the eye at dead center,
the wild, white-rimmed eye of the bull
that bulges back still, the longing surge
of that eye—it seems

about to be in the way of a naming, except
that what might be spoken outright in such a place
would seem instantly untrue. The bull
still struggles in the green muds; he seems the earth
borne upward half into an ornate,
outraged flesh, hurling itself
at the barriers, frantic to get at us.

From CARDINALS IN THE ICE AGE

(GRAYWOLF PRESS, 1987)

To Vincent Engels,

companion on the stream, intimate to the ways
of trouts and salmons, prophet of E. Subvaria,
bookman, poet, journalist, historian,
uncle, father, and extraordinary
friend of a lifetime:

this book, with love

A Watercolor

The paper was too wet—the colors ran.
Greens went olive; blues turned flat
in ways I'd not intended. Blacks and browns
bloomed in little soft rosettes

which bled into the lesser densities of hue;
for lofty in the hierarchies of my error
there stood great readiness to let
water do the work; nor had I learned

to love transparency, nor yet
to hold the paper's whiteness
in correct regard—therefore
such failed renderings: dull trees around

a cloudy pond. I turned away the better to see out
over the field to where the woods should be.
The woods were night-ridden, though a voice
rose at the field's farther edge,

something like a rush of leaves.
It was too dark to see, but when I turned
the air shone for a second where my hand
had rested, then transformed itself

into a membrane of green fire that traced
my moving arm . . . so for a time
I paced, gesturing about the room
to see complexly flare and fail the light

though soon enough I tired
and came again to the window, wanting air.

—at Breadloaf, 1960

Apple Trees

Among the cherry saplings in the spring
I see the lichenous dry trunk
of the wild Spy, its one-limbed

blossoming. Then, in fall,
the McIntosh turns black of leaf
after one thin bearing of a dozen fruits,

and I am obliged to fell it. But in May
it springs up in a hairy vigor of new shoots,
and I cut them back, and they

leap up again, and again, which I admire—
though I know you will be bound to say
how neither the dying back nor the splendid

rising from the dry wood is more
than merely the dumb way of things;
which I, bound long in the orders of Desire,

will say I have understood.

Foote Brook

for David and Roger

At the foot of the slope down which
we faltered, the night roared, the brook
being in full spate. Unbalancing,
we leaned into pliancies of birch,

caught ourselves against
pitchy hemlocks. Then,
before we had expected it,
we breathed spray—

we were almost there. Because the moon
had excited to light the edge of a cloud,
the brook at the falls leaped for an instant
with radiance—though elsewhere

light did not abound, nor could we
at that moment have said
night had by ordinary canon come
upon us. The brook was no more

than a minor brightness, yet its voice
was a powerful spasm of the night,
and the large world everywhere
so bountiful an irregularity of surfaces,

we could scarcely keep our feet.

Sunrise

Throughout the night the sky
had been wild with stars.
Then in the morning came an instant
when the hills sharpened, and grew shadowless,

and the world seemed no casual
enterprise of creation. From beyond the hills
rose soft pillars of light,
until, as if caught by high winds,

they wove and interwove, and became
the bright, close fabric of sky.
Later came a burst of warm rain,
but by sunset the light had cleared,

and at the tip of one needle of the white pine
that shaded the porch, a drop of rainwater
trembled. It was clear
as ice. It contained a fierce,

quivering image of the sun.
The light drew back, and back,
and with no further evidence of breath
the sky was precisely as it had ever been.

Goldfinch

After the goldfinch
had in a spark of panic flown,
the stalk of timothy went on
shivering. Overnight had come wind,

and the world had given way
by half, at least—the trees
nearly bare, the woods admitting
good measure of light.

As for the goldfinch,
nothing remained
except its small impulse
lent the grass, sustained

far longer than one,
moved to consider so small
an evidence of breath,
might rightly have expected.

Orchard

By late afternoon the light
had given way, and the air
cooled. Mists welled
from the warm ditches,

spilled over, and merged.
We drove through the topmost layers
of a growing cloud.
From the doorsills up our house

greeted us, though directly enough
we found the steps and walked
sure-footed in, the rooms
settling a little as we entered—

this after a gilt September day
in celebration of itself
spent picking apples
in the Early Transparent orchard,

the air beneath the young trees
a dust of green light, the apples
a fragrant windfall,
so wherever we looked

there seemed to have occurred
in the grass among the strict
rows an exuberant error
of season, a great yield

of sudden yellow flowers.

The Marshes at Suamico, Wisconsin

At the edge of the marshes the cattails leaped with frogs.
One of us found twined on a sedge twig a tiny green snake,
a vigor of grassy light burning its slow way out,
picked it up, let it coil in his palm,
wave its head, flick its coral tongue—

carried it so for awhile until it grew frightened,
tensed, and gave off for so small a thing
a remarkable high-flavored reek. He flung it away,
and none of us ever could find it again, or another like it,
though we kept on the lookout. Then, deeper,

the marsh smell began, the air clean enough
till we stirred up the mud, slogging through
to the blinds, our trails filling in with a fetid
thickness of oozes, only the pale
swath of bent reeds to show how we'd come.

The lake leached in from beneath; where we walked
was something less earth than water, swelling
with bubbles that burst through the duckweed and cress,
our faces at intervals swept with clean, stony gusts
from the open lake. The mallows were springy

with redwings. Everywhere flashed the green bolts
of dragonflies; snakes and turtles cruised
the channels; feathers of mud braided lakeward. At dawn
came the ducks, the sky awash to the feathery roots
of its undersoils: flocks of mallard and canvasback,

teal that swung in over the blind, or flared
on some sheen of the wind. In the marshes at Suamico,
watchful, we felt the world borne down
by its own abundancies. Wherever we broke
through the pursy earth, there billowed about us a quick

exhalation of soils, a rich, recognizable stink,
while over us there in the dawn shone the bird-ridden sky.

Clearing

One day together walking
careless beneath the refractive canopy
of the October woods,
we were stopped, hurled back

by solid light, our minds,
unready, flung
to the clearing's farther edge.
There we turned,

looked back to see
across a barren of ferns
our empty bodies, lost,
bewildered, sick with ignorance

and fear—but light
had intervened. Up
from the saturate heart of the earth
it sprang and flooded,

rose sulfurous in the living woods.
Everywhere about us bled
the raw, seasonal edges.
There we stood.

Fixing the Furnace

I had been no more
than repairing my old furnace
which was inconstant, and would not,

when most I required it, burn;
for I had anticipated frost,
though the season was yet summery.

And having turned one bolt and pressed
the reset, I lurched back
as without warning the furnace

startled into life,
and by God and uncommon grace—
for I had with ignorance

and the wrong tools approached
the task—from the spy hole
dazzled forth, and white with fire!

Mist

This morning some scarlet maples on the hill
were muted to pink by a mist,
and by that masking of color and the warm air
I was put next to tears,

for which I was unprepared,
being by fall beyond all other seasons
made quick and joyous to note how the blushed
yellows most enlivened the delicate woods,

that the reds and oranges close up
were fragile, dry and brown,
how among the marigolds a foot
above the ground, the frost

had touched and killed, while close
at their roots the earth was warm,
loose-soiled, as summer long.

The Ash Grove in October

October has always seemed
an error of time—who will not argue
that in this place it is the freshest
of the seasons, the loveliest, most

to be loved? Yet in one night
the ash grove deposits its leaves
in a litter of gold about
the grey boles, which sight

startles, this failure of leaves, the perennial
astonishment—though I should know,
and well enough by now,
there is nothing about the ash tree moderate,

gradual, or considered, as with the maple;
or obstinate, as with the oak.
I have learned to expect
that around the middle of October

will occur in a sudden night
the storming of leaves.
This year I see it again in the way
I have never understood,

as if the given day
were to be the last on which
I might perceive such a thing
as the unlit brilliance of ash leaves.

during the time of the failure of leaves,
when it still seems possible
that winter will not come
and the warm hazes of October will lie

forever in great, breatheable fields
about the open-windowed houses
of our neighborhood—in which
it still seems possible

that in a single night the leaves
might burst up from the grass
like a flushed covey of small yellow birds,
and rearrange themselves on the branches,

so that in the morning we would find
our lawns to be shaded again,
yet a brightness beneath
the reawakened, light-feeding trees.

Cardinals in the Ice Age

When Louise called to tell me
a pair of cardinals was at her feeder
and had been around for days,
I was, besides envious, reassured,

not having at my own tray seen
a cardinal in years. I had grown in fact
to fear I might not soon again.
I had thought they must have fled

the growing inclemencies of this place
to somewhere farther south; and it was clear
I had not the strategies to lure them north
again. To me this was in the way of a most

considerable loss. But here were cardinals,
or at least word of them, and any time I chose
I might cross the road and see them for myself;
and yet stayed home, for while it was a short walk,

the day was cold, the road a difficult course
of icy ruts, and they were not my cardinals,
but hers. Besides, was it not enough to know
the birds were back, there in my neighbor's yard,

bright on the vivid snow? I took this
to be rare and necessary evidence that still
some time remained before the first lobes
of the great oncoming ice on its long probe south

awakened the neighborhood one night
to the sounds of our mountains going down,
screech of rock on bedrock, huge
morainal wave of houses, trees and boulders,

and finally the dull moon reflected
from the still face of the ice cliff
looming two miles overhead
into a birdless sky.

Snowy Owl

One day, stopping at the barn, we looked
and simply he was gone, and has not
to the common day of any of ten winters
journeyed back. We recollect

how everywhere about the barn the world
had grown wary, quieted, and hid. But never
did we see him fly or hunt. Never
did his lonely and terrific voice augment

the neighborhood. Though overhead
had squawked and stormed a fury of crows,
he did not move or blink,
but governed there, unflawed in stillness,

except once briefly clashed
the blue hook of his beak. Oh, we
admired that wonder! but he left,
being not indigenous, and starving.

Barking Dog

From down the road and near the landlord's house
his terrible dog, whose fierce and guardian voice
kept us all close upon our boundaries,
warmed up with a few preliminary snarls,

then barked, savage, incurious, and untiring
the whole night: two sharp yelps, a pause,
and then unvarying two more—nor could I sleep.
Therefore, though I disliked at night

to walk through my over-dark and speechless house
where I must pass a room in which lurked
some uncommon terror that once
had come to someone who lived

there in that room, and died; and then to walk
along the cold, light-feeding road;
nevertheless I ventured out
into the dog-voiced night, angry to be afraid,

when just at the corner of our properties
the world fell silent, and a great black dog
charged across the yard. He was silent,
he seemed not tentative, he carried

his head low. Of all the dread forms,
most I dreaded that! Slowly I backed away
afraid to turn, our eyes on one another's, till
I thought I might be safe, and flung about and ran.

Thank God he did not follow, only
all night ranged the bench marks of our yards
and barked, and barked. This happened long ago
when still I was wary of malice, large and small,

convinced, though nothing could I see, that I was seen,
and had not journeyed far in understanding
whichever way I turned was always something
at my back. How was it they who lived

along the landlord's road and in his house
had borne it that long while, that voice
which overwhelmed the world,
strict of measure and extensive of dominion,

and they lived nearer than ever I lived? *Thus
in the large world peace has not yet visited!*
For his voice which troubled me was strong and large,
and carried far, and nothing drowned it out;

for so was set his measure in my head.

Unfocusing on Window, Tree and Light

At first the amethyst vase, then
the screens and moldings blurred.
Dust flecks flared on the window
and dimmed, upon which entered into view

the branches of the black locust
sharp across the drive, the fabric
of leaves and limbs coiled
around burls of light. Next,

darkness against light, then blackness
against color, height, shape of crown, bulk
and density of bole. In early June
appeared the delicate, paired leaves

like fern fronds, then from the long
trailers of white blossoms
a ponderous, streaming scent
gone visible. Later, the flowers became

dry pods. Thorns sprang
in rosettes from every
crotch and joining of branch
and bole. In one of those odd and idle

gestures of reconciliation
I have accustomed myself to make
toward the world I have through God's disfavor
lost, hoping to justify it

in the fullness and perfection
of a single word, I have proposed to myself
the locust tree against the sky,
its thorny branches enclosing light,

to be a figure of loss. Over the years
often and unaccountably I have become
aware of myself moved to forlornness
and have seen it is because

without considering,
with no preparation at all,
I have found the locust sharp in my eye,
so that to spare myself

I have unfocused, and in time
the tree has receded, appeared as if it were
some element of sky, turgid
pattern of cloud or constellate

lightlessness. Just now
I have postured to a friend,
saying how it is (gesturing at the tree)
that I cannot with certainty name

nor even wholly acknowledge what I see.
But she has gone,
and holding at shorter and more proper focus
I add the event to the list of those

that this week at the oddest of times—
while peeling an orange, opening
a car door, walking across the highway
for the mail—have moved me

to the nearness of tears,
to speak out of something
like the surfacing of convictions
to say aloud *there will not*

after all be time
enough! and having said this
nevertheless begun quite helplessly
to refashion the image of the locust,

once more to charter the light
into starry islands between its limbs;
to draw it back into clear shape
from the deep, retentive sky.

Cardinals

1

I saw the cardinal
from the kitchen window
on one of the first warm days:
a scarlet puff at the center

of the holly bush, a red,
beaked, and black-eyed berry.
His crest lifted
to the wind. I tapped the glass,

but it was only when I walked out
and reached into the bush
so that I was no more
than five inches from taking him

into the circle of my thumb and finger
where I thought he might burn
like a small, beating flame,
that suddenly he sleeked

and flickered low across the yard
into the heart of a dark cedar.

2

The lawns were full
of green light. There was
a scarlet litter
of windfall holly berries.

Five feeding cardinals
bloomed in the grass. It was
a day for the felling of trees,
the butchering of animals,

the capture of great fish.
But I looked into the cold
blue iris of the sky,
I saw that although

I had been set upright,
I would be permitted
to fall back.

Avocados

for Julie McDermott

Into the serene leaves
of the last tree of the last orchard
in La Habra, I looked up, trying to spot
avocados. I tried

a dozen angles, lay on my back,
looked over my shoulder to one side,
and then slightly to the other, stared
between my fingers, until

from the vantage of some
unplanned stance, there they were,
dozens of them, dark, pendulous,
rotten-ripe where they had hung

for days before I took it in my head
to look for them. I brought out
the long-handled snips and cut,
trying to catch them as they fell,

a couple ending in green, oily smears
in my palm. I cut them, cautious,
careful of angles, there in the green
deep shade beneath the tree,

only a yard away the parking lot
a flat of dry light, but the avocados
precisely the color of the leaves'
undersides, ready to draw back

on the inmost darkness
of the inmost seed.

Traveling

Afraid, I was always afraid:
we would be late, our seats
stolen, that once aboard

in the close compartments
someone would light up, and then
should I object, in anger

and contempt he would rebuke me,
on hot days require the windows
be closed, play music

too loud, pretend
to not understand when I enquired
where we might be, how far

we might have come, where we were
bound, had yet to go. That ours
might be the wrong train

through inattention
wrongly boarded, and we were lost,
irretrievable, unticketed; that we

had long passed and repassed
our destination, that the intolerable
delays on the dark sidings

required firm looking into, though
to whom I ought to have addressed myself,
according to what tone and stance

I did not know, and so continued
restless, weary, and impatient;
that there had slipped my mind

that which I from the very first
had been cautious to remember; that outside
were truly nothing but dull fields, smoke,

black snow; that it was certain we
had been rerouted, given
no notice, would not arrive,

and should have, hours ago.

Derailment

Though five cars of the morning train
to Subotica careened into the river
and a man was drowned, a woman torn in two,
it happened too far from where I slept

for me to have heard. Nonetheless
I started awake, crossed to the window,
and looked out to see the road asteam
in the warm morning, a brown wash

streaming in the ditches. Lights flashed
at the crossing, and kept on. But what
had stirred me? The room
was still, I had all night

most calmly slept, no more
than ordinarily stirred, though it is true
that in my sleep I had thought myself
aware of a sky enormously thundering

and the world to its mountainous rimstones
in paroxysms of fire, and from this
had been moved to wake (to a cry,
to a rolling of thunder?) shaken

to a power of unease as if myself
caught and rent in the first instant
of casual dismemberment, not yet
awake, terrified and aware

that for the usual generous brightening
of the world, for my ordinary commitment
to its authoritative light,
I had waited overlong.

Slovenj Gradec

for Alenka and Saša Rainer

That close to the mountain
at that time of year
the frost came early.
Any who cared to look

could see how close at hand
it had all along
been gathering. The mountains
rose luminous as clouds

above the gibberish color
of the October woods.
In fact, there were no clouds,
but something intervened

for the light did not
make shadows. The planet
had long been cooling.
Already it was beyond comfort.

In Bohinj

We stood together on the lakeshore.
The water was slow with cold.
It bloomed in soft storms of mist
that rose and joined and dazzled

around us everywhere.
We saw flung out over the lake
the streaming plumes of the mountain.
There was behind it all, we knew,

some cold power of the sun.
The sky froze and unfroze
its green veils—yet neither of us
was persuaded of the cold,

for the sky engendered a light
by which from the beginning
had we thought to look
we might plainly have beheld the world.

The Hunters

for Mira and Miša Stanić

Traveling, our plans in ruin
by reason of the unseasonable snow,
the day gone sour with the silences we kept,
through the dark afternoon impatient

for the Belgrade train, we waited
in the bitter restaurant
of the Vojvodina Hotel,
of our poor and cold room dispossessed

to favor the Italian hunters who complained
one table away about the dogs, their guides,
our room, the moldy bread, a cup
with a chipped lip . . . or so Miša

translated for us, saying it was "normal," this
was the way in this place at this hotel
at this time of the year, anyone
ought to have expected it to be.

But we had not so expected it so to be,
for oh, but the yellow grease congealed
on the chill, unhappy restaurant plates,
upstairs sat empty our room we could not use,

and all the while far out on the foggy plain
pheasants preened and crowed and crowded
in the stubbles of the maize fields, hares
played in multitudes beyond imagining,

roebuck bellowed and leaped at the forest's edge
in herds, in herds! Everywhere browsed and rooted
fallow deer and boar, the marshes were raucous
with geese, big pike and carp threshed

the shallows into foam. Had we
the inclination, we could fish and hunt.
But we were cold and tired,
and yearned for sleep; besides,

against the windows rained a slush
of snow and fog and coal smoke; our weapons
lay disassembled in their sleeves; and whatever
remained of the light, it did not count.

Chestnuts

for Katha Pollitt

Nothing so imprisoned the young light
of the fall afternoon, or with such urgency
returned it, as the ripe chestnuts
by the river wind shaken from the trees

to scatter lustrous in the grass,
in the beds of winter roses. They rained
onto the parked cars all day along
Lovdenska Ulica, exploded

on the boulevards, and we dodged
and covered our heads against
the bounty of dangerous sweet chestnuts
in October, in Novi Sad.

Taxi

From over our driver's shoulder
in the rear-view mirror I observed
the angry driver of the scarlet Zastava
with both hands rend his head and lean

raging into the windshield. Traffic was hot
and solid to either side, and close
the red car followed, swerving
and desperate to pass. Our driver, loud

in his power, sang joyful to the radio,
and I—I huddled, certain we would die,
and begged him to slow down, but lacked
syntax; so there we were,

hurtling terrified along
the very center line
of Marsala Tita, and God knew
what lay ahead. Once I thought

to leap the seat and wrest the wheel away,
but saw that then we were the more inevitably
doomed, being travelers, strangers, lost
and insufficient, unable

with clarity to see enough ahead
to mark our proper turnings
and prepare for them.

Homesick

Never before had we seen leaves
shrivel on the very trees, apples
harden and fall before they were ripe.
But at last, after five months

without rain, it rained. Streams thickened
with mud and scoured
the valleys, and what remained
of the village gardens vaguely greened.

In the bus terminal at Skopje,
because the floor was tracked
with a grease of clayey mud,
a woman from Bitola skidded, and falling,

scattered a hundred paprikas,
citron, red, lime-gold and green.
Helping her gather these up, I was brought
to think of the garden I had left behind

in order that I might discover myself to be
precisely where that moment I knelt
scrambling for her spilled fruit. I thought
of pepper plants in the cool mornings, flowering

melons and pumpkins, carrots
bulging the soil. I did not doubt
that care would not have been taken
in my absence; therefore also that

all must by now have yielded
to a wilderness of moonflowers
and bindweed, the onions
maggoty, the eggplants

fallen nightly one by one, soft
in the soft mulch. None of it
could I confirm, for I was traveling, and far.
But there, from the smeared floor,

from beneath benches, from out
of the thickets of shadow, from among
the careless boots of strangers
retrieving bright peppers, I considered

the orders of husbandry, rubbed
one yellow fruit against my cheek,
thought somewhere in the dank corners
of the windowless and evil-smelling room

might yet reside fair evidence
of the love and wrath
of the creation; went
on looking; longed for home.

Ohrid

Within the month we had swum
at a green height in the warm lake,
while only yesterday,
black and ashy to the knees,

we'd bushwhacked the burnt slopes,
come down to the groves
where bees clustered at the jellied masses
of almond sap, and the earth was sticky

with windfall figs . . . whereupon
arrived an unseasonable cold, so bitter
that the sour watchman in the orchard
would not suffer himself to unpocket

his hands, not even to brandish
his rifle when he surprised us
looting there. Lizards clung to the tiles
and fell. Against all advice and reason

we had come, too late in the year. What
had made us consider we might be
exempt? Only that each night
in the final days before the cold,

the lower the sun had fallen
on the horizon, the brighter
the lake had shone.

The Recognition

Before the photograph of the hostages
milling in the snowy yard I lingered
until the guide called out,

and could not for my life
think who might have been the one
listless in the middle rank,

propping himself against the pocked wall,
featureless, white-shirted, bald,
among them all he so stood out to me.

The Revolutionary Museum in Ljubljana

Row on row of double photographs, before-
and-after, images so direct
as to invite study before horror,
a dozen or so hostages (some women

in aprons, an old man scratching
his thigh), all fairly
casual, for perhaps
it was the first occasion, and none of them

chose to know what it was all
about, or did not understand
the protocol, or figured it
for a bluff, or simply

went on thinking about the taste
of bread still in the backs
of their mouths, the smell
of cooking fires, autumn leaves

everywhere drifting. Crowns
of big chestnuts flowered
in the background. Dogs
yawned beneath wagons, children

clambered on the walls. But then,
in the interval, some huge
and unrecorded violence would have taken place,
and next they would all be lying

as in the throes of a terrible dream,
legs and arms wracked
askew, heads flung
back, wrenched sideways,

all of them their mouths
sprung wide. The children
would have vanished, and the dogs
would be looking at the camera, friendly

and attentive. I had to take on faith
the trees were ripening
their fruits. It is not too much to say
I came to know everything

we know against ourselves.
But I had not expected
in horror such dispassion, seeing
how nothing followed from what I saw

because I was alive.

Night Cry in Ljubljana

Everywhere around us as we slept
little vacuoles of noise flickered
in the dark, small sparks
of sound, no more

than wind might make
at an edge of paper. Then from deep
in the courtyard warrens of the Slon
they configured a single voice which rose

and wearied, rose again
and fell. It came to no regard
but mine, though pale light
which might have been reflected

from a face came through
one window. That night,
the next and next, I searched
and found among the bottle crates

and sour middens of cabbage leaves
nothing. I had hoped
to pick out some nameable shape
with hair and teeth and eyes

from the noisome clutter
of that yard where I feared
whatever cried lay dying, crushed
under rubbish, leg caught or collared

and strangling in a snarl
of wire—failing that,
then have it expire cleanly
into silence. But on it went, and on,

as in the exile of nightmare a voice
uneven, everywhere and unassigned,
lacking tongue, without
capacity. What cried in pain

from the dark and the rank mazes
of rubble? How was it
that ever I had forgiven myself
warmth, stupidity, anger, love, regret?

I thought that in the terrible
and very instant when it ceased,
all with it might for love and justice cease,
and the world so quiet itself

that, wary to think the cry
might any time resume itself,
we would never hear more
than the fearful silence that required it.

Picnic

for Ivan Gadjansky

That night the sky
had brightened with a storm
no one expected; but at dawn
it grew dark. Everyone had sat

in rows on long benches in the park
at the edge of the river, the tall
grandfather, fingers thrust
through the gills of a large carp

held aloft for the photographer
to admire; the grandmother, younger
than anyone living
could possibly remember her

to have been; children, aunts; uncles
in shawls; a dog,
a pet crow on a pony's back.
But everything in that photograph

is long since dead, even the children, the dog,
the pony; even the light
clouding the lake and the bright
grass. Patches of damp

had spread on the women's skirts.
Not a shadow was cast, and every object
shone with some manner of light.
How they assumed their lives! The brim

of the old man's hat blew back, his beard
ruffled, her skirt ballooned
a little in the wind. By now
they have forgotten the light, the river,

the occasion, each other, everything.
Had I known them
they would have forgotten me as well,
and I would have lost

even that little store of breath;
for I would have come upon them
unexpected, as they arranged themselves
on the benches by the Danube

and stiffened in the required poses,
no place in that close order, and no time
to spare a traveler, a stranger at that,
requiring direction, lost

and strangely grateful for his need,
but lacking the tongue;
and though inclined
to fail at the most familiar truth,

stubborn in the manner of travelers
to discern and name it; moreover ready
in his abominable accent
to persist.

Dead Dog

At the edge of everything that moved and spoke
was the smile of the dead dog
which for days had lain vividly crushed
into the coarse grain of the road.

No, this was not the first time
we had surprised ourselves coming on it,
for this was our usual way. The sea wind
buzzed in the dry beards of the palms,

the trees bent sharply inland. The air scoured
our windows with powdery sand,
though at times less voraciously,
upon which we ventured out, each time

freshly startled to come upon
such dispirit of form, lacking
the usual engagements of beauty.
We went on, though it was true that at times

we were at night afraid, standing
on the seawall, our eyes
grainy with salt. We feared
the seething space before us

from which we knew the sea
crawled blindly in,
just as we feared the face
which some nights we discovered

glaring in from the pelted darkness
outside our window, claws fanned wide
at the ears to make the figure
of the fanged and resurrectionary skull.

Oh, then we drew back against
the headboard, and held
to one another. Meantime, our room
emptied itself of light; meantime

there was backrush of light
on that discountenance.

Badlands

We came down into the dry bottoms,
a scorpion mangled in the knuckle
of the wiper blade, yet struggling.
At every intersection grew huddles

of fussy crosses, yellow and pink,
fretted and scrolled, garlanded
with hibiscus. We saw to the east
the shriveled sea. West, the mountains

spilled to the sandy basins. North
was a visible heat, and over everything
spread blue, membranous dusts. But ahead
the road ran empty, except

for a crushed iguana, skull crested
and agape, straining a little
from the green, leathery shred
of its body; once, a dismembered dog;

on the windshield at eye level, at near
and particular focus, an arc
of strawy venom dried
to crystals, where the scorpion,

wind-crushed and clawless, had struck
and struck; the skeleton of a cow,
there in its belly the heaped,
incorruptible turds.

Cobra

for Julia Alvarez

I fear the cobra that the keeper
has teased from its box, which has reared
and spread its hood, hissed, lunged
at the keeper's yellow boots, gathered,

struck, regathered. I shudder back
from the edge of the pit, gather myself,
for though the keeper desperately has tried
to distract him, I have been singled out,

he has fixed on me, he has broken loose,
in a flash is at my feet, rising there
in the terrible display. And like no one before him
and nothing I have ever hoped to know,

he is so eagerly alert to the quick
lick of my blood that, though he does not
immediately strike, I feel spread
from the clenched heart I find I have

until this moment only indeterminately borne,
a paralysis of exaltation, a long
shiver of acknowledgment so powerful
that suddenly I have found my hand

to have extended itself, to be wavering
only inches from his open jaws,
thumb and fingers fusing into the glossy plates
of a snake's head, becoming eyed, intent, fanged,

and then lengthening into a scaled body
that unroots itself from my shoulder,
falls and coils, spreads the eyed hood,
rears, readies—so that there at my feet

I see them look back
each at the dreadful other, I see
each stare both ways
in the wary, commensurate longing.

Flicker

for Syd Lea

Spotting the road-killed flicker
on the center line, I stopped the car
and walked back. I saw
the black crescent of his breast,

the folded wings, head broken
to one side, the red nape, a bead of blood
bright at each nostril. I picked him up
and found him limp, warm, the membranes

not yet milky on his eyes. I pinched up
the papery blue skin of the saddle,
slit it, peeled it from the bone
and bright fascia, cut off the wings, the claws,

the brown-barred cape, detached the skull
at the first cervical vertebra, and tossed away
what was left, my fingers coppery
with blood. And just then

as I cleaned my knife in the sand
beside the road, out of no instance,
out of no warning at all,
there came over me so urgent, so dizzy a swell

of longing that I with the bloody feathers
in my hand raised my hand to my face,
touched my eyes, brushed at my lips, thinking
that with the next deep undulation of pulse

my chest would tear open and my heart
fly out to roll at my feet beside
the sandy carcass of the bird.
I did not ask what I loved—only

by some fierce necessity took up
the knife and wrapped the feathers
about the bone handle and traced
the clean cutting edge along the blue

channel of a vein until my chest
was running with beads of my blood—
and lost courage, could not
cut deeper, not knowing what it was

moved me, that I would
in time over and over,
never expecting it, leap
to the recognition.

The Silence

for John Engels, jr.

The one child having in manner of speaking fled,
his brother ran out on the porch to call him back.
"Philip!" he cried out, *"Philip!"* I caught him up,
thinking if ever the dead were to be recalled

it would be in similar voice flung confident
into raving light. Since then
each fall when the woods darken with color
the horror has been absurdly to wonder

if I in my sternest father's voice
had commanded into the bloodied gullet of the day
Come back! Come back! he might have heard.
But on the hill

the pines had strained to a power of wind.
Come back! I might have cried, but I did not,
and silence stormed. Meanwhile
he is speechless, dark, of no intent.

Patterns of Sleep

That man—photographed in sleep
by red light so that the green blanket
had gone black, and his face seemed scalded,
bedclothes tangled around his legs and spilling

onto the floor, head wired and taped
(but for all that clearly agreeable to it,
easy enough in mind to have gone to sleep
in a strange room before a camera, under

an unnatural light, likely even dreaming)
—that man without knowing it, and before
our very eyes, came close to dying: abruptly
stopped breathing, reached out without haste

one arm into the vivid light beyond the bed,
struggled up onto the other elbow, raised
his open mouth as if to drink rain, and then,
after a long time during which he was,

as we could see, calmly, motionlessly
struggling, everything resumed—first
the slow folding of his body back
onto the bed, next the breath, finally,

it may be assumed, though we
could not be sure of it, the dream—
all this, as the narrator assured us,
common enough, each of us the moment we close

our eyes at great and common risk, no matter
where we might be, nor the character
of the light, our dream
which we cannot except in rare event

remember, replaced for an instant
every night with nothing,
or with some slow upwelling
of fiery light we discover

we have all along deeply
enclosed; and then, an instant
before we awake, giving way, drawing back
into itself, leaving behind

the red stain of light
by which the camera sees,
and of which upon awakening
we remember precisely nothing,

though we feel something must have escaped us
and wonder what it might have been,
and why we are wherever
we may be, how

we could have agreed to this,
why after all these years of taking breath
and before that of breathing like a small
translucent fish the warm salines

of blood it should suddenly
seem difficult, something
about which it seems possible,
even necessary, to make a decision.

The Raft

for Hayden Carruth

His father told him
to be careful, to go no farther
than the boundaries
of the lily cove. His father

told him again about his cousin Archie
who had fallen into the scalding water
of the switchyard sump, because
the cinders floating there between the tracks

had made it seem to be
dry ground. "He wasn't thinking
where he was. He wasn't watching, he was thinking
of something else," his father said.

And he agreed he would watch
where he was going, wanting badly
to get down to the lake and out
to where he could not see

the bottom any more and where
it would not be evidently safe.
"That day he never came home
to eat, he never came home, he was dead,

and nobody knew or cared, they just
went on with whatever it was
they were doing for themselves!"
His father was going on and on

into the room like that
when he ran out the door and down
to the old dock, and found the raft
hidden in the reeds along the shore,

splintery pine boards scummy
with mud and moss; and when
he pushed it into the knee-
deep water at the end

of the dock, and stood, it ducked
and wavered and nearly
heaved him off . . . but held,
an inch awash, instep-deep.

He sprawled down onto his belly
and paddled out with his hands,
and it was like swimming—
from the house his father

looking out might have seen him
confidently swimming, buoyed
onto the surface, heading out beyond
the safe boundaries, but in fact

more safe than ever he had been
or ever might hope to be, even
should he range beyond the cove
and the dark line where the wind began—

though it was strange
to cup his hand about his eyes, lean
close to the surface of the lake
so that his nose touched water,

and look down to see, inches below,
the dense golden field of the weed.
It was strange to want so much
to stand up on the raft, step boldly off,

and walk over the feathery tips of weed
to shore, his father watching him,
walk straight on shore and call up
to the terrified house,

that he is safe and has come back, and the lake
has borne him up as he had known it would,
and there had been from the very beginning
nothing to worry about, nothing at all.

Staring down into the pale water,
still bellied into the raft, he saw
the thin skin of the lake thicken
with fiery clouds, because the sky

had thickened with fiery clouds
and become opaque, so that there
as in the end, this time in the blazing lake,
in the pale cloud of his unwary face

was the awful issue of the looking back.

The Photograph

for David and Julie

From the line of young birch on the far shore
crows called, erupted into the sky
out of the yellow leaves, flurried there,
fell back. The sun was high,

everything in perfect order on the raft,
the anchor rope in a tight spiral, weighed
by the red coffee can half filled
with cedar-smelling loam

from the edge of the swamp. He spilled
a handful onto the rough pine
of the deck, threaded a worm, and let it down,
careful it didn't snag, until the line

went slack, and he thought the lead
must have touched bottom, drew it up a bit,
then waited, leaning over, trying to see
into the shadows among the twists

of pickerel weed, the light
where it touched the water going green,
slanting down into the weed beds, silvery
with water dusts and pollens. Over the clean

sand bottom schools of yellow perch,
bluegills, redeyes, lavender and flash
of shiners, waver and ripple of light,
short bursts of gold and green

where the young bass fed. But nothing
happened, nothing. He waited for a fish,
and when he looked up, his eyes
dazzled at the sky. It was as if he still

were looking into the water, for the sun
was low, and a green light rose
soft from the cedars. His mother stood
on the beach and called, but he chose

not to hear, though she called and called.
At last he looked to land
and saw her farther off than he had thought,
her dress blowing, her feet in deep sand.

And so he began to paddle back, the raft
wanting to turn in circles, the wind
against him; so he stood and leaned
into the paddle, dug hard, looked up again

and saw the beach was empty, the lake
ruffling, the water going dense
and steely. It took him more time
than he'd thought he had. It was not

as if he'd truly had a choice—the wind
had turned against him, and when
he stared into the water, his face
did not stare back. He felt the rain begin,

and while he struggled toward the beach
his mother returned, and took a photograph
that caught the raft low in the slight chop,
seeming a powerful distance from shore,

and him, paddle in hand, his knickers
drooping, the birch on the far shore
bristling from snowy sand, everything
badly overexposed. It frightened him to see

how far out on the lake he had been.
He was frightened that he could not see
his face, but only a dark shape
under the hat brim. Even though

it had been in Klondike, in the general store
where he'd stood to hold and see the photograph
under his early-summer feet the plank floor
dry and gritty, it hadn't at all

been certain that the foolish one
in the photograph was not slowly sinking
into the pale lake, endangered
and alone, calling out

to the mother who stood intent,
her camera to her eye, framing him there,
catching the birches, the crows overhead,
the lake rising on them both—somehow

even the fishy air gathering, and the sky
gathering, and around him the deepening smell
of cedar before rain, the blue surge of lightning
for an instant withheld.

The Sea at Long Point

In early morning from Long Point
the sea became indistinguishable
from light. By midday
it had breathed upward,

infiltrated the air,
become luminous haze.
But in the deep part of the night,
when, time having given way,

not rarely would I start awake
grieving and angry
at how it had overridden me,
there was no saying what shape the sea

might have rendered itself to be,
that outside among the rocks
chopped soft, whose breath—
heavy with sea lavender

and beach plums, rank
from the aspirate granite,
rose so thick it clouded the room.

The Planet

for Jessica, June 1996

Through binoculars last night, my arm
braced on the porch stanchion, I saw
from Long Point over the aura of Portland
the bright disc of Jupiter, behind it

the old light of Cygnus. Brilliant,
the images wavered, yet clear at first
as otherwise and elsewhere the world
did not seem clear, nor the sky

above the world . . . two little moons
to my east of the planet, or three, the huge
discrete motions of the body
frozen there, nothing moving except

by blood tremor my hand shook so
over that time of distance that the small
trembling magnified itself, and the planet
danced, and nothing

would submit itself to focus.

Comet

In memory of Vincent Engels

In 1910 when I was eight,
mother took me from my bed
and out into the yard and pointed,
and there over our house it shone, higher

than the trees. It streamed
and billowed light, in the sky
terrible as an angel of God hovering,
about to stoop,

trailing long hair and robes
of fire. I was only eight,
and felt terrified to see that sight,
and privileged, and never have

forgotten it. None of us
on the lawn that night,
with everything else just the way
it always was—the tree frog

that sounded like a small bird dreaming
peeping away in the low crotch
of the chestnut, the drone
of crickets, across the street

somebody hunting night crawlers,
his lantern moving slow
along the edges of the flower beds,
the scarlet or yellow of a tulip

flashing out of the dark from time to time—
none of us knew how to take it.
Even today, talking it over, we're still not sure
we could have seen

a thing like that, though our minds
are clear, and we remember it
as if it were the night before.
And that's not all. Early next morning

the yard still dark, from the holly bush
a cardinal was singing, and from
the hickory, a mockingbird,
and for a minute there, not quite

over the line to wakefulness
and probably by what I'd seen
still blinded to the usual ways of things,
I thought the trees were singing.

In my long life have not been
many times like that one, first
a huge firework in the heaven,
a slow explosion that stayed alight, then trees

singing. But soon enough
I was awake, and knew better,
and for years
have known better. For years, till now,

the comet has held
the other recollection down.
I don't know why
it comes back to me at all,

for of that night I can't recall
anything of any person there,
not even of my mother, who held me
and spoke low, not how

she looked, or what
her voice was like, her words,
it was so long ago. Probably
I used the dream of trees

to balance off the terror
I must have felt, being only eight . . .
the wonder of it, allowed up late
beyond late in the face

of all that light. The trees sang
as if the world had taken in
and changed and was returning
whatever sweetness might have lain

buried at the heart of all that fire.
Though it was the smaller event,
by far, it burns
powerful in my memory as the sight

of that thing in the sky.
I'll take it to the grave,
though I don't know why
I should remember it at all,

for that trees might sing
had seemed, in the face of so wild
a presence, no equal wonder,
had borne with it nothing of terror

or disbelief; and surely
there must be things I ought
from duty of love better
to have remembered for being

dearer to me, and yet
are lost, gone out and lost
forever, and forever
have not sung back to me.

Winter Flight

In memory of Norbert Engels

1

Just now, here on the runway at Milwaukee,
already three hours late into Ontario
by way of Denver, which is filled
beyond all possibility with snow,

my invalid father, who has always feared
to fly, comes back just long enough
to ask me, who is shepherding him west,
are we airborne? an hour yet from taking off,

and he, the whole time here beside me
so far as I can tell, half-dead,
mouth agape, a dark stain down
one trouser leg, eyes rolled into his head,

asking so as to display some shape
of interest, staring out the window
into the garish nightmare of blue runway lights
each in its pool of blue snow, that snow-

flood in a cold place neither of us
is likely to see again, nor cares to see;
then, sagging back into his seat on the dead
leg, dead arm, sour smell of the old meat

giving way, asks *how high are we?*
goes still, tries himself once hard to shove
himself upright, and fails. And I cannot help or speak
for being one who, wishing to move, moves.

2

In the thrust and vigorous angle
of the aircraft when at last
it rises, and we enter the black sky
of winter that arcs from here and west

306

and east of here to as far as we might
in order of safety wish to go—when
at last it rises, piercing the night clouds,
entering the watery currents of the high wind,

it is as he has been promised he should fear:
earth-pull as he could never have
imagined it, stony masses of the continent,
power of water calling after him come back!

flesh of belly, breasts and balls
hauled at, even the smallest
of his small bloods hauled at,
and in tumult to the east and west

the great seas he has never seen
about to spill out over the cold land,
below him the angry shallows of the lakes,
below him the forests of Wisconsin

lashing away, and ahead the mountains
sharply in wait, rising and hardening, ahead
and beneath him nothing with much
in the way of promise to it. Half-dead

he is for the first time flying,
and the last, over the calm flowering
of the moonlit clouds, torn loose
from the entire beloved matter of things,

moving himself to move, fearing it is
in any but the most formal of descents
nothing but annihilation, flesh strewn
about the icy fields of the blue-lit planet,

which, as it turns out, falls away,
thrusts up, billows with snow and salt, surges
together, calls after him, boils up
at its ravenous verges.

Two Days

for Paul Zimmer

In the Metro station from the foot
of the dead escalator, uncertain I looked
five stories up into the eye of daylight
and wondered did I dare to climb those stairs?

But tried, hoping to outlast my body, which
in recent years had not precisely raged
against me, yet had come
precisely not to love me. Then

something intervened between the light and me.
That part of myself that wished to breathe and see
did not with grace respond, and in my breast
raw shadow unshaped itself, and tore away.

Abruptly I emerged into the wintry day
coughing and blinking, gasping for air and light,
and on the pavement at my feet rolled bright
a dozen yellow apples, one

crushed into white pulp turning brown,
together with a scatter of bronze mums.
It was cold, and nothing moved. Beneath
the pavement stirred the coiled world.

The sun illuminated as from within
the yellow apples. The flowers dully flamed.
Thus was lovely and composed the day
wherein resumed its light. Therefore

I was casual with Zimmer, and I said
that by all the evidence I might soon die.
But he condemned the thought. Thereafter
it was never more than simple favor to a friend

I loved, neither to die nor further speak of it.
But one day later, driving north through fog,
with little trust I safely would arrive,
I saw some fool of sounder heart stop dead

in the southbound lane to read his map.
And frequently I was passed by drivers
free and joyous in their cars. But I
had grown timid for having seen

deformed in me the voluntary and intentional—
with hours to go I felt not in control:
how readily my car might slide
into the ditch, and trap me there

where helpless I would die, remembering
how only one day before a light
of which I had been unaware
abruptly had gone out, and I,

astounded by pain, had slumped
against the wall, and felt
the back thrust of the lively soils beyond.
But though I lacked the strength to raise my arms

and to either side reach out and touch the stone
and could not therefore join to myself
that power, at least I did not fall.
I might have thought,

what is diminished here? how long
before no light remains to be used up?
but had seen instead that in my need
I was not to be forsaken by the massive world

which theretofore I called unyielding.
For the care I felt, the steering wheel
leaped lively in my hand. The driver
close upon me following grew wary, likewise

who followed him. We were alive.
It had been from the very first that close a thing.
Speeding along just south of Albany,
into the orotund, whole-hearted weathers

of the north, oh we were but a whisker from
annihilation, and we knew it! Shrubs of fog
bloomed wild in the right-of-way. And yet
perhaps not wholly out of reach

did Exit 13 offer fuel and food,
while at 14 was maybe lodging to be had.

Revisit

The clear disk of the sun
was dim on the horizon as the moon.
I could by its light discern
less than prospect, for nothing

described itself except
it was rendered out of loss
or loneliness. In my tracks
the snow smoked and swirled

as if fire were on the verge
of breaking through.
Light had begun to penetrate
the ice on the windows,

to drift over the floors,
climb slantingly the walls.
I imagined how in late afternoon
it might free itself once more

to the bitter yard
from which I should by then
have for hours been gone—
though for the moment light sustained

the deep, familiar rubbles
of emptiness. In the wintry yard
I stood to reclaim right
of property, and looked

up at the windows, one of which
I recalled to have opened
onto the fragrance
of the lavender lilac, the other

onto that of the white.

From WALKING TO COOTEHILL

(MIDDLEBURY / UNIVERSITY PRESS
OF NEW ENGLAND, 1993)

Newborn

The world displayed itself simply enough.
There were portents, of course,
the mirrors smoky and slow.
But I had no choice,

I was unpreventable.
A minute old, I was one history
of ten billion conflagrations,
my heart a chimney.

I was nothing
if not interested.

—for Henry Matthew Amistadi

The Naming

Watching for Animals

Had he been quicker, less
unbelieving, more willing
to look up, he would have seen

bears rise on their hind legs
from the tall grass
along the lake shore, elk

go skittish and alert,
swans flare from the rotting ice—loons,
whales, martens, everything

abruptly alarmed and winging,
sounding, clawing back
to the thronged hideouts, the bull

abruptly unkneeling to buck
white-eyed around the fences, cows
in the milk barns commencing

to bawl, sheep scared
into antic, trick and caper.
Instead, at dawn

his narrow window, by night
a mirror, began to clear,
and gradually revealed

the shorn world, empty
of the animals which had bounded
into being and out again

in the one teeming instant
between his glance to and away
from an odd agitation of some

meadow grasses, which, scarcely
grazed by his eye, and without
mediation, resolved to a nibbling hare.

Night Bird

At moonset the stars
flung themselves apart
from one another, the frogs
which had rejoiced all night

at the river's edge fell silent,
and from the deep mulch of shadow
underneath the spruce
commenced in its turn

a night bird of some kind,
which until morning
called two hundred times
and more, though surely

it was nameless to itself.

Love Poem

How definitely, for once,
he spoke! And indeed
she seemed moved, even
thoughtful—though also

she looked at him as if
he were some especially unterrifying
apparition. And when at last
they parted—oh then

he could not say he was not
without regret! In fact
at that very moment
the doors of the sky clanged thunderous

and final overhead, and night
took charge,
formal as always—but as always
quick to close everything down.

Details of the Frozen Man

At the pole the sun circles
and circles. When at last

we raise his casket and open it
his face unclouds

from the ice—first, blue skin
of forehead, knuckles, nose tip,

then the sodden wool of the shroud,
thin shadow of red beard. Finally

he is melted free and lies
curved as a sleeping man

at rest in himself, spine flexed
and tapering to the lively

roundnesses of skull, his eyes
blue-white around the in-pitched

irises, one staring as if
to recall itself, lips drawn, tongue

in the tight beam of our little light
so fixed as to seem willed

to its perfect silence. Something
soft-welling, heavy as oil, overflows

this catchment. Circling
the casket, milling about,

on the verge of ceremony, we glance
at one another and away and down

into the grave, where his hands
cross on one another

like a living man's, the nails
torn, yellow, sad.

Locked Out

"Why don't you call the landlord?" one of them said.
The afternoon was cold, the window ledge
just out of reach to the left, three feet away.
I had to stand precarious on the narrow rail
of the hallway balcony, back to the wall, reach out
with my left hand somehow to find a hold
among the mortar joints, and then,
hinging on hand and foot,
pivot, right leg swung out
over the yard, fingers desperate for
some catchable roughness. If
everything worked, I'd end up spraddled

in the ⊗ of the circled man—
breathing hard, hanging on to the window frame,
screwed flat to the round casement,
goggling scare-eyed through the glass
at the yellow fish that schooled
the sunny curtains of my shower stall.
I could not spare

an instant of misbalance, for the earth
awaited twenty feet below, disguised as a layer
of crumbling concrete, the floor
of the courtyard oozing and pooled,
trash in its corners. I faltered
on the rail. I needed more courage
than ever I had. Next door

the gardener leaned on his rake and stared.
The mail man, fanning a sheaf
of yellow envelopes, craned for a clearer look,
while from the kitchen door directly underneath,
the landlord's cook stepped out to shade
his eyes at me, and stood
foreshortened, arms erupting
from his ears, feet in white sneakers
fringing his chin. I stretched
and reached and inched along a bit,
fearful and overbalanced. I could barely touch
the window frame. Some one of the watchers said,
"You're going to kill yourself!" Another said
"Get a ladder." I hadn't thought of that.

"Or a locksmith." Nor of that.
"You're going to kill yourself."
Inside where I could not see
dwelt his shadowed, breathable air. Books trembled
along his mantelpiece, eggs dreamed
in the fridge. Everything slept silent
in its chartered place. I wavered there.
Inside his rooms a silence grew

and grew; I had the sense it might accumulate
so greatly as to burst the door,
like a powerful wind boil down the corridor
and tear me from my holds. Locked out,
ready to fall, I shouted down at them, at all
the watchers, to whichever one, *"As for
the landlord, he's never to be found!"*

Turtle Hunter

Fingers and forearms terrified and chill,
I grabbled blind in the murky water
for the sawtooth edges of carapace,

caught desperate hold, tussled and flung
into the boat the raging snapper I'd trod up
from the cobbled bottom, scabrous,

spraddled and pissing, stony jaws
agape, plastron a fringe of leeches,
the one stone that of all

the dark-enclosing others had humped
under my foot, in the dangerous throb
of startlement thrust back.

Feeding the Swans

for Vince and Betty

Far across the lake we saw through snow
shadows of mountains. Nearer
milled rafts of canvasback, flaring

and edgy at dusk. Our buckets empty
we turned home whereupon
the three swans, cygnet, cob and pen,

that had hung offshore as long as we stood there
came wary up the beach to feed.
With what elegant hesitation

they'd refused us as we tried
to lure them in, handful by handful
broadcasting on the sand

the yellow corn, yet failed—
meantime, the first skin
of the first ice edging in.

Olduvai

Glance down at your feet
stop, kneel and scrape
with bare fingers in the red, abrasive soils

until it is loosened from the matrix,
then take it up, hold it, smooth
the polished vault, peer close

at the astonishing checks and crazings, pause
for a good while,
little dry cascades

of red earth dribbling
from every aperture—*skull!*
skull! Look up. Everything

will have changed, except
for the faint, diminishing
heart's aftershock.

Hagfish

Behold the swimmer, afloat between
a staring sun and the dim oozes:
he gazes down through a lustrous sea
which, as it deepens, closes

on its green light. His shadow might be
a wreck, or a deep reef. All at once he feels
the soft blow at his groin, cruel rasp
of jaws, long slither of entry.

He is frightened, loses strength,
declines to the peaceful sea bed
where there is light enough so that
when in green murk he half awakes

he cannot keep himself from the sight
of the bulging wound from out of which
powerfully prolongs itself that length
of ropy body, the blind head, and working jaws.

Clearly it has not been a mere
unhappy dreaming that the swimmer
should have felt that strange
surge in his belly, knot and odd

emptying at heart. Now he lies helpless
in a place he knows nothing about.
He does not wish to give up
what he feels slipping away.

This is the fate he has expected,
and managed thus far to escape.
But he has been unwary,
and without warning he is inhabited,

the inhabitation is complete. Light
will never brighten or deaden
more than this. Above, at its great depth,
the surface softly glitters.

Pigeons

I don't love the fat rabble of pigeons
that from my first day in this place
has swarmed gluttonous from distant neighborhoods
at dawn and dusk, hooting and babbling, shitting
the yard, the eaves, smothering
the few green spasms of new grass. And this morning

for the third day in a row they
wake me up, fluting at dawn from the ridgepole,
scratching at the roof slates, rousing me to fly
enraged to the window to terrify them off
with shout, handclap, window-bang—upon which

they flurry and burst from the filthy ledges,
each time—I admit it—beautifully,
as if a hundred silvery shards of roof
have in an irregular wind torn loose, feathered risen.
But scared to merely one orbit of the neighborhood,
each time increased in number, they return, stall

over the house, descend, immense
filthy fluttering, greedy seethe of wings,
derangement of green and coral
iridescences, and in less than a minute

have overrun the feeder that on our first day
in this new place I'd planted
at the center of its treeless, birdless,
gardenless back yard.

Silent Film

for David Huddle

We come around a sharp bend in the road
    and there unbalanced on the top rung of a ladder,
arms flailing, stands a man
      with a comic mustache,
   while from the open window strains to him
        a girl most delicate, hands clasped
   at her right ear, bright hair unbound, her bosom
heaving and her eyes cast up
   for the help that is certain not to come.

        Another man, the father in his outrage,
   braces himself akimbo at the ladder's foot,
     stroke upon stroke lopping it away
         until, still climbing and intent,
        the suitor stands upon the ground

ankle-deep in splinters, whereupon
   he pauses uncertain, bewilderedly aware
     something is not right, and just in time

   leaps to the bright sweep of the blade,
     then disappears at double speed
        around the corner of the house, knees high
and pumping, the terrible parent
   hot on his heels, the girl

in the last and bitter sag of her defeat,
        fallen out of sight. Neither of us
   finds it necessary to restrain
the other, the thing is concluded, no use
   to interfere. And so together
     we wander off, each
        uncertain whether he has not
   discerned within himself some small
         ignobility of sentiment before

the sorry spectacle. Each knows in the other
   singular capacity for Love,
    for Pity and Desire, likewise
     for Righteousness, but also
the clownish hitch
   in the fundamental plasms . . . therefore
will neither of us
   risk ourselves outright to laugh.

With Zimmer at the Zoo

From the very outset
we'd thought we would be late,
from the very first

thought the zoo would soon
be closing, when in truth
it barely had opened, then

through an entire morning
did nothing but stare
at the bull giraffe in his slow

floating run about the moated
enclosure. About noon
a bellowing and caterwaul

arose from the far side of the park
from what must have been
a fierce, considerable beast—

the truth was
the singular animals we were keen to see
were but recently removed

from exhibition, and in
their expensive compounds slept,
and would not be awakened. The truth was

we would not in the short remainder of our lives
have opportunity to pass this way again
and feared that in our final hours

we'd dream how, just at closing,
had we possessed courage
and the art, we might

have slipped inside, evaded
the keepers till deep at night
when the zoo awoke to roar its great

and varied chorus to the moon, then stood
close by the shining fence, and loud
in our solitudes mooed with the Bongo.

The Waiters at the Park Hotel, Belgrade

were unavailable, however urgently
we called out to them, beckoned, displayed
irritation. Their backs

turned, they paid us
no mind, never spoke, but again,
and again, flushed

and cursing, hurled themselves
into the infernal kitchens, returning
spent, to brood over the bitter

aperitifs, the very
and fragrant coffees, breads,
rich soups for which,

before the chill import of their disdain,
the icy choirs of their plates
and linens, lustres

of cutlery, stern shinings
of crystal, we suffered ourselves
powerfully to hunger.

—for Katha Pollitt, September 1985

Dead Pig

Not drunk, but sick
from bad fish or fowl or some
several other possibilities, in fact
almost to dying on the landing

in Marseilles, the liberty boat
long gone, the carrier
an occasional shudder
of green running light far
to sea, the sea between us
a shoaling of whitecaps
otherwise stormy with darkness,

desperate, I found a hotel
and to the night clerk tried
to explain, and say my name,
and failed, but he gave me a room,
and just barely inside, the door
still clicking shut, fallen
helpless to hands and knees,
I spewed out
everything, everywhere, onto

the floor, into bidet, toilet bowl,
sink, potted fern, then fell
on my face somewhere, half
underneath the bed, slept there until,
cheek and hair crusted
to the dusty rug, bitter-mouthed I woke
in a sour, webby light that could have been
morning, early evening, any time

of a bad day, brown
clouds, a brown sea
spitting phlegmy spray. The carrier
hours out of sight, I anyway
came down to the empty slip
and hung around awhile, nobody
to see me or ask

why I was there. Birds screamed
everywhere. I let it sink in
that the ship had sailed

without me, and there
I was, not sure
exactly where I was, but pretty sure
they'd hang me once
I got back, if I did, for how

could I explain, and who
would want to listen,
or, listening, take my word? Once

glanced into an angle of the pilings,
saw there richnesses of trash: oil sheen, clots
of fish guts, tar balls, churnings
of orange peels, turds, condoms,
then abruptly recognized
beneath the flash and swerve
of schooling alewives the delicate

pale wavering of drowned flesh,
sat up, said on the instant to myself
"Dead pig!" just like that, just that
clear-sighted, that
definite—even though

I was in plenty enough
of trouble, AWOL
and fugitive and still
a little sick, even though

the corpse was headless,
bloodless, so long awash
as to be not much more finely dense
than the harbor water, said
triumphant and aloud, *"Dead pig!"*

Walking to Cootehill

It has been a long walk to Cootehill
and back again, heel and big toe
blistered, the traffic both ways impetuous
along the narrow lanes.
For a mile or more the journey
stank of ditches, at one point
of a sheep's carcass, three weeks
powerfully dead, already on the way
to almost bones. In Cootehill

at Paddy Boyles's Mens'and Boys'
I purchased for its jauntiness
a new cap, gray wool houndstooth foxhunter,
and on the way back,

in one field spotted an old ram
dangling a hoof. Moved on his account,
I shouted to the farmer, who,
beating dust from his cap against his leg
and wiring shut the gate,
threw over his shoulder *tis only*

a thorn, no more'n a fookin thorn!
making it clear
he believed I had reproved him,
and coming back a little way

let me know I was less by far
than halfway from Cootehill, hinting

I was maybe even losing ground.
Behind me, the lane narrowed
onto distances from which diminished
the monotonous, pained bleatings
of the ram. Whitethorn and wild roses

were in raucous bloom. From everywhere
in the hedges came great chirrupings
and bustle of chaffinches,
cattle lowed, the sky
sputtered with light. I limped
along the dwindling lane,
wary of cars, suspicious of the ditches
out of which some skittish creature, the instant
I least expected it, likely
would flush—as on my way
doves had erupted in wild flight,
hares skidded
on the macadam, and from deep
in the roadside skullcap had come
little angular breakneck skitterings. Now,

at last safely back, and wearing
this new cap, I posture where
my images converge between
the four mirrors of the Music Room,
before and behind and to either hand
grinning and scowling, cocking
the cap over one eye, then the other, alert
for the least anterior glint
of bald spot—in fact, I look,

wearing this cap, my age,
and consider returning it; in fact
I so greatly fail to be pleased
that it rockets up on garish exhausts

of question marks, exclamation points,
asterisks, arrows, stars,
to shudder, hover and bare
to the general mockery
my unbecoming skull.

—Annaghmakerrig, August 1990

Proofs of the Withholding

Down on the shore
big black-winged gulls
slide in from nowhere
to swarm the bluefish guts
I've just flung onto the rocks,
gasp and mutter, feeding—
and together with the onshore wind

and the small surf make another voice,
the only fit name for which I can find
is *laughter*. And though it's early,
the sun risen barely clear of itself,

there's all this young light on the verge of fire,
sea and sky reflected, imagined
and reimagined each
in the other so powerfully I almost doubt
the prospect of darknesses

to follow, and go on trying to look
to where the sea has become
not clearly itself,
to where it continually vanishes
past the black headland:

At Dawn on Gun Point

I wake with a great start. I've overslept.
I haven't dreamed. I've seen the sky
coldly rejoin the horizon.
I've seen the dawn erupt

from the chill soils of the sea,
and the big oak black
with roosting crows—it's seemed
a mighty formulation of rebuke,

for certain nothing in the way
of an answering love. I'd thought
there must be things
one is required to forget.

The Unnaming

Aurora

for Richard Dillard

I climbed Ledge Road on up to Prospect Street
from which I planned to look out across the lake,
over which the night before occurred
the red aurora I failed to see. I was cautious,

fearing the dull ache in my chest and arm
that warn me when I've climbed too fast,
but soon enough reached the top where
only days ago snow brooded, and while I slept

unrecollectably dreaming,
out of cold silence arose showers,
veils, fountains of red light—
never mind that next morning

the road sign cautioned that at the slow,
dangerous dip of Prospect might linger ice.

The Weather

After ten days of rain, the heart
cannot tell if it is too young

or too old, is unwilling
to decide, does not know,

refuses to say.
After twenty days it learns

that even in daylight, if only slightly,
the window reflects the wallpaper

and that to lean toward the glass
is to see it whiten and go dead.

Landslide

for Don Sheehan

By first light the pines struck down into the meadow.
Only an hour before the clouds had been heavy, shadows
buried the rafters, and light scurried
window to window. But then
the snow began to flicker, clouds to deform,
and from the incandescent line of the peak
proceeded a ragged scrolling of light, finally
the sun itself clearing the highest ridge,
bearing with it a wind so violent
that nothing in the stunned world knew more
than that something must have changed. At 5 a.m.,
the house cold, cold light billowing and the hibiscus
abloom in the north window, dark clouds low,
gold-bellied over the snowy yard, the sky
paling and bold against it two engorged blossoms
back-lit by snow shine, star-hearted purple-to-vermilion
where the petals overlapped, I looked up at the mountain
and from just beneath the shoulder of one shimmering ridge

occurred an abrupt enlargement of shadow
from out of which the mountain stormed,
bearing before it colossal froth of mud, boulders, trees,
bright explosions of brooks and ponds, snow clouds, all
soundless, therefore suggesting nothing of danger
so that I felt no need to run
before the landslide until at last
it cascaded over the head wall into the valley
and crested in a roar of dust and snow
at the road's crown and overran
the house where I had been standing at the porch window
brave with amazement. Too late
I discovered myself to have failed
to escape, to have been borne down
by house and mountain, my cheek
crushed into a sour linoleum, my breath
irretrievable, on my eyelids ant,

earwig, spider, the house above me still
        and orderly in ruin that theretofore most ordinary
            of all mornings when merely to have looked
up at the mountain from the swollen buds
and blooms of the hibiscus, of all things red
        most red, had been enough
to commence the overbalancing
           into that swirl, billow, upheaving dome
    of ice and shadow where I was about to die,
      or was already dead, or must describe
which it was to be.

                                  —*at the Frost Place, 1988*

Waking from Nightmare

My timid cat, unhinged by something—
shadow of door frame, fringe
of comforter—claws free of
her dream, hisses, flies
scrabbling across the floor to squat
and calm herself by pissing the rug, as is
her miserable custom.
I gasp upright,

stare out into a sky
shattered and made wild
by treetops threshing in the orange light
flung up from the GE parking lot. Once more
I have dreamed badly
of what loomed irretrievable
even as I dreamed it,
remnant of some appalling consignment

of remorse and blame. I sit till daylight
braced wary against the headboard,
while underneath the bed, exhausted,
recomposed, the cat
purrs and licks her fur. And when finally
I can see, there
is the neighborhood just
lightening, just
settling, of the last shudder
of the dream just barely quit.

Devil's Hole

for Saša Rainer

The story goes,
said Saša to me, *that in the great past*
right there in that cave
you forever inattentive fail to see,
himself the Devil came to wish to die,
forgot about God, forgot
about you and me, wished to die
from ordinary pain from loving
a woman did not love him, which problem

he have not anticipate, being Devil
and used to his way. Oh,
but the terrible whore of his predicament
assails him yet! cried Saša, *after this*

he is no worse than us, was nought
for him you know but keep on
loving, him being as we know
one stiff in his convictions!
Then, as we swept

into the big curve, Saša hollering
There she is, Devil's
Hole! I missed it yet again, the dusty
roadside foliage everywhere alike,
black stumps of guard rails
flashing past, dust
and rusty cables, shadow

on shadow, the cliff
a powerful green surge, and somewhere
or other Devil's Hole. *This time,*
cried Saša wrenching the car
onto the shoulder, *I stop*

and you will see! and urged me out
into the dusty roadside brush
into the green shadow of the cliff
to see for myself could I catch out the Devil
who had forgotten not only me,
but also to hate pity and to cherish envy
and likewise horror of roundness
and abundance, in the full

mortifications of love skulking
in his elusive roadside hole
yearning for her, forever beyond

the disposals of mercy. So I stood
quite possibly close by, peering and staring,
but hard as I tried saw precisely
nothing, only drab camouflage
of hawthorn and alder. The sun

low over my shoulder, I squinted
into my shadow, alert
to its diminishment into the thickets,
up on the roadside Saša pacing and pointing, the car
idling on the road, the light
by the dusty leaves broken, broken, and rebroken.

Black Dog

Just before dawn today
the yard is empty, no sign
anything prowled there
as all night and every night,

beneath the window
loll-tongued and grinning, in
and out of the long shadows,
any time could have leaped

through the moony glass,
been on me in a flash,
and what might I have done,
who would have feared him more

than ever he loved me?

Wakeful at Midnight

Do you pray to be safe,
rendered without interest
to whatever in your house, hiddenly at play
and otherwise incurious, might pause

in its doings, consider, sharpen its notice, horribly
attend you? How readily on stairwells
do you turn your back? On cellar doors,
on the unlockable closets? Do you live

in terror of the coldnesses of attics?
Midnights, certain the unearthly light
moves room by room closer to where
you have failed to sleep,
how can you not believe

that the darkness flowering about you
will soon pose limits to itself,
that you will be sought out?

—at the Frost Place, August 1988

Ghosts

The looming thing
that moved against me all night long
still lives in the hallway when,
shoes in hand, I limp to the door

and peer out. Then through the wings
of sluggish shadow that it is
spread bright fragrances—
sweet breads, bacon, eggs frying

in the sunny kitchen and I
cannot go down, am frightened to go down,
seeing I have dreamed all night

of birds, of the dogs
of my growing up, my mother
at twenty, my father

among soldiers, thinking
I would hear their voices
for the last time; and hearing them.

The Warning

Every morning there is a conflagration
of twenty peaks
and the sun flies up from behind them
growing hotter and smaller,
straining to disappear
into its vehement heart.
Nearly as old as my dead mother

I cannot keep myself from warning her
she is about to die. All day
I consider strategies, suspecting the dead
to be set in their ways, difficult
to warn, and warned,

probably scornful. Though I recall
no detail of her face, only
a smudge of eye or of nostril, perhaps
the shadow of a hand,
I am desperate
to be understood. But at night

we are caught between existences.
Though she does not fail
to listen, she seems not to hear,
and speaks to me at all times

in her most ordinary voice
about nothing at all.
Whereas the knowledge I propose
lacerates my tongue,
her calm voice answers *nothing*
nothing nothing

A Little Night Music for My Mother

The tasseled lamp shades
      tremble. Far below the house
            water is on the move. Every surface

         is peaceful, except for the mirrors.
             To west and south blank sides
of a neighbor's house,
           long downpitch
of hillside, dimness

beneath lilacs, increasingly
    an eye which sees

      and what is worse knows

Nothing here
          remembers, nothing
      believes the dead can truly
        have loved us.

    They are nearly forgotten,
        yet everywhere the darkness

of early winter stirs aside
      meantime
    the telephones, cords trailing
         over sad, flowery carpets
call faintly
    as if in distant rooms.

Long Ago

one fiery halt dawn
my mother lay by our wrecked car,
still in the savage roadside grasses
a scarlet sop of linen
to her forehead,
and in a soft,
embarrassed voice said

oh please
don't look at me!

           said that
to me, her fragile own, in whom
close, close to the rendable surfaces
our like bloods perilously kept.

I Dream of Roy Hanna

with whom one morning at a crossroad
outside Peoria, hitching east
from Reno to South Bend, I fought,
then traveled on with, parted from,

and never saw again, until last night
when I dreamed of waiting with him
in that cold dawn, exhausted, stranded
hopeless for a ride eleven hours, the sky

reddening, line poles and wires
taking shape, his face
resuming shape. I dream
of the night-long shrilling of wires,

the two of us, no more
than silent clumpings of shadow,
furious with waiting,
lurching together,

bumping, one or other thrown
off-balance, in an instant
enraged, swinging, glaring,
dawn light spilling everywhere—

of the slow revelations of place,
of us in our slow emergences,
who have not met since then, except
this once where the road is empty.

—for Syd Lea

Lonnie Peterson

Right here in Guthrie's house, directly
in the middle of trying to light
a coal fire, distracted, it's true,

my guard down, Maeve
for the fourth time since breakfast
at the first phrase of *Für Elise*

in the music room next door,
Owen careering up and down the lawn
dragged by a roaring runaway mower, Bernard

hurried and sharp among
his man-high, ironic foxgloves,
his composts from the bottoms up

transfiguring themselves,
here in Ireland, fifty years after the fact,
Lonnie Peterson presents himself,

pushy as ever, out of some imperative
of coal smoke, green smell
of a cut lawn, gas fumes, flowers,

the insistent tune, fitting time
badly as once he fit his little desk
far back in the classroom, directly

behind mine, where, farting
into his lunch box, prolonging belches
beyond the heroic, beyond

even my huge capacities
for admiration, like clockwork
every morning puking

onto his desk top, pissing
his knickers, he refused to cry.
I poke at the clinkery grate

where the sullen coal no more
than smolders, but once or twice
flares up, as abruptly dies.

—Annaghmakerrig, August 1990

The Ghosts at Red Banks

. . . small hissing rain, white stone
at the pond's edge, clump
of yellow flag—I've stood here
in front of this house under its big cedar
fifty-eight years ago this very spot
in another understanding. Looking in
at one window I see the spring's
first hatch of spiders scuttling
on the sill, leaf dusts and fly husks, at another
a gray over-brimming light pooled fanwise
on the floor. High in the tree

a widow-maker snaps, brief eddying
of wind and the pond water
clouds and curls, the day thickening
with passage—for I have come to believe
they are returning or even
that they are somehow still here
though more and more with nothing
on their hands but time, and having
forgotten altogether
the gorgeous syntax—they fail
at being remembered—*what*

has happened? Why
were we never warned? Where are we
now? How was it undertaken, how
rightly undertaken, all this
which is left undone? But I
cannot answer, being practically
wordless, seeming to have forgotten
the name for everything, while I suspect
they remember nothing else.
Directly enough

a blossoming of yellow flag.
From a third window, house smells
cascade over the sill—*closets,*
cellar mold, cedar, kerosene—
and across the reflective water, overlaid
on a dull film of sky,
falls the general shape I've made
wherever I've stopped light.

The Morning News

A village boy is down
on the white road. Beneath him,
at first glance his shadow,
is another boy, already dead.
The first has reached out
to intercept the bullet,
in the instant of this photograph

just fired, so direct a gesture
as to be invisible, fixed nonetheless
by the camera as the boy's hand is fixed
light ruddy in the webs, palm clutching
a pulp of shadow, pink rinds of fingertips, fingers
a fan of bones. Day springs up
in trees and flowers of scarlet light,

and I think of the unmemorable small violences
from which mostly I have healed: forehead
bloodied on a tree limb, palm
thorn-gouged, cheek ripped
by a twig, once my right foot gashed
by a sliver of glass hid deep
in the narcissus bed, left breast

crookedly incised, why, when
and according to what process
of small correction now escapes me, but stitched up,
then deeply knit, then knit
ragged, edges overgrown
to proudflesh. For just now

a bearded figure in a jacket
dark with this morning's rain has risen
from among the gravestones one hand
brandishing a wreath of red carnations, to hurl
into a flower-wielding crowd

grenades, then stand intent and curious—
so little general skill have we at resolution, and he
surely one among us, wondering
how many of the bastards did
I get? So that this morning
praise blossoms difficultly,
while scarcely beyond the thinning edges
of the particular light creation snarls.

A Reading

Looking out through doors wedged open
onto a descending lawn, hard green
as in the final hour before a thunderstorm,
then beyond through a half-arch of willows
framing two cedars, past which

at middle distance rose pines
blue from the first opalescences
of evening haze from out of which
reasonably I might have expected deer
at any moment to advance, confident, grazing
and staring about, behind me

a woman fanning herself, at the lectern
his hair rumpling in the wind
from an electric fan set loud
on a chair beside him, the poet
whom over the fan's clatter and rush
I failed to hear; above all

beside me delicately shifting
a girl breathless to listen,
ardent to set down in a small book
word, line, sentence I strained
to see, finding
the room too dark, her hand
too small and light, and that she smelled

sour, of old clothes, and besides
as if everything
were plain between us, definite
and understood, she
with her forearm tenderly
or fiercely, I could not tell
for certain, shielded the page.

The Garden in Late Summer

Who among us can truly say
he outlives the thick matters
of cold? Meantime
the world flowers: foxglove,
hollyhock, calendula wrenched
sunward, cosmos by its own weight
downsprawled, cumuli
of marigolds, beaded lily stalks,
curl and shrivel of peony leaves,
lightburst of gloriosas,
and from the beds of alyssum, pink
and white, shastas, dahlias,
all grand manner of rose. Thus
summer arrives, bedizened, decorous,
old, male and uncertain, riding
conclusion, unwilling to last.

Mountain Road

Low on the mountain road
this year as every year
since I first came
to set orderly the new place,

too early in August
and plain before me on the mountain road
overnight erupts
from the same tree
vermilion leaves shaken

with light, at the same time
a lesser light falling
on the road as along
a body of still water.
In such a climate
contradiction lacerates the heart:

I must be innocent
of everything, and yet
somehow exasperate the season
for there before me
is discourse plain enough,
and I continue unwary.

After Alcuin

O my cell, my sweet
beloved dwelling place: farewell
forever! the pines
are resonant with wind,

the peach groves are in flower,
and the fields bloom with wild marjoram
for the free gathering.
The river, its banks brilliant with daisies,

surrounds you, and the fishermen,
as always, are tending their nets.
The cloisters are fragrant
with apple blossoms,

roses and lilies mass
scarlet and white in the gardens,
and one of every bird God ever made
sings morning praises to Him, as once

in this holy place I am about to leave,
my master prayed from his book
aloud, and we novices followed,
joyful, with untroubled hearts.

But clouds double
and redouble. The world shudders
through the slow coalescences of soils
and lights, and prospect

is not sustained. Now
my prayers and songs are full of tears,
for with no warning at all you are lost
to an enemy whose face

I will never know. Never again
will the novices come to sing praises with me
beneath your bright roof. Oh, it is thus
the beauty of the world ends,

and all is swept away: for nothing is forever,
night descends, winter in an instant
destroys the rose, and the young, passionate hunter
who once chased after the stag

across the fields, is an old man
staggering on his crutch. Why
should it be the special nature
of our wretchedness to love most

that which most eludes us, that
which is stolen away?
Why should it be
that in even the most luminous

arrangements of memory,
the bitterest of winds
come to torment the warm
green sea, only an instant before

flowering with sunlight,
an instant before
leaping and flashing with fishes?

Meadow

Once in late summer I walked into
the tawny deer-tramped meadow, found

in a crushed-out hollow
evidence of disport, scatter

of clothing, joyous
stink of the bruised grasses—so turned

in sad confusion back, tried
to disperse myself, but everywhere

along the meanders of the brook
arose the warm reek

of cedars, and the willows
flickered with green light.

Walker Mountain

All day and night outside his window
the gravel trucks skirt Walker Mountain
                    thunderous along the little road
          uproars of loose chains, tailgates,
          downshift, catch
                    and strangled bellow
          of big breathing—outside his window

nothing pauses
                    but labors on,
          at times the earth
from its clangorous epicenters
          buckling to spring back,
                    his bed lurching.

Night after night along the road
                    skunks and groundhogs
          scuttle too late for the shoulders
                    raccoons double on themselves, he sees
                              green eye-fire of the dazzled foxes
                              masks and guard hairs bright
                    in the truck lights, standing their grounds,
                              interested to the end.

          And just where the light not quite gives out

          at times an ungainly bird shape will flush
                    from some horrible blot in the median.

     Night after night the dog's red brush,

the vixen's belly fur,
          are felted to the pavement. Mornings he sees
                    long smears of gut,
          tongue-blot, eyes
                    strung out luminous and green, the clouds
          on Walker Mountain

                masking the sun,
                            sliding down to mix
                                        with the meadow fogs, masking
                            the road. Thus
the agencies of ruin that morning

                        early and loud outside his window
unstoppably declare themselves—

            nor does he leap
more vigorous with age, nor his life
            resolve itself in beatitudes
                        of consonance—moreover
his heart has begun
                        the traitorous fat ripening. It seems
            that everything confined
                        to the terrestrial duration has begun
to shake into its separate dusts. When at last

            from out of the chill landscapes
                        the pines of the east ridge have begun dully,
                                    dutifully to glow, he leaves the road,

                slogs through the marsh
                            forces his way chest-high
                through cattails, tightropes
                            the slippery logs bridging

                            the little springs, unties
            the painter, pushes off and rows
                        clear out to the lake's center
                                    drifts there awhile, the sky lightening,
                        withdrawing shadow and reflection,

            the woods commencing
                        to scream with crows;
                            leans over the gunwale,
            face bent so near the surface

                            each breath softly forms itself
                            onto the water,

                    then stares
            into the clarities of shadow his head makes
        stopping light, finding there the downward sparkings
of stars, abrupt deepenings,
            mantlings of oozes, bedrock, then
                    reboundings or
            upwellings of the green fire
            he has never failed to believe
                    burns close on the clean center,
                        his face close

            almost to kissing the warm
        surfaces, each breath halt,
        excited, roughening,
                    each more than the fragile last.

Emergency

The morning wind that blew from the south
through Cedar Grove across the golf course,
carried the stink of winter—the day
nevertheless warm, sweetly proportioned,
a fat, upwelling sun, a ripening light

though now it is all about to be taken back
that never was freely given
because his heart, swollen to movement
it seems not in disposition to sustain
has called him, and he has awakened

terrified, and awakened the night man at his desk
who has sent for help, which has come
and extracted him to the dark passageways
dazzlements and blindings of corridors,
and rolled him off gaping stare-eyed up
to the intent regard of the head-man's clotted nostrils,
perceived through the pale V

of his own perplexed, embarrassed feet,
the leapings aside of the lobby-dwellers
from the crook of the foot-man's arm, the wakeful
makers-way, nimble
getters-out-of-there—likewise

respectful flingers-wide of doors
beyond the last of which he finds himself
removed to a cold night, moonless
and unstarred, a parking lot excited
to pulses of red light—behind him

the dazzling lobby, at his desk
and registers the night man, those
terrible courtesies, that sorrowful
vast breathing of doors

—South Bend, February 20, 1992

In a Side Aisle of Kennedy Bros. Antiques Mall

When I stumbled on the oval print
I was shaken, for it was mine,
having hung at the head of our stairwell
twenty years, before
I sold it. Beyond counting
the times I paused before the very girl
on her beribboned swing, that boy
spying on her from behind
the flowering bush. Nearby

stood the big green demijohn
with its seigniorial seal,
brought unbroken all the cold way
from Wisconsin to Vermont,
likewise cleared out, sold for nothing,

and for a moment I thought
I must have come on the whole of the old consignment,
long auctioned off, and retrieval
might be in the question after all.
But search as I might, I found nothing else, everything
was gone, lost for good, got rid of

in some stupid crisis of muddle and cumulation.
That day, years later, suffering room enough
and to spare, surrounded
by middens of china, clocks, chromos, everywhere
clutters of old glass ringing with light, I stood

in a dusty aisle of Kennedy Brothers' Mall
in the midst of those sad dispositions,
amazed to discover myself

so staggered with loss; at so
desiring everything, all of it,
back again, appalled.

Epitaph

I recall the whole of my life, brief
and hurriedly attained, daily live
through everything again, by turns

unloving and aggrieved, yet not
beyond sorrow, repentance,
shame. I think of all

who have outlived me—most
I was not loathe to leave,
a few I was. One or two

were crazy, them perhaps
I loved, though
stayed away from.

And with none was easy.

Naturist Beach

Arms wide to the terrible sun,
                dewlapped, lavender
      and hairy,
             passionately luminous

                    against the gray sea, belly

      broad powerful brocades
            of fuchsias and purples, breasts venous
      dun-haired, tipped with dun,

                      before which spectacle I,
          far lesser flowering, bleached
                and flaccid, pray, though

I know it will not be
          what saves me, may I be
              reborn like that, to such
          ferocity of color
      as that, naked,

          ugly, fearless
                before light, un-
abashed.

                          —*Hvar, 1985*

From
BIG WATER

(LYONS & BURFORD, 1995)

Preface: Gutting Bluefish

Down on the shore
big black-winged gulls
slide in from nowhere
and swarm the bluefish guts
I've just flung onto the rocks,
gasp and mutter, and together

with the onshore wind
and the small surf, make
another voice, the only fit name for which

is laughter. And though it's early,
the sun barely clear of itself,
there's all this young light
on the verge of fire,

sea and sky reflected,
imagined and reimagined each
in the other so powerfully, I almost doubt

the prospect of darknesses
to follow, and so go on
trying to look to where
the sea has become
not clearly itself, to where
it continually vanishes
past the black headland.

PART I

Looking for Water

Looking for Water

A river is supposed to be nearby, and reachable
and since in a strange place the first thing
is to look for running water, I ask, and discover
that no one knows exactly
where the river is, though
there's plenty of speculation,
they think it might be somewhere back below
where the hiking trails used to run,
beyond the old bridle paths, probably
overgrown by now, as they recall, a difficult

tangle of distance over steep descents
through grapevine, blackberry, alder hells.
I have to make my own way, following
in the hardening red clay the beautiful tridental tracks
of what turn out to be a dozen
wild turkeys that a scant ten yards ahead
take wing in the watery dusk,
flap up and glide back over the road, slow
as big, bronze, iridescent fish,
the whole time wind like a minor surf,
and while I'm still breathing hard, six deer
exactly the color of hickory startle and crash off
through a sudden general reddening of the day,
and staring after them I see
a white gleam through the trees,
not the river, but a headstone—I've come

on the old graveyard,
where the turkeys must just
have been feeding, and the deer
running through, leaping the headstones
of Cheatham and Goode, *Asleep
in Jesus,* and the Glasgow sisters, dead

at ten and two and eight,
reason enough to give up and head back,
and I'm home after dark
where a globed lamp in the farthest dip of the lawn
I mistake for the moon on water.

Aquarium

I hadn't touched it for months,
the water had long cleared itself, the plants
flourished and thickened,
and at the end of my room
it seemed another room
pouring out light.
Daily the red oranda
came up for food, likewise
the bubble eye, ryunkin, black
dragon eye. But something began
to go wrong—quite suddenly
one of the buffaloheads, though desperate
to feed, could not swim up
from the bottom,
and the great calico veiltail as I watched
capsized, and swam upside down
no matter what I did

to the beautiful water, changed it, warmed it, cooled it,
measured out medicines
and salt, no matter how—
everything having failed,
and in the last extreme helpless—
I tried to cure it with light: dimmed

the aquarium, brightened it
to something like
morning, made it night again,
then morning again, then night. . . .

At Night on the River

When night comes in, wary
as a trout, ready in an instant
to shrink back
onto the kernel of darkness
from which it hatched
I've thought it might be worth dying
just to drown and be buried here.
You need to stand
at night all night
to your knees in the Winooski
in wait for the back flow
of darkness, the river meantime

crushing waders onto skin, muscle, blood, bone.
Among other things you'll find
that at night the river smells sour and steely,
the air burns like a coin on the tongue,
that the water bears past in drift lines
of light. Nothing is enough, something,
probably the tedious songs
with which we've tried
to replace ourselves have kept us
uneasy. But lean close
to the water. At night standing in the river
the name you spoke all day
will give way to another. You'll forget
to bear in mind how little
you'll resemble what you see.

Falling In

At my age gone awkward
having forgotten everything
I ought to have remembered
about keeping balance, I fall
from the boat trying to board the dinghy,
like in a Buster Keaton bit, the dinghy
skidding away and swamping and my legs

spreading, till in I go, and come up
kicking and sputtering, then find I can't
make it back into the boat, grab hold
of the high gunwale, and heave, but can't
get leverage, chin myself
a dozen times till I think
I've lost my breath for good, and end up
clinging to the rudder, exhausted, beginning to feel

the cold, the knowledge dawning
that I'm in trouble, big trouble. But I wait,
thinking something has to happen
to get me out of this, though I can't think
what it might be. But I'm wrong, nothing happens, time

drags, and it's cold, it's cold,
too early to be swimming, too far to swim,
too deep to wade in, nothing happens and I try

waiting it out, but it goes on too long,
and nothing to do but after a long time
give up—whereupon I yell, holler,
bellow for help, loud
and bitterly ashamed. And after all

there's some guy working on his boat
who hears me and comes down
to the end of the dock and spots me
and rows out and saves me, and that's
the end of it. After he's gone,
I stand here on the dock,
dripping to a cold puddle
thinking it over, trying to name

how I'm feeling—not
relief, no remnant fear
or after-fear, but mainly
embarrassment, the tag-end
of something like boredom, a growing cold,
most of it left over from out there, and still growing,

but give it up and go out
to retrieve the dinghy, retrieve
some of the duffel, find one oar,
and a floating glove,
but I'm cold, and leave the rest
to drift in in its own time,
and all the way home, the cold
hanging on, my calves knotting

with cold, the world
ashiver, I begin
thinking to myself, *I'm*
in trouble, this
is going to take
a long time, what do I do
until it's over?

The Storm

I will myself not to despair
when I wait by the sea for good weather.
Even on the brightest of days
the storm has been a continual
awful hanging in the air,
and comes often, and endures,
longer each time, sometimes early

after a windless night that has been calm
with moon and stars, a fog
hanging low and close into the coast, soft
against the window, then
clearing, then

a line of big thunderheads advancing
from the north where last time
I happened to look nothing was, only
the broadest of daylight. And then
the sky breathes deeply,
and before I can think

the whirligig in the yard has spun itself
to pieces, the sea is shuddering
to its floor, and the sea
has flung itself at the window, the window
has bulged inward
and the beach plum and beach roses
have blown flat and seem about
to uproot and fly away,
and it is here, just at this spot
where America stops

thirty feet over the long, unhappy reach
of the ripped Atlantic, that this
is being written—in Maine
looking north from a streaked window
toward some black, savage rock of an island
I have never seen before and swear

wasn't there before, and that seems at this very instant
to have at once fallen from the sky
and boiled up from below, and is being
devoured by its surf and can be reached
only by swimming.

A Photo of My Mother and Grandpa Lighting Out

Look at that, blood
to blood, my grandpa used to say,
at sunset or sunrise, *that's all it is, one's*
the back end of the other, take your pick. It's 1912,
July, after dawn, and they're looking to take
some brookies from the Little Beaver, lighting out
on his bike, in overlappings of fog
though underfoot

little brightnesses explode
from the flinty gravels,
likewise from the handlebar bell, the earpiece
of his glasses, what might be a ring
on my mother's hand. They're lighting out,

but posing too. It's so early in the morning,
my mother's thinking
the little trout must be asleep
just as she'd like to be,
that dew is still settling without brilliance
onto the cattails, and the redwings
haven't gotten around to being
awake yet, only an occasional dazed cheep
or whistle from the ditch, or from deep

in the marsh grass. Skunks
and raccoons must be still up and about, the sun
is the barest of reddenings over the spruce
from east of Joe's Island, and just beginning to pink
the first frettings of wind on Bawbeese Lake. The world's

fragrant—marsh mud and cedar, a faint
fishiness to the air, dust that smells like dust
one minute after rain. I get this, all of it
except for the color and the smells, which I'm obliged
to make up, sounds too: birds,
the scouring of bike wheels
over gravel. And one or two

small motions: dew falling, the tiny
surgings of grass, unfoldings
of violets, mallows, wild roses. I get all this
from the murky photograph taken
too early in the morning, not near
enough light. My mother's young,
she's hanging on to my grandpa's checkered shirt
with one hand, with the other
a Prince Albert can which must
be full of worms, the old paper
is cracked across her face which she turns
to look back at someone
or other's camera. She's wearing

white stockings, high shoes, gray cloche, gray
gloves, my grandpa's got on
a boater, he's carrying the rods
across his handlebars, he's troubling
to keep upright and still
be slow enough for the Brownie's lens,
and the bike is listing, front wheel sharply
angled. Ahead of them the marsh
is a low gray hedge of shadow readying itself
for light, for birdsong, for a fullness of sun, for all
the various blossomings they probably expect—and that

is where they're going to, that
is where they're lighting out for,
ready to follow the long
slow leap of their shadows before them,
the night distending into dawn.
Therefore I hold the picture
at a certain angle to the sky

and my mother and my grandpa disappear
in a little square of light, a dull fire
that from somewhere deep
in the dimensionless old paper
has stirred, found fuel, surfaced, ignited.

East Middlebury

With small confidence in skill, gear, or tackle,
years upstream of us, inattentive
and restless to renounce
everything we might have failed
to remember—on that day
of more than ordinarily dank sun
thigh-deep in the familiar river in which
we no longer capably believed,
each pointed out to the other
where at the pool's head had occurred
one tiny rise, upon which came another,

more vigorous, and so on, until before long
the river from bank to bank was lively
with splashes to a hatch of little yellow mayflies,
which at this time of the afternoon at this time of year
we ought to have expected, and to which
short and late we cast, raising at once
three minor trout, then waded ashore to rest
in the strangeness it was to have undertaken

from little hope the old rubric, and by the agitations
of an inert surface to have been restartled.

Dead Pool

Never in all my days on this stream
have I taken a trout from this pool
under the black willow—a good place
for big fish, the current deeply undercutting
the bank, a good cover of foam
on the eddy, caddis always, shifting
schools of dace. Still, once a year

I wade the riffle at its head, move
into the shades of the clay bank
and fish the run—a nymph
to an expected hatch, though nothing
has ever come of it, nor of a dun
cocked prettily in the drift line. Today,
the same. I lie in the sand

by the oxbow and watch, imagining how
one day my fly might ride
true in the feeding lane, and in a shimmer of spray
the river will burst and I'll be staring
into the ravenous power
I've always known
to be holding there. I know

of other spots like this one, where
in some fluid congress of the general dark
something heavy takes
secret breath, by reason of
its sheer bulk wary, and at pains
to conceal the breaking
of surfaces. Here lies in wait
what feeds by night, but only then.

PART II

The North Branch

The North Branch

We took the train to Lakewood.
There'd been fires in the old days, swept
the North Branch country,
but over the years we fished there
most of the land recovered itself
in second-growth popple and wild
cherry, scrub maple
and birch. Blackberry
and raspberry bushes got thicker every year
in the clearings, and in the shadow
of this scrub, here and there, you saw

seedlings of hemlock from the few
remaining stands, even a few
white pine that came
from god knows where. And fern, may apple, winter-
green, coral mushrooms, the big red *russula,*

and everywhere you looked
the charred stumps of the old pines,
some of them too big for the two of us
to join hands around. Made you wonder
what it must have been like
before the fires and lumbermen. It was
hard country around that river, killing frosts

by the middle of September, in October
snow began, lasted
six months, by the third week
of April you might see
a little grass again. When my brother
and I fished those rivers

we found a farmer let us sleep
in his hay barn, we'd pull together
a four-foot mound of hay
and sink into it, and get waked up
by the mice stirring in the hay,
and know by that it was daylight
and time to get up. No rats, thank god,

big pine snakes underneath the barn,
saw them lots of times
sunning themselves on stumps. Used to be

that river was something, read once
in the files of the old *Green Bay Advocate*
of a party took seven hundred
and eleven trout in three days
of fishing. This was

at the end of August, 1871. Another time
some years later four hundred
and sixteen fish that ran
a quarter pound to two and a half. Nothing
like that anymore, of course, and of course
that's why. But I tell you

it was still a beautiful stream,
the North Branch, in the upper reaches
wild, but lower down
a river for swans, maybe
forty feet wide, in places, and running deep
between the banks, and a powerful

current, so that even in the glides
it was punishing to wade
upstream, and then below the highway
it spread out in
a still water, but still

with lines of drift that went
past us quicker than we could wade
or walk the banks. We'd come
to the stream with the wet brush
in our faces, and sometimes we'd stand

on the meadow bank below
the oxbow and see
little grayish blobs of insect shapes
bobbing to the surface and fumbling

themselves airborne, and twenty feet out
the neb of a trout showing and gathering
one in, and then a hatch or spinner flight
filling the air, swallows by the dozen
hawking among them, cedar waxwings
coming out of the trees to take
one fly, and every square yard
of the stream with a feeding
trout. Black flies

could be bad, especially around
the pilings of the cattle bridges,
crawled down your collar, into
your ears, up your nose, your cuffs, bit
like a sunuvabitch, I used to think we'd maybe lose

a pound of meat apiece to them
some days. But we'd stay at it
no matter what, until almost sunset,
when the chill at last got to us,
and we'd come off the stream
shivering, bleeding, exultant.
In those days that was a river
where unless hot prairie winds were blowing in

from Kansas, or the Fox
had opened the reservation dam
and sent down a head of muddy water,
we felt we could take fish

somewhere along it—even
on the worst days we used to take
a lot of brookies in the riffles, small,
but by god they'd brighten the day!

Hatch

Another month
and the fly-making season
is on us, just barely time
before we're wader-deep
in May, and the Clyde runs clear again
and the bats begin to fly,
and by the end of the month

I'll be back in the meadows
where some years ago
near Decoration Day there came
a hatch of little gray flies with yellow
egg sacs, dense over
the river, and great

red-sided fishes wallowing
all around me, to which I passionately cast
all day with the right hand
until the right hand gave out, whereupon

I used the left and wore that out, too,
but never struck a fish—and didn't I have
a very bad moment when at last it occurred to me
they might be suckers, and struggled down

to the riffles at the tail
of the pool, and kicked some out,
and sure enough they were, big
five-pounders, striped bloody red

as a North Branch rainbow—since when,
the end of May and that hatch on,
I travel to some quiet place
where I figure trout
must be rising to it—nevertheless
can't help myself but look
more than twice at any
surfacing red sides.

Green Bay Flies

Two deep rivers ran
through the heart of town to the Bay,
and in March I watched the ice break up
and the big floes go tumbling, splintering
the piers, debarking the oaks and pines
along the banks four feet up their trunks.
In April, the first thunder
in six months, proclaiming
spring, and in July
up from the Bay, from beyond
Peet's Slough and Long Tail Point
and the marsh meadows blue
with sweet flag the hatch came,
a fly or two fluttering

to the street lights, then a few more, then
before you knew it
the mayflies of Green Bay would be swarming up
the Fox in huge rustling clouds half as wide
as the river, so many they darkened the arc lights
on the Blue Jays' field, covered
every window pane, clustered the screens, clogged
car radiators, covered your hat, your sleeves,
sometimes even brought traffic

to a halt. You could feel their wings
brushing your face with little breezes
that I swear were enough
to cool you down on a hot night, the air
adazzle with wings, and high

in the evening sky swallows
by the hundreds, cedar waxwings
darting out from the trees to meet a fly
just perfectly in mid flight, one second
this little fluttery dab of golden light,
then the flash and hover
of the bird, then

nothing, like a flicked switch, the evening gone
minutely the darker for it.
If it had been raining
the streets and sidewalks in the morning
would be slippery with a green slime
of eggs, the flies having mistaken
the wet concrete for a surface
of live water. But nothing

like it anymore, the hatch
is over, probably
forever, the Bay a soup
of silt and sewage and sulfides
from the mills, not even clean
enough to swim in anymore. But back then,
those summer evenings—I can still
hear it, the sound
like a long train
way off in the distance,
a sort of humming rumble
wrought up by those millions,
billions, of delicate wings

that caught up every last scrap of light
left to the day in that last
half hour as night came down
and the street lamps
came on. I've never forgotten
how it was those years in July
the night stepping in, slow

and deliberate as a heron, the sky
softly darkening like it does
even now, evenings
in late summer, a smell
of lawns and dust and the steely
scent of the Bay drifting in, the air

still hot, but a growing softness
to everything—at such a time
you could surprise
yourself catch sight of yourself
in a shop window, if the time
was right, and the mayflies
hadn't yet swarmed the glass, and depending
on how you wanted to look to yourself
in such a light you'd look it.

A Fly Box

In those days when even the beaches
of Green Bay were clean enough
for swimming, the marshes
had muskrat houses and dogfish minnows
and snipe and nesting mallards,
and the wild blue iris that we called
sweet flag—in those days

we fished Queen of the Waters, Ginger Quill,
Coachman, Grizzly King, Brown
Hackle, Gray Hackle,
White Miller, maybe

a Parmacheene Belle from time
to time, Cowdung or Beaverkill,
but I favored
the Professor for tail fly, Silver Sedge
or Pink Lady for the dropper,
though nowadays

such dressings won't do,
the trout are all entomologists,
they don't find the idea
of a hatch of Professors
or Queen of the Waters especially
credible, and so

if you want a dressing
that seems to appeal to the large
modern trout, here's one, copied

from the Peshtigo's
Hexagenia limbata: wing—dark
brown hair, bucktail, raccoon or mink, upright
and divided. *Tail*—hair fibers, as above.
Body—yellowish spun fur, ribbed
with bold spirals of brown. Rib the body
with brown hackle stems. *Hackle*—furnace, all this

on a 6 or 8 XL. With this dressing
I've had much luck across the years, even when
it went by the name
of *Dark Michigan Mayfly.*
Then, of course, there's the Red Quill,
Ephemerella subvaria, a great standby
throughout the early spring,
and at other times as well, and good
for several other flies common
in Vermont, one of them
an *Epeorus* of dark
complexion. *Leptophlebia*

cupida, this
is the Whirling Dun, although
you are likely to find it burdened
by almost any name, depending
on what fly the angler thinks
he's imitating. We have a writer
on the *Post* who called it last spring
The Barrington because
that happened to be the fly he was using
during the hatch, and he caught
a few fish, and so he wrote

"The air was full of Barringtons." A difficult fly
to dress, for the wing
has lost its richness of slate,
and while almost transparent has
something of a brownish-bluish shade
lent it by the veins. As for the March Brown . . .
no comment needed. He won't often

be required, but when he is
you'll be sick if you haven't
a supply. *Stenonema vicarium,*
an admirable fly. If he
were an angler, he would be
wise, witty, clear-spoken, graceful, never

ponderous or opaque, never, or at least
not often, given
to ripe philosophizing,
forever observant, colorful, full of abhorrence
for the quaint and admiration
for the truly strong of character
and personality. Most authors say

you can substitute the March Brown for
the Gray Fox, when the gray *Stenonema*
is hatching, and *vice versa,* and no doubt
they are right, but I
have never tried it, and why should I, because
it's a great entertainment
to dress them both, no better waste
of time I can think of, and besides

if one is going in for imitation,
why do it half way? So I say
make up a dozen of the Gray Fox, and you'll be delighted
when you see the natural, abundant in Vermont,
Stenonema ithaca by name, dressed

in grayish mode, legs
handsomely banded dark
and light, very lively, quick

and independent of disposition,
with a personality that seems
developed, at least compared
with other mayflies. The Light Cahill is another fly
it's a pleasure to make, and lovely
to use when the eyes
are not as sharp as they used
to be, and even when they are, because
no matter, you can always see it
on the water. And to it I owe

one three-pounder at the head
of Healy's Rapids, and the memory
of one of the same size lost
when the hook bent, and many smaller.
Black Gnat, Equinox Gnat
or Mosquito, these I employ
on the upper meadows of the Clyde, though seldom
on the Connecticut, where they have not
proved useful. The big idea
is to keep them small, no more
than two-thirds the size

the hook will accommodate, and even then
they'll look hopelessly too large. As for
the Blue Dun, an important fly
for the smaller hatches, I don't care
if you dress it as dark blue or iron blue,
in either case keep it small. Sometimes

in the rain the trout will be slashing away
at the hatch of this fly,
and the gnats will be attacking
the little sails as they come down
the current, and you'll be able

to see the natural better
than the artificial, though if
you're wearing glasses,
you'll be hopelessly
up against it, because
in such weather the lens

fogs over the no doubt
already fogging eye, and I've seen
more than one angler gone thus blind
say the hell with it, clip off

his fly, sit down
discouraged on a rock,
and fish breaking everywhere!

White Miller

I'd watched him tie the fly, then catch
that fish, had seen it slurping away
in the big Clay Bank Pool on the South Branch
of the Oconto River, had tried for it myself,
slashing away with a floppy tip-dead castoff
South Bend nine-and-a-half footer someone
had dredged up for me from a far back corner
of the woodshed in Green Bay. I laid out

slashing casts, floated a soaked Brown Hackle
everywhere but over the big fish, for some reason failed
to put him down, finally gave up and yelled
for my uncle. I'll never forget
the wondrous calm
with which he looked things over. I've modeled
my aspirations to collectedness

on the way he stood
that evening on the edge
of the Clay Bank Pool, on the South Branch
of the Oconto River not far
from Suring, light dimming, a late hatch

of something big and pale and vaporous
coming off the water like slight
coalescences of mist, mosquitoes
beginning to hum in my ear, a light breeze
in the overhanging branches of the white pines
on the far side of the stream, and just at the edge
of a midstream V in the current, over
and over again, that great, loud, leisurely insuck
of the big fish. I itched

for that fish, my mind was scoured clean
as a riffle by floods and freshets of desire. But Vince
just stood there, humming a little
to himself finally said aloud

OK, in the half-dark sure-fingered tied on
a fluttery-looking white thing
the size of my thumb, and with his old-time English
elbow-to-the-side-strictly-wrist-
and-forearm cast laid down that fly three feet above
and two inches to the right
of the rise ring, upon which the rainbow came
to the White Miller, and at that instant
arose in me that day on the North Branch
in that fourteenth year
of what turned out to be
my life, this great, persistent yearning,

to possess that fly, to have it for my own, study it,
hold it in my hand, feel what vibrancy, what
radiance of blood it must have been
brought that big rainbow a foot
out of water, to hang blazing there
in what seemed to me
foreordination of fury!

Letter

The eyes burn and the hands tremble
at your letter about the evening hatch
last Saturday on the big bend
of the Winooski, and it's
pure envy upsets me, no, regret
as much as envy, that I wasn't there
with you. What you tell me makes me wish

to change the subject, otherwise
I won't be able to get on
with what's left to me of my life. So

here goes, I've
kept busy, among other things been digging
into the history of the St. Joe valley,
and lately have made the acquaintance
of the Chevalier de La Salle,
likewise of Hennepin,
who, after nine months
on the lower Mississippi, and forced
to spend the winter at Michilimakinac,
thought to pass the dead time by preaching
on holy days. I remember

there was a stream not far
from Mackinac, I'd visit
it in July for a week, and every night I'd go down
to the river at six and fish till dark,
sometimes till after dark, and it
was gorgeous, standstill, one spot

did you for the night, you caught a trout
and waited five minutes till the others

started rising again, then went at it
again, or maybe walked
ten yards, in those days, though,
sometimes a little static for my tastes, I used
to like to move more. And I've discovered

that the Miami used to kill
as many as two hundred buffalo daily
near here, on the river plain
which is now the city dump, and that
a pioneer woman once killed a deer
with a pitchfork in the Kankakee swamp. Most recently

I have spent one entire Holy Day
of Obligation killing,
skinning and pickling
a large French rabbit,
for *hasenpfeffer*. And what else? My old friend

Peaches Granfield
is dead, who used
to camp with me, we'd camp
at Idlewild to fish for trout and shoot
at bats. You might

have liked that—with a full
stomach and the supper dishes lying around and the bats
swooping out of the darkness of the spruces
to circle over the blaze, and Peaches
with a strong flashlight
cunningly held on one of them
I'd pepper away with the .410. Peaches

was a noble fellow, most perfectly
certain of his place in the world, in consequence
utterly insensitive. You may not know
he began as a butcher, but the trade

proved too dangerous
for a man like him, who could not talk
without waving his long arms around,
and one day he rammed a piece of chuck
into the grinder, and his hand
along with it, straight
into the hamburger, then retailing
at 18¢ a pound. Well, against

all reason I persist, keep
busy, can still
use my shop, handle the tools
quite as well as before, it seems, thank
God, or wing
a *Duchess* or a *Childers*
or a *Dirty Orange,* though when
I tire, I really sag, my legs
get cold and stiff, and even
the wood ticks don't seem to want me
anymore. I'd love
to have seen it, love

to have been there with you
with all those rainbows coming up
and eager for the fly, even if I had not
been able, as surely
I would not have been, to fish. Mayflies,
against all reason, persist

on the St. Joe, a handsome
dark gray one lit on my hand
only yesterday, despite the fact

that this July the river
seems to be sweating, or at least
it's the color of sweat—you'll have
to imagine for yourself what I mean—lately,
though my eye for them persists,
the resemblances have begun
to resist my saying. This letter

is disorderly, I'm afraid, but things
are changing for me, therefore

for the world which over all these years
has accustomed itself
to being seen by me
in my particular way
and discovers it a grievous business
to have to reset itself, so that often
I wake up these days
in a confusion of recollection, maybe
on the North Branch, when I was young and just
beginning to fish, and could be on the water a week
and be alone, never see
another angler,

and there'd be wild rainbows rising, leaping, flashing
all over the pools, from bottom
to top, sometimes
the entire river seeming to go
green and crimson
with them, and I knew nothing
about the dry fly, though later

there came a couple of wild evenings
in the Oxbow when the March Brown
was on, and once on the Dugway Pool
with little olives, but mostly

it has been a slow
hard work, as we all
have come to know.

The Little Beaver

The turbines at Johnson's Falls
up on the Peshtigo would open,
every morning at seven and the water
would come up three feet in thirty minutes, first
a few twigs and leaves, then a slight
muddying, and then before we knew it
we were having a hard time getting back
to shore, where the rocks and logs

we'd been sitting on an hour before
would be covered, only big V-shaped wrinkles
on the brown surface, and what had been a little riffle
would be a rapids filled with noise
and crazy water. At four

the slots would close, the water fall, and by five
the big river would be a series of clear runs
and riffles between pools. Where one tip of granite
had stuck up, now
a reef of bare rock and sand was drying
in the sun, a few trout would be making
neat swirls near the ledges of the far shore,
and along the banks where we walked
the sweet fern giving off smells
of verbena and sage. So midsummers

what with all the risings
and fallings, I used to give up
on the Peshtigo and seek out

the small rivers, like the Beaver, near Pound,
a little stream, two men fishing it
one man too many, yet
it yielded many a three-pounder,
though to look at it you had to wonder

how such a trout could find the room
to turn around. Try to get to it,
you had to crash brush so thick
you couldn't always get your arms free
to swat mosquitoes and black flies, and once

you came to the water's edge, you like as not
found yourself trapped in some alder hell,
black flies up your nose and in your ears, wood ticks
in your crotch, one foot
on a root above the water, the other
caught in a tangle behind you, or up
to the calf in a mudhole or quicksand, trout
darting away in every direction,
Little Beaver brookies,
spotted crimson in pale blue
halos, spotted lemon
and white, backs
moss-mottled-to-black, bellies
shaded off to a golden ivory,
fins striped orange and anthracite
and white.

Try wading it, you had to bend
double to keep under the arch
of the willows, and there would be
blockades of logs and roots to be stumbled
and scrambled over, and at every step you flushed out trout,
there in the brook like sardines. But finally
I had to give up on that river, got a cramp

in my back one day, stooping
under the alders, had to crawl out through the swamp
on my hands and knees, was two hours
getting to my car, bad hurting all the way,
out of necessity took to fishing from a boat,
a real comedown I felt it,

going out with Fenske, who
isn't always too certain where he is
or what he's about, one time
when he looked up at the comet
fell over right on his back
in the marsh mud. A man

like Fenske's no good on a river
like the Little Beaver, goddam
pike fisherman, that's what he is,
hardly ever shaves, smells
worse than a skunk in heat,
drunkest man I ever saw,

if you were to give him two dollars
for telling the truth and twenty cents
for lying, he'd take the twenty cents
every time. He used to bring
two tons of gear along in his old GMC
when we went out, his feeling was
it was easier to take it all
than to have to figure out
what he needed. That was Fenske, he had what it took

to make a good pike fisherman—sorry,
Great Northern Pike fisherman. Fish & Game
and the Tourist Bureau people,
what they did was they took our sorry old jack pike
that nobody would carry through the streets
and want to be seen with, and gave him
a brand new name, Great Northern Pike, and made
a million-dollar fish out of him. Wouldn't
of made fifty cents with *snake,* which is what
everybody called him when we was kids. Hell, that's what
I ought to do with carp, Great Copper Bass,
how's that? Make my goddam fortune, which God knows
I could use. One thing I've learned in an otherwise
pretty useless life, the name you give a thing
makes all the difference in the world. Oh, I loved that brook,

the Little Beaver, such beautiful
gliding water. When finally I'd break through to it
at the heart of that awful snarl
of swamp willow, cedar,
alder hell and mud, the world in thickets
between me and the road,
it would be trembling in the sun.

Big Water

My brother and I never caught
one of the big rainbows for which the Soo
was famous, though he hooked into something once
that smashed his rod with one run,
and left him swearing
like a sonuvabitch. Oh it was exciting
just to know they were there, the big fish,
and when the water was low

and the light was right you could look down
from the top of the dam at the head
of the river and see them, long
gray shapes lying easy in the water,
almost still, maybe once in a while
a little curl of a fin. One year
we heard of a local had been arrested
with a thirty-three pounder
that he'd speared. That kept us coming back
five years more at least, though between us
we caught exactly nothing, *half
of nothing apiece,* my brother said,
and we worked hard for it. We'd cross the locks
and fish all day in the tail race below

the powerhouse, edging out into
the heavy water to where
we didn't dare take another step, or turn

around even, and had to back
into shore over stones round and smooth
and slippery as you'll imagine
skull bones might be. Or we'd fish
from the spit of land beyond the tail race, in the rapids, bell
ringing behind us, horns bellowing and whistles screaming
from the ore carriers warped in to the big bollards
on the locks, men in foreign-looking caps

yelling up messages
to the crews on deck: *If you see Georgie McInnis
in Duluth, tell him Oley
is working at the Soo.* Other men

on the approaches to the locks
fished for whitefish with forty feet of line, and two
large mayflies on the hook, and you could look down
and see shining schools of fry, thirty yards
across, and suddenly
they'd melt away as a big trout
came cruising by only ten
or twelve feet down. It was good times, that's for sure,

when my brother and I
could get together at the Soo, big trout
on our minds, we'll be together at the Soo,
where we stayed at Mrs. Letourneau's Boarding House
every year in August for fourteen years
because it was cheap, and there was a tub
set on lion paws, and long enough
for a tall man to straighten out his legs, and deep enough
to bring the water to his chest—stayed there

in spite of the bugs. I remember
the first night there, I dreamed
I was covered with specks
of fire, woke up, there was a bug
working on me, I jumped up and pulled
the covers off the mattress, there they were,
half a dozen things big as potato bugs crawling up
the bed board, and I woke up my brother

in a panic, I said "There's bedbugs, the place
is crawling with bugs," but in the war he'd served
in India with the Brits, with kraits and cobras and bugs
could swell your balls
to the size of cantaloupes, "What of it,
go to sleep!" he said. So what the hell, I went out
to the car and spent the night
in the back seat. Every year for fourteen years

my brother and I went back to work
the rapids, our heads aching with what
it would be like to hang into one
of those fish. Never did. Last year I went
back to the Soo alone, stayed one day, first time

in years, everything changed, my brother
dead, wife and daughter
dead, nobody talking
about big fish, the whitefish
long gone account of the lampreys, likewise
the lakers, everybody's mind
on something else or other, though lots

of guys out fishing on the docks
because of not much work,
and nothing much else to do, sitting there
waiting it out, bored and cold

in a sheeting rain that day, water pouring
off their hats and down their necks and into the sleeves
of their jackets every time they raised
their arms, and to top it off
the day I was there the turbines
were shut down, and the slots closed, the race
no more than a series of riffles and runs
between pools—though in the taverns
the proof was there, up on the walls behind the bars,
over the mirrors in glass cases, there they were, the big fish,
a little the worse for the years
they'd hung there, dusty, varnish peeling, paint
pretty garish in some cases, nevertheless for all
the bug-eyes, cracked and missing fins
there they were, mounts

of twelve- and fifteen-pound rainbows
come to the fly out there
in the rapids, the guides
straining at their poles trying to hold the canoes
upright and steady, the canoes
still pitching and rolling plenty, the sports
rolling out their heavy lines, the flies
floating down the feeding lanes
of that demented water,

and the great trout coming
to the fly, breaking water, suspending themselves
over the rapids, an outburst, a levitation
of high-leaping rainbows, striped scarlet, striped
cherry-red, green-
gilled, brilliant
in the ripe, sun-smelling day!

Thunder River

I used to love coming onto the dark pools
of the Thunder to find
a school of dace skittering
crazily along the surface, then everything

going still again, so that I knew
something big must be at work, and it might pay me
to walk upstream and bait up a small hook with a tiny piece
of redworm and catch me a small dace and cut the tail off
and throw the rest back into the river where
it would turn and bump downstream along
the bottom giving back

little golden measures of light, then to thread
the chub tail onto a bigger hook and drift it
down into the pool and let it swing
in short silvery arcs, the sun meantime

rising higher, maybe a deerfly
buzzing in narrowing circles
around my head, the air
going heavy with the sweetness
of crushed ferns and warm hemlock.
But usually nothing

would happen, though once
in a while a big fish might flash
deep in the pool, or boil
at something I couldn't see, the thick back
porpoising, rise rings spreading
to splash the edges of the bank.

And always before I expected it
the sound of the woods would be rising
everywhere around me, the hour gone abruptly late
and dark having come on, wind
booming in the hemlocks
and behind me somewhere

where I'd never find them again
the runs and riffles of the Thunder
would come alive, the great pools
and oxbows flashing with big night-feeding

rainbows, swimming against the press
of the river, cavernously
gaping, flaring out ruffs
of scarlet gills, the water
storming about them, stony
in their throats, and the skin of the pools ashine
with schools of frenzied dace.
Exhausted, fly-bitten, muddy, hungry,

and sweating, I'd look up and see
nothing, no stars even, only the dark lock
and interlock of hemlocks—until
once on the road, I'd look up again and meet
the cool eye of the moon just
swum up from the deepest poolings of space,
for the rest of the night to poise itself directly
over wherever I might find myself
in my long walk home along County Z,
to hold itself steady and head-on above me
huge in the huge current of the sky.

From
SINKING CREEK

(LYONS BOOKS, 1998)

"Sinking Creek drops gradually down to the town of Newport, Virginia, then crosses under US460. Something remarkable happens on this last stretch. The flow becomes sparser and sparser. Then, finally in a meadow just above the New River, Sinking Creek lives up to its name and quietly disappears."

—Harry Slone, *Virginia Trout Streams*

PART I

Death Trip

Fleeing Monaghan

The rhododendron overmastered
everything, nettles
flourished, the composts
steamed, and in the rank hollows
at the foot of the drive

the spawn-ridden fill
from the mushroom barns
daily thrust up a thousand
pale heads,

and so I fled,
holed up at the dead end
of the line, and found one day
somewhere outside Tralee that rat's-warren
of a graveyard, rats

at the old graves, bits and pieces
of casket handles, satin scraps,
medallions, something I took
for a finger bone and something

likely worse had I cared
to look more closely or venture
further into that Christ-awful green
and dripping place,

its only light a Traveler's cart
citron, scarlet, orange and blue
for hire at the gate.

Stove Cleaning

The stove
lies on its side in the snowy yard,
spilling rust-flakes,
scale and cinders. I figure it

for seventy years
since last it held fire,
and scrub at the cold flowers of soot
which bloom three inches thick in the firebox.

Cracked hob,
missing grate and one
fire cover shattered because
my grandpa used it as a base plate

for a twenty-ton hydraulic jack.
Rusting ailanthus leaves
frame the doors, combers and crests
support the clawed

legs; posts and finials, rosebud
handles, a stag's head
on the fire door. The mad white eye
of the fire gauge glares

from a field of lilies, and ridges,
ledges, scrolls of nickel-plate
ascend the silvery pillar
of the pipe. Once it's clean

it will be one goddamned glorious
beauty of a stove, and I can't wait
to fire it up and see the needle swing
from COLD to HIGH HEAT, to move

the damper knob from KINDLE to BAKE, and feel
the room get summery, though it will be weeks,
weeks, before the old residues
have worn themselves from my hands.

Night Game in Right Field

Lord, but that ball would rise
high in the flare of the lights
become like something always there,
round, full, shining little moon,

float longer than it should,
and then decline to exactly where
I ought to have found myself
camped under it, casual, easy

—instead, scared
and staring blind into the lights,
born to retribution of mismeasure,
I always froze, my last hope luck,

or absent luck, then somehow
revelation, would pray
that this one time, just this once,
I might know exactly where

on the field to set myself, might
reckon rightly the convergences, hot glove
waiting, ready to make
the play, lovingly to gather in

that elegant curve
of the falling into place.

Death Trip

1

For a long time the family kept it from me,
later said they'd thought I'd had it bad enough
the baby not yet even six months dead,
so that by the time they couldn't put it off

for one more day, and finally called, and I'd
bullied the Credit Union to open up
at 9 P.M., and made the loan, and bought
the ticket, managed to get out

to the airport onto the last
flight to Chicago, then barely caught
the commuter to South Bend, she'd died,
it was over—or probably just

about Pittsburgh it was over, me
forking up cold eggs from a chilly plate,
listening to the stewardess announce
she was sorry, no help for it, we

were a little behind, nevertheless
thought there was a better than good chance
we'd make up our lost time, said we had
a powerful tailwind, didn't see

how after all we could be too very late.

2

Back in South Bend after twenty years,
first thing got the cab to swing by
the old place, knew every corner, every
tree, saw one or two

might have been neighbors once,
turned onto East Napoleon
Boulevard, and there it was—
or something like it anyway,

house numbers gone, porch pillars painted
some godawful blue, the willows, grown
from slips she'd brought
from Mt. Vernon back in '42

gone; lilacs, flame bush
gone; got out, stood there
by the cab, our meters
ticking, engines cycling—

some plastic drapes kept me from seeing in,
thank God, perhaps.

3

At the wake, my dear
old fluttery grandma who through it all
kept busy, anxious that everyone
be fed sufficiently and well,

quite suddenly, both hands full
of plates and napkins, stopped
dead to cry aloud into
the convivially feeding crowd, *oh*

my . . . oh

my . . .

4

At the funeral home the old man said
it was a good thing I'd missed her,
hadn't seen her like she was, she was
so bad, the pain

had changed her so. My sister said
she wouldn't have known me anyway,
my brother explained
several times in his most reasonable voice

how she wouldn't have wanted me
to see her that way, he
was sorry, though, took all
the blame, should have called me

sooner. Next day came
the wake. I urged myself
up there to stand beside her
in her coffin, though in the end

neither of us looked the other's way.

Mud Season: My Grandma Mourning

In Memory of Laura Perry

Spring being always a joy for her,
the April she was eighty I drove her
into the hills around Lincoln, scraping
the oil pan, lumping

through ruts and potholes, the roads
as they say in Vermont in the spring,
twenty foot wide
by three foot deep, I began to think

we'd never make it out of there.
But my grandma was looking out
at the little farms in their poor fields,
the maple and spruce

and juniper stealing down
into the pastures, mullein
burdock, milkweed
everywhere, likewise everywhere

the cellar holes, empty as graves
the day of resurrection, fringed
at the north ends with lilac, south
forsythia, and where the front steps had been

the first rusty shoots
of the peonies, sometimes
a dustiness of little blue
flowers, maybe forget-me-nots

carpeting the family cemeteries
where the men lay dead
in their forties, the women
their thirties, the children

their first or second years. *"The winters!"*
my grandma whispered,
"the poor things!" That was all, she
wasn't one to be word-struck

much beyond occasion. Once she wanted me
to stop, "Only
for a minute," my grandma said
"I want to see

the names." Though it shames me
to recall, I didn't dare
slow even a little in that spring mud,
too much afraid of bogging down,

knowing those roads too well,
knowing you had to anticipate
trouble, that above all else
you had to keep good headway on.

Elegy in the Third Week of November

In Memory of Joanne Rathgeb

Snow driving in from the Adirondacks
through full strong sunlight, first snow
of this summery fall still abloom
with cosmos, geranium, calendula

—though the maples
were never fooled, and clattered
bonily night upon night
from the south winds

that should have smelled
like snow. The snow
held off, though earlier by far
the butternut saw it coming,

and gave up, and started dropping
slippery, unsweepable leaves
all over the driveways and decks—
this in the middle of September

when it wasn't yet clear
that the weathers would turn
against us, though of course
we ought to have known, and we did know—

meanwhile the late flowering
that astonished us to hope.

PART II

Suicide Notes

Question

One time it occurred to me—walking
some back lane in Monaghan in a fine rain,
rain dripping from my hat brim,
the edges of the woods aflame

with the alien rhododendron—
one need not go home. I stopped dead
in the road, rejoicing, shuddered
with delight at the truth of it,

but then was astonished at myself,
for surely I did not love where I was,
and longed to be from where I had come—
though not for the life of me could I remember

a thing of that place, though I imagined
it might have been in a flat land, among flowers,
or beside an ocean somewhere, in either case
white clouds shaping and reshaping themselves.

I thought I must have believed
that in those places the earth
truly loved me, and probably
could scarcely breathe

waiting for what was to come. What was it
memory clamored for? After all these years,
I have forgotten
the familiar language of questions

Now I put them wrong, nothing
about them is necessary,
so how shall I answer
what I cannot ask?

Instances of Blood in Iowa

for Calvin Kentfield

1

That year at Iowa there were with me
Calvin and Veronica and Karl,
and Gail, each thinking we loved the other—not
that it matters now, for Calvin leaped

from the cliffs at Palomar, and broke, and died
on the sharp screes at the base, and I
am as slow to memory as to love:
of Gail, Veronica and Karl I no longer know.

2

I make a picture of that year:
the engraving shows
the locks at Keokuk, about to close
on a black barge; a yellow mist;

and overhead, too high
in the orders of memory to clearly see
and give a name to, a giant bird
hanging in the sky, wings wide.

3

I try remembering how blood
beat in my wrists the day I stared
at the fat model, whose big breasts
were the first that I'd seen bare,

or the night I chanced on Veronica,
surprised, transparent, naked
as a ghost upon the stairs, clutching
a white cloth to her breast. But when I tried

431

to make a picture out of this
the burin leaped and cleanly
tore my palm—whereupon the proof
displayed itself: red meat and yellow fat,

the white shine of the mortal bone before
blood welled and streamed
onto the copper plate, and dried.

4

Once, when I asked him why it was
he bothered to write poems, Karl sighed,
laid wrist to pale forehead, closed
his eyes, and cried: *Because I must!*

Blood deeply etched
the plate. For days
I scraped away at the dried crusts
with a palette knife, and meantime tried

to get my belly flat with fasting, but
it broke me, every time. One day I woke up
still full of blood and fat,
and was briefly considered for Suez,

though in the end Ike spared my life
to such mean evidence of breath as this,
beyond which circumstance
not much. The ruined plate I sailed far

into the woods. The nameless model hides
her breasts, like Veronica, and holds
a supine pose, all thigh and mottled
buttock. My hand is scarred. It shows.

5

As for the rest:
I mostly think of Calvin
who gives me back the lean and distant look
from far beyond return of favor for

the night he wrestled down drunk
crazy Karl, who'd run
a bread knife through my hand, with one
knee held him there, and took

my wrist and turned my hand palm-up,
his fingers streaming with my blood, his feet
in blood, blood everywhere. And I
still can and do

largely mourn for Calvin, who is dead,
and carried with him everything we knew—
how in the last good days of that last year
we nearly fled,

took to the boats, jumped ship
in Borneo, stayed drunk
in Peleleu, but in the end
did not. Blood leaps

in my wrists. I think
of Calvin with his arms like wings
stretched wide to hold him steady
to the air, and I

am standing on the sharp, receptive rocks
and looking up, the cold sea
at my feet, and he—
too high to clearly name

in the last free instant, arms wide,
hanging there.

The 20th Century Limited

Close at the edge of the platform
already terrified
to ecstasy, waiting

for the enormous winds
of its approach, smash
and wallop of drive rods

smoke billowing
everywhere—
my brother, my parents,

everything from ten feet out
gone spectral
through steam, so joyous

an uproar
of steam, of steel-
to-steel so fine

a hullabaloo
as I haven't known
since but ache,

crave and hanker and itch,
pine, lust for and thirst and
yearn for still, that

great suck and inrush
of vacuum,
power of in-pull, that resistless

horror of the edging in

Suicide Notes

1

Maybe when we're dead
we talk to those
we loved, and they hear us,

but they don't understand,
and what they hear
seems so alien

they're frightened by it,
and maybe then they talk to us
to say they're afraid, but we

are too troubled, too wrapped
in our troubles, to listen,
we still wonder if we're done,

if we're done with everything,
in the world we cared for,
if we're done

with the world—I think things
like this, and they seem
to come from far

back, far, far back
like they've been catching up on me
for longer than I've lived,

suddenly this night-soaked
fear, a scratching
of who knows what on some

surface in my room, and I wake up
in my bed, next instant
there's nothing at the window, I mean

a window where nothing is, where
just as I must have thought to look
had to have been something looking back

2

The dead suddenly
have regained their voices.
They have opinions. They are not reluctant

to express them—yet incautiously
once more they are leaning
toward that silence,

though it had not come to them
with anything like ease. Now their voices
mumble in the dark halls

of my dreams. I know it's best
to not answer them, even though
I cannot keep myself from the question.

3

I found the air
between the high surge of the sky
and the earth alive

with a few snowflakes.
Mornings when I waked up
I felt a tightening

behind my knees. I used
to narrow my eyes
at the dead—*they were*

so elegantly poised!
I was sick
of the skin of my voice,

found every dream
a dead loss, though never
omitted to take notice. I damned

the obliquities, tried
to persuade myself
from the act of retrieval.

I believed it was truly
*dogs to their vomit, crows
to carrion!* Dead leaves

were always whirling
at my feet.

4

I imagine that in the death by falling,
the dreadful giving-way,
there will be time to see

the slow flowering planet
open to me, and to think
with what power, how shatteringly

I will be embraced—or even that
I might with safety
penetrate the grass,

the cold rock, somehow survive
the fire at the center, then fly
through the green, lightening seas

on the far side—but knowing, knowing
the whole time how I will in fact
bloody the hard edge of the world

with what there is of me that even though
it may fall lightly, does not wish to fly.

5

Every morning breath
comes indisputably slower,
the heart assumes this certain

slight reluctance, and my eyes
hide themselves from light
till the last possible moment

when I awaken toward
the next possible morning.

6

This morning, the first of February,
the water in the dog's dish frozen,
cold air knifing in from every crack,

I remember how last night I'd thought I'd leave,
but didn't, seeing there was no place
for me to go, lacking besides courage

for anything but threats, conviction
about everything but fear. The sky
like water frozen in a deep

blue-bottom dish, backed me down.
And being this coward, I thought I'd die
if death came free, if there were no

pain, nothing I'd have to admit to,
be sorry for, think I might
have handled better if only

I'd taken the time to reason it
out. So now, this morning, driving to work,
I'm invited by telephone poles, bridges,

maple stumps, but not wanting to die
under the ice of a river, or in any cold way,
not liking to think of the instant before

when I without hope might suddenly
wish for it not to happen, the ragged spear
of the spruce pole piercing windshield and chest,

my heart convulsing on the wood, lungs
full of splinters and creosote, myself
probably trying to say

one last thing into the air of Vermont,
some word to whatever at that instant might seem
to require recognition, but lacking

a usable breath to discharge what I
even at that moment will consider
a duty, and hesitate.

7

In this tag end of the bad weather to the south
the garden blows flat . . . petals and leaves
fly everywhere, without falling,

until the rain begins, and then
become a sodden confetti on the lawn.
Then thunder, then lightning.

The house is dead calm. I think of it
as the space it displaces in this black
foaming of the air. There is no place for me

in all this tumult. I am unsuited.
It grows darker and darker. The lamps
break into something like speech. They dazzle

and deafen. I go around
shutting off lights.

8

With poems it's much the same
as with the dead and me. I mean
that with the dead and me

only this little
of all that's forgotten remains.
We've been invaded

by this love of silence.

9

Against my will the dead
return to me, crystals
advancing in their eyes, grey

lesions of hand and tongue. They come to me
one by one, their breaths
freezing on the walls. They think

love can resume
its complicated pose,
and they affect, therefore,

a garrulous blood, they pretend
to a raucous, inflexible heart, in this
outrageous embrace in which

on the coldest nights the rooster's crow
freezes like thorns
to the branches of the heart.

10

This body has built itself
out of its own memory
which has been marked by fault

of disproportion.
Already the dying organisms
have begun peacefully

to unite among themselves.
Soon they will believe
they never existed, soon

they will understand
how they have added up
to a body shameful with sweat

and troubled with accumulation.
Soon everything will remain
simply the small suffocations of matter.

11

The windows open.
At the locked heart of the house.
The mirrors tremble—no way to tell

if it's night or morning,
the sun shudders so
at the far edges of the sky.

In another room,
a window slides itself open.
Maybe in time

the mirrors will remember us,
but our reflections
will be a trick of the eye.

Be wary, keep watch:
they are bent on reentry.

PART III

At Summer's End

A Few Words from the Septuagenarian Proprietor of This Establishment

for Bill Dunlop

In the great repose of evening
after the fat reds of the sunset,
space seems joyous. My right leg, knee, hip
are undecided as to whether

to support me. But I'm standing,
I'm still standing
on the world at this place in this time,
in some assurance

that trout are in the brooks,
quail, pheasants, grouse at large
in the corn rows, prairies,
woodlands. It's true

that sometimes I feel
preserved as a ham,
that at such times my body
begins to hunger

after itself. It has turned out dangerous
to have thought of the body
as enclosing the heart
in benediction or caress,

for now have begun the swellings
inward, the uproll
of blood, the devouring. My legs
which have for the most part loved me,

despite their best efforts
persevere in uncertainty
to the very point that movement seems
most times a destiny. They have begun

to separate themselves from me,
and my feet from my legs,
however hard I try
to fall in and march.

Such a suffusion
of yellow light tonight, such
densities of sky and cloud, the moon
preparing to establish itself, the comet

expected. My eyes
are in my head for aesthetic reasons,
my ears too, though
I cannot account

for nose or mouth,
or bare skull, or beard.
When I smile,
it is because I have come

to love, no, to desire,
hats, I wear large sweaters
loose as chasubles, I've begun
to accompany myself

almost everywhere. I talk
to myself softly, seriously.

—*from Hollins, February 1996*

Hummingbird on a Telephone Wire

On this dank mosquito-ridden road on Gun Point, up in Maine
wondering just how far I can go and still get back, without someone
having to call the rescue squad, I happen to glance up, and see
this vivid little dab of color on the telephone wire, a hummingbird

perched there like a little sleeked-down bunch of green
and scarlet petals—never saw such a thing before, thought
they weakened and fell dead if they didn't eat their weight
every ten minutes. I watch it for ten minutes, and it doesn't move,

gets me worrying, and as usual I start to think it's up to me, I'd better
do something, call its attention to itself, maybe
it doesn't have sense enough to know it's hungry, maybe
it's already too weak to fly. So I try,

but can't scare it off, it won't move, won't be saved
though I think it sees me, for it turns its head
side to side a little, shifts a little, but will not fly, until
the very instant I quit all my cane-waving, hooting,

gingerly hopping on the one good leg, give up yelling
at it, fly, go find a flower, eat!—and then it gives me a look
and takes off flying strong and definite in the direction of the sea
where no flowers grow, and I look after it for a minute,

then work myself up to limp on another hundred feet or so,
but give up on that, too, turn around, walk home head-on
into the rich stink of the sea that this whole time has been building up
behind me—kelp and fish-guts, clam shells, salt and gull-shit,

the islands just offshore white with it, the beach adding
something cold and stony, just under it all a powerful sweetness,
roadside leaves and flowers—in this place wild roses, mostly,
though also beach pea, lupine, cow-vetch, even the occasional patch

of pink or yellow lady slippers, not to mention
maybe five varieties of goldenrod, nor the singular fern
I'm on the outlook to encounter, and which
I'm almost certain never to have seen before.

Japtan and Long Point

I waded the reef through a building surf,
wary of morays, trying to keep dry,
the ledger I'd used for a plant press stuffed
with pandanus leaves, hibiscus blossoms,

some other flowers I hadn't got round
to figuring out just what they were. Now,
thirty-eight years later, this July day
on Long Point up in Maine, the sea beyond

the white oak ridge smells exactly the same
as on Japtan that day in '54
when I'd quit my botanizing, waded
in from the bombed-out Japanese half-track,

where I'd sat in the commander's cockpit
from which ten years before he'd faced the low
rise of the beach, the line of palms, and next
instant was nothing, just old blood bound up

in rust the color of old blood. I stare
back at the morning sun above Long Point
into which the sky's emptying itself.
One gull slides, swings, and sideslips overhead.

The sea's aswarm with sunlight shot back from
the little chop, and the bird up there plays
this wind for all he can get out of it,
never, so far as I can see, glancing down,

though surely he is hunting.

At Summer's End

Early August, and the young butternut
is already dropping its leaves, the nuts
thud and ring on the tin roof,

the squirrels are everywhere.
Such richness! It means something to them
that this tree should seem so eager

to finish its business.
The voice softens, a word becomes air
the moment it is spoken. You finger the limp leaves.

Precisely to the degree that you have loved something:
a house, a woman, a bird, this tree, anything at all,
you are punished by time.

Like the tree,
I take myself by surprise.

Poem and a Near Dream on My 65th Birthday

The shadow of the big dead elm
shines blue as a peacock's breast
against the snow. It's not enough. I've loved

nothing, nothing, nothing
about the weathers of this place:
the summer stink of mildew

in the basements, thin mosses
and lichens blotching the pickets
of the garden fences. Now,

more than ever, the language
eludes me, my tongue's
gone strange in my mouth. Tonight

for all the birthday food
that glues my guts together, for all
the grammarless dream talk,

at this close edge of sleep, I can't
sleep, out of somewhere
bring to mind white fences, an excitement

of beetles clumsy in the weeds, wing-cases
like oil-sheen on water, clambering
eagerly the seed-heads, disposed to fly

straight into the huge
shining beetle-shape of the sun.

—January 19, 1996

Booyah

Whenever he got to feeling emotional my father
would cook up a mess of chicken booyah.
He'd get out the copper boiler
and hose it out, and fill it half full
of water, then another quarter full
of Gettelman's Thousand Dollar Beer,
and into this throw two pounds of onions,
tomatoes, a pound of carrots, some turnips,
a dozen big potatoes
with a little Bay Settlement red clay
left on for the flavor, then bay leaves, salt,
and peppercorns you had to watch out for

later on, and six or seven cut-up fryers, all this
boiled down, for seven or eight or ten hours—depending
on how time had begun to present itself
to him—over an oak and maple fire
in the back yard, so that everything

transformed itself. For the first two hours
it was beer, and the next two
Hungarian wine, cheap stuff, *bikéver* "Bull's
Blood" was what you called for, a shot of it
at the Golden West Tavern on Highway 64,
chasing it with a seven-ounce Gettelman, and after that
Four Roses all the way,
so that by the time the booyah was ready,

he wouldn't be hungry. I took a job
out of state, and being as how it made him sorrowful,
he scheduled a party. When I said
I just wanted out of there,
he told me I owed him that much,

at least, a proper send-off, I could forget
the rest of it, whatever he meant
by that. The family came,
aunts, cousins and uncles and some others

he said were relatives but who
I couldn't remember
ever having seen before, but had no particular
reason to doubt. A half dozen
of his tavern buddies, came and started drinking
and played poker dice on the picnic table, slamming
the leather cup down so hard
the glasses jumped and the silverware
clamored. He got drunk
pretty fast, there were plenty of signs

I knew to look for, all the time
the booyah richening
over the fire, cooking down, getting thicker
and darker, the air
smelling as good as anything
ever likely would smell. When my mother died

he threw a booyah party and after the boilermakers,
just at the start of Four Roses, he gave a speech
about how he wanted
to kill himself and if he'd had a gun
he'd do it that very minute,
and if I'd had a gun

I'd have given it to him. I still recall
that smell—wake up to it sometimes,
out of a dream I can never wholly remember,
in which the air had taken on
a complicated texture, an extravagant design,
and the world seemed a glorious concoction, a commingling,
of everything into everything
else it could never have been before
some one instant in the long course
of the long fire.

Cranberry-Orange Relish

A pound of ripe cranberries, for two days
macerate in a dark rum, then do not
treat them gently, but bruise,
mash, pulp, squash
with a wooden pestle
to an abundance of juices, in fact
until the juices seem on the verge

of overswelling the bowl, then drop in
two fistsful, maybe three, of fine-
chopped orange with rind, two golden
blobs of it, and crush
it in, and then add sugar, no thin
sprinkling, but a cupful dumped
and awakened with a wooden spoon

to a thick suffusion, drench of sourness, bite of color,
then for two days let conjoin
the lonely taste of cranberry,
the joyous orange, the rum, in some
warm corner of the kitchen, until
the bowl faintly becomes
audible, a scarce wash of sound, a tiny

bubbling, and then
in a glass bowl set it out
and let it be eaten last, to offset
gravied breast and thigh
of the heavy fowl, liverish
stuffing, the effete
potato, lethargy of pumpkins

gone leaden in their crusts, let it be eaten
so that our hearts may be together overrun
with comparable sweetnesses,
tart gratitudes, until finally,

dawdling and groaning, we bear them
to the various hungerings
of our beds, lightened
of their desolations.

Vertigo

Often I start awake
in the middle of the night,
sweating, spread-eagled
on the bed, and it seems time

at the bare edge
of some dream, and I confess
to embarrassment
at being so

outmatched, my heart
so endeavoring from me.
And to get up at night in a dark room
is, I tell you, to work hard

at balance, to fall
into doors, trip
over things. Again
tonight without thinking

I jump up and feel
the quick twist of a darkness
not the room's, reel,
catch myself, try

to steady myself, and then
still giddy, feel my way
to the window to see
what could have come over me

through the locked window,
the tight blinds.

Stink

My father, I don't want to, won't, can't
talk about him, know it's wrong of me, isn't
Christian, I've confessed it
once a week now my whole life,

but he was a bad man, and I
hated him—so this
is a punishment, that I can't wear
my glasses anymore, the sores

on my nose won't allow it, I can't
read the *Blade* anymore, can't read
anything, can't see to get around
the house, though you'd think I'd know

my way blindfolded after seventy years
in this one place, but my shins
tell the story, a mess of blood and scabs,
and I blacked an eye last week

on the bedroom door, can't see
the garden, only smell it, of course
the garden's another story, I know
where everything is, remember the layout

perfectly, it's where I really ought to live,
and I'm aware I always cared more
for five months of gardening
than a year of housekeeping, cared more

for those smells and colors, and if
I were all blind I could still find my way
to anything, give you all the names
of the big smells—lilacs, of course, but alyssum, too,

and iris, and the rose, the climbing Blaze, only
the one, never cared or could get interested
in any but this old climber, takes no care, I spend more time
propping up the trellis than on feeding & pruning & all the rest

you've got to provide those delicate, fainting
hybrids. As for me
and my own trellis, well, I never
was much of a bloomer even

when I was young, but never delicate, either,
and occasionally you could have found me
easy enough by the smell—I carried peanuts
in a pocket every day for seventy years, smoked Holiday

pipe tobacco, sweetened myself up
with witch hazel or Mennen Skin Bracer, produced
my good share of sweat, made fragrant
more than one shirt, hat, pair of shoes, have given off

more than a faint stink of sin, I'm sure, only one
truly big one, though, not prideful to say I always tried to be
a good man, good to my daughter, now dead, to my wife,
now dead, my friends, most of them

dead too, and to the world in general, as much
as I could be—with failures plenty, of course, plenty
to be ashamed of, but I tried my best, my best gift
the garden, full of good smells and colors. But I never once tried

not hating him. I won't list the miseries he made
for me, but it does go on, this anger, this
sinful hatred, I'd make him die
every day over a lifetime if I could, toothless

and weak and helpless in his bed, and all of us
out of cold duty in the room, that stinking
room, old sweat, the rot of his old meat breaking down,
rubber tubing, piss and shit and through

the window, faint as anything could be and still
be said to be, that contrary
fragrance of the lilacs, big hedge of them outside
the sickroom window—now

I can't get the smell
out of my nose, I think it's coming
off of me, even in the garden
on the warmest days of warm soil, the greenest days

of the fullest blossoming, I can smell myself
beyond hope of washing it off. Damn
to hell these sores on my nose that keep me
from seeing, the cankers eating in, almost

to the bone by now, every morning
I expect to see white bone each side
of my nose, under
my eyes, except of course

I can't see, not the rose blooming, not the bone
baring itself, I'm here sort of in between, squeezed
between the sweet scents of rose and iris and lilacs
and my own rising stink, my own slow ingrowth

on the trellis, so to speak, or maybe
the trellis is coming out, whichever way
I need to look at myself will do—this day or that one,
the blur in the mirror, scaly, thin, hairless, blind, its insides

breaking out or the outsides drawing in, sucked in, I think
it's that latter, like something at the roots
feeding, the gopherous soul, anyway
something that's been in there so long

it's forgotten the differences between
itself and the darkness
it gives off and thinks of itself if it thinks at all
as a power of hunger, pulling

everything that's outside
in, swallowing, a non-stop feeding,
a horror of piss and shit around it, under
and inside, the bone

gnawing its slow way out, the meat
shrinking in, in the end
each neither one
nor the other, and here it is

starting on my nose, pretty soon will follow
the cave-in onto the hollowness,
the skull flooding with a true
circulation of sweet air, with garden

smell, no in and out to it, only
a fullness of rose, iris, lilac, fine
slow rot of fall leaves. He beat me,
took me out of school, made me walk

behind the buggy all the way
to town breathing
the dust, sweating, stepping around
the horse turds, but that's

the nature of my complaint, petty, not near enough
to account for eighty years of rage and hate.
I could say
he went at his food like a pig, came home drunk

pissed under my window, stank, most of all stank, never
washed, stank like feet, tobacco, stale
drink, mud and cowshit, old clothes,
soggy papers, hair

and rat-bones, stank
like he rotted where he stood—you can see
this can't be true, I've been out
of control on this subject for seventy years, that's why

I won't talk about it, can't talk about it, it's bad enough
to know I'm going to burn for all this hate.
Meantime I'm given
to making myself smell good, colognes

and after-shaves leave a trail behind me
through the house—I don't care,
after that last shave
I want the undertaker to slap it on,

a good big dripping palm full
of Mennen's Skin Bracer or lacking that
a good Jamaican witch hazel, provide me
the best smell that can be managed, given

the circumstance, then close the lid on it,
though probably something will linger
out there, along with the roses, or lilacs, or maybe,
if I manage to check out at just the right time

of year, some *nicotiana*, sweetest of all,
maybe will linger a faint
sour edge to the place, some whiff
of what they used to call *miasma,*

or *noxious vapor*, but for lack
of a proper term, *shit*
I said then,
and I say it now.

Blaze

In Memory of Leon Perry

I have to be careful, if I stand up quick
getting out of bed, or up from a chair,
I get so dizzy, hands full of sweat,
mouth full of spit—always had

this cool head for numbers, now
I'm satisfied if it doesn't
heat up and knock me over when I
stand up quick, or unkneel myself
in church, or up from in front

of this rosebush, to which
despite appearances I'm not
praying, only
feeding it some overpriced and purified
commercial cowshit—always had this head

for numbers, but nowadays
can't add two and two with any assurance
it'll come out right. But this rose, I don't
forget its name, this climbing rose,

"Blaze" is its name, is old as me, older,
even, brought it
from Hillsdale to Toledo in 1934
and it's been happy
ever since, every year
more blossoms and bigger ones.
I don't think anything

can kill this rose, what attention
I give it doesn't much matter, I spend my time
anyway just trying to stay
upright, nothing to spare
for a rosebush. I admire

this rose because it's not
long and thin and windy like
that ivy there, or sloppy
like that stand of hollyhock. That blaze red

takes over everything, I admire that,
by God! *God,*
but I'd like to see it out to the end,
the two of us using up the last breath

of this tasty air, this fresh
sharpness, this coolness
of earth like from the corner
of the ell where the hose
leaks into moss
and leaves and the rot

churns in the old sills, and mixed in and yet
somehow strong over everything
the smell of the rose, though it's blooming
more than twenty yards away
towards the front of the house, every April
deader than hell, then in early May

a little nudge and rustle
of green way down
among the roots, and in a week
a foot tall, and in three weeks
up to my waist—anyway the both of us
using up the last of this sweet air
together, with sometimes a little
sunshine on the leaves and walls, the day-smell
taking me off guard,

and it comes to me
that this is exactly how it was
one day a long time ago,
which I must have noticed

and marked down in my head
for future reference and may
have that day been
reminded of another one, and so on,

and backward to the first day
of the first rose. But I
catch sight of myself in passing
in a mirror or shop window, and I have
this stale look to my face, and I may not

be sure of two and two, but I'm dead
sure—like when
five times a night
I lever myself out of bed
to stand and pee in the dark,
aiming by sound, sometimes
on target, sometimes not, but hanging on

like death to the towel rack
over the tank, barking my shins
on the toilet bowl, listing left and right
as if strong winds were blowing, the ones
that howl in from the wild old gardens
out there, every time forget myself

in this thick rose-smelling world, remind myself
of something I should never
have forgotten, and jump up too quick to greet it.

Rat

At first it was a mere suspicion
of a smell, maybe an onion
or potato gone rotten under the stove,
but in three days grown to a rich, sourceless

crescendo of downright stink,
that came to fill the entire house, though by
month's end it had dwindled
to a more general atmosphere, and been

forgotten—at least until
I ripped the ceiling tiles away
and the leg bones,
still strung together by a little skin, leaped out

in a rain of teeth and plaster dust and ribs and straw,
and clasped, for an instant dryly passionate,
my face, sprang free, clattered
down the wall, exploded, slid and scattered themselves

everywhere, explaining
everything, or just about.

PART IV

The Cold in June

The Cold in June: After Claudel

for Svetlana

When you speak to me
it is not only to you I answer,
but to everything
surrounding us:

the mortal spasm of a poem,
entire as a single word,
sprung from my mouth,
and caught there, held there

between us, held there
by the simple pressure
and weight of our breaths.

Ste. Jérôme en pénance

The lion is sour and disapproving.
He seems to be guarding the saint's scarlet hat
at first glance a pool of blood,
streaming ties like rivulets that knot

then separate. Jerome floats
from his toes which barely touch
a stony sand. At his feet
scorpion, asp, lizard, scatterings

of bearded stones that might be stones
or might be spiders, buoy him
in his slight ecstasy. The mountain
rises behind him, weathered

to sharp splits of flint. In the tree
at the saint's right shoulder the tercel
shivers its wings and screams,
the kestrel at his left elbow

perches calm on a sharp blade
of the cliff; and five dark trees—
baring between them a frozen patch of blue
unquestionable sky—rise sheer

from the stone. The dour saint,
bald and old, scrapes at his heart
with a stone the shape of a heart, but his breast
sheds merely a scant blood. Nothing

quite looks at anything else: the lion unfocuses
on the scarlet hat, the scorpion,
vaguely imploring, raises claws
and stinger, the snake

interests itself in a patch
of cool grass, and Jerome himself, at once
bored, furious and dutiful, his white robe
improbably pristine, glares beseechingly

into and beyond the upper right-hand corner
of the frame, where, he has come to suspect,
most likely continues
the bitter, incurious sky.

Koi Pool at Sunset

I had only to raise my empty hand
over what seemed an empty pool
to draw from out of nowhere

a frenzy of greedy koi
a hundred of them, maybe two, or even three,
to churn, boil at my feet

and gape to be fed—as if something
of the inflamed sky had inverted itself
to a tumultuous ignition

of the clear water, orange, gold, red—whereas
similarly to gesture at the sky
made nothing happen, nothing

at all, however much something
ought to have been made
to happen, and I waited—but the sky

serene to the last deep of its void
recurving gut, and, utterly without hunger,
declined the transformation.

Carving the Salmon

I shape this piece
        of curly maple into the rough
                form of a salmon on

my bandsaw, a fine, sour smell
        of sawdust, a hint of scorching and smoke
                because the blade is dull, cut

the side shape first, then the top.
        And then it is recognizable, a fish,
                and ready for finishing. It quivers

a little at the skew chisel, flinches
        at the spoon bit. With the straight gouge
                I give it eyes, and with the veiner, gills,

and it leaps a little in my hand. Now
        that it sees and breathes, it starts
                to flop and suffocate. It becomes

much harder to hold. But it will be
        a long while before I learn
                to fashion the blood.

Waking to the Moon

When I wake up
the moon is slanting
over the cove and through

the pines and then through my window
and crosscuts the room, and on
the far side climbs slowly the wall.

I know I won't sleep again
tonight. What pleases me
in my old age is to awake

to light—never mind
the past, useless as regret.
I go out onto the porch,

and the sea sounds magnify themselves,
also the stars, Portland's aura
to the south. The moon

is motionless and calm
in its place, confident
of many more risings.

If you have to grow old,
it might as well be
by the shore. Tonight

I'll stand here, swatting
at mosquitoes, and try
to wait out the moon.

Mosquitoes

The long curl of the surf
subsides into itself
so soft against the rocks
as barely to lift and stir

the kelp. The ocean
is clearly intent
on this old stone.
It swells with an in-

tolerable slowness
against the scoured cliff. Surely
it will spill over.
Surely it will recede

gently as it is about to flood
this mosquito-ridden
place in which I find myself,
so overbrimmed with blood

as not to be able
to leave the house
for fear of the swarming.

Snorkeling in Fog

I am greatly defended
against the cold—wet suit
gloves, booties and helmet—
but cold. Close in,

I see bottom, but not much
there—one small school
of sand eels, flashing and shifting,
a lobster half under his rock.

I turn over to look up
into the fog no less
dense than the sea, but
nothing at all.

From beneath
I feel the upsurge of the ocean
rebounding from the sea floor
from above the noiseless weight

of the sodden sky. By some stern law
I seem to have become attached
at once to sky
and sea and fear both.

Afloat at their coupling,
I've never learned bravery.
I've been this way. But today
in a heavy fog—the trees

on the cliff edge far less
than outlines—I swim all the way out
to the first line of lobster pots,
and watch the cables, greenly hairy,

diminish to the darkening.

The Cold in June

The moon lies like a white stone
in the glassy cove. It chills

the water, though June
is well along. Frost flowers

on the rushes, a little ice
begins to crinkle at the shore.

It is an uneasy time—the wild roses
have begun to smell like snow,

and if I doubt my senses,
it is after all merely

one more doubt.

Drowning

Diving on the fouled anchor
in the murky, mud-bottomed cove,
with plenty of misgivings, afraid

of not finding the breath I'll need,
I pull myself down the slimy rope
and find it snarled like a turk's head

around the shackle, turn to come up
and find it's fouled itself
around my ankle, more

than a couple of tight turns, in fact
knotted, and I can't loosen it,
and Phil on the boat can't quite reach,

and so I tell him to winch it up
a bit, but that only cinches the line
tighter, and by now I'm exhausted

and lie back, the wet suit
floating me o.k., but I'm anchored
in both directions, the cold

of the cold ooze climbing
the line, and the big boat
starting to drift over me,

and I lever
on my caught leg just enough
to hold it off, but gradually

it bears down on me, bears
me down, and I begin
to go under, utterly relaxed

and curious as to how
this will turn out, what
it will be like, floating there

caught tight to the ocean,
the shadow of the boat
beginning to slide over me, my face

raked by barnacles, the line
biting into my leg, and though
it may be it's my duty to escape

I can't believe
I'm not afraid, here
at the boundary, utterly

relaxed, my eyes tight
on the sky which has dried
into something like a yellow skin,

a dim radiance behind it,
only curious as to how
this is going to turn out,

bound tight on the one hand
to the planet, on the other
the big shadow of the boat

about to press me down
to where I can live forever
with this feeling which

will never return—for who
after all is able
to call me back, call after me, unknot

me, beg me to return, and why
should they? And why
when this concludes itself

will I not? And why should I?
If I am called back
it will have to be

as if you are speaking
to me just now.
I had not expected

the water to come over me,
like sleep, or to find
that one has to remain

somewhere—but after all,
that is how things
like this are made.

PART V

The Garden

Iris

Overnight the great bronze bearded iris
have bloomed, and the spikes
of the orange lupine as well are opening
from the bottoms up. The azaleas

are gone, but the peonies
and rhododendron are only a day
away. If I didn't know better
I'd think that in my little plot

the earth had focused all its joy.
But then toward afternoon
from over the lake comes
a darkening, and the underleaves

of the aspen flash white and silver.
There is a narrowing and lowering
of the entire density
of the sky—the flowers

of course are oblivious.
It is up to me to be afraid.

Raking Leaves

For the second year in a row
I've let things go, neglected the leaves: the huge
golden leaves the maples discarded
all through golden October, that layered themselves
to a four weeks' deepness, the days and long nights of October
dense with the soft undertones of their falling.
Another year over, another year,

and confronting accumulation, I hang back
from raking the leaves, inert beyond
all inertia, until with the late rains they've thickened
and swelled, grown sodden and thick—I've assumed the guilt,
excused myself from the task for the sake of my hands, hips,
knees, and also from sheer laziness, yet
all winter accused myself, foreseeing the labor
of raking them up, heavy and wet,

dreaded the work as I dreaded
the thought of it. Now, at last, unwilling
I've brought myself to it and found,
this warm, sunny day in mid-April, crocuses
blooming and in the few beds of the garden
not smothered in leaves thrust upon thrust
of lilies and peonies. I've found
the first layers soft with the first

sun of the year one might call truly warm,
wet, soft almost to crumbling,
already commencing the laborious turn
toward mold, though still
with something left to them of the gold
of the down-drifting light they were; and then
a few inches down I come to the frost,
the durable cold at the final layer. Suddenly

there's a sense of bulb and rhizome, root,
runner and seed reclaiming themselves, thrust on thrust
into the crumbling cold of the leaves, a sense
of a million, a billion burstings of buds, a great
discharge of green light, everywhere the garden
making me think of the trees
of October last, prophesy the leaves
of October, the building of leaves that goes on

till only the name of it stays with me, rather the sound
of the spin and downwhirl of the golden leaves
beyond any name, the sound of the leaves
falling over the dark silences
of the infolding bulbs and rhizomes, runners, roots,
all the luxuriant frills of the gardens
receding into themselves, all night the soft
falling of leaves overwhelming my dreams, the leaves

building and building. In the final days of October the leaves
build on themselves, build and build,
deepen and burden the soils.
Let all who doubt the resolve of accumulation,
who all their lives have wanted the world
neatened and cleaned and bared to the sharp
definitions of boundaries, despair. Here, under the leaves,

even stone is fragrant, the gardens
breathe underfoot. The chill
cover of leaves bears down on the gardens, the gardens
bear back. I honor the leaves
that bury my garden, I surprise myself to find that I love
the gorgeous debris, what requires removal. Disheveled
and breathless with labor, I swipe at the frozen leaves, I foresee
I'm destined to live a long life, letting things go.

Bird Song

for Jack Beal and Sondra Freckelton

First the crow, then
the mockingbird, and as I watched
leaves unfurled themselves

from the dogwood. For days the shadow
of the tree raced around and around it,
and the cardinals in its branches

flashed out and dimmed, flashed out and dimmed
like bloodbursts—or, since this
is a poem that does not seek

to breach the skin of the world—
as if little windows were opening
and closing on fire.

Hollins, March 7, 1996

Cardinal in the Cross Hairs

He flickers scarlet in the cross hairs,
there at the feeder. He doesn't
have a chance. He is so close

in the scope that his wings
brush my face. Everything
withdraws, and when I shoot

it is like a song,
the bullet delicate as the feeding bird,
as cleanly singing.

Gloriosas

Coarse hairy-leaved, un-
killable, maroon-hearted
in a golden corolla, they can be

counted on till November, year
after year, growing everywhere, even
in the chinks of the driveway. But

I have to stop here. Categories
lose their meanings. When I stand among
the gloriosa, the seed

goes dead in my tongue.

Tending the Flower Boxes

Pick off the dry crowns of the geranium
deadhead the pansy and petunia,

the wilted rose crepe of yesterday's hibiscus:
and you awaken in them the old voice of necessity,

and they are deceived into generation,
to bloom and re-bloom, though something

still sings inside the beheaded stalk.

PART VI

Fishing the Source

Crossing from Killimer on New Year's Day

Crossing from Killimer,
first car onto the ferry, bumper
snug up against the chains, foul
weather, the ship rolling a good

twenty degrees, and the Shannon
slopping over the bow,
to splatter my windshield, the bow
driving into the chop, then three, then six

inches of green water sheeting side to side
over the foredeck, and me thinking that at last
it was now, it was now, that I'd know at last
the watery breath I'd dreamed of often enough

to bring me up in the storm of my bed
gasping and choking, the great sea
of the dream ebbing fast,
till nothing was left but the drowning

—though here I am now,
dry, safe and awake, in another
country, another year, the river far off,
only a dream of the sea, and its ferries

foundering just only enough to alarm
such as myself, so that years after
it shames us to think of the fear,
fear of it, fear
being the remains of it all
to remember,
though the whole time
there under it all, there
the river's salmon were forcing

the current, beyond even
urgency, just as now, as forever, just
as then—above them the awkward
keels, the blathering screws the green seas burgeoning,

mounting against us
in our perilous crosswise run
and we hung on, hung on, hung on.

Quarry

Trying for one of the big carp, I heaved
my father's brand-new pitchfork like a spear,
then lost hold of the running line, and when
I looked down into the bullseye

of the settling green water I saw it there,
the white tip of its new ash handle growing
out of the pickerel weed. I knew
it had to be dived for, but I

was no swimmer, and feared
water. Still, I stripped and stood
shivering in the cold sun looking down
into the water, stood so

for a long time, the pitchfork
seeming not entirely beyond reach. But I
was worried, I was afraid, there was no way
to predict if I would grab it on what was sure to be

a clumsy swipe of my hand I knew
I needed badly for swimming with,
and I thought what it would be like
for my feet to tangle in the hairy weeds,

but suddenly for no reason I can now recall
I dived, green water breaking on my face,
and I remember only the terrible breathless
threshing of silence as I groped

for the handle, somehow caught the string
and pulled the fork to shore. There I sat
for a long time, catching at breath, ashamed
to have been frightened, watching

the slow bronze shapes of carp nosing
the bottom, where, I knew, my young bones,
white as an ash handle, ought to be settling
in the blue mud clouds I'd stirred up, until

far out on the surface suddenly there burst
what I took to be the bubble of my last
held breath, as if some great fish
had risen from the bottom, and rolled there.

Sinking Creek

This river leads nowhere.
The earth soaks it up.
Shore and water and stream bed

disappear,
but the river's there
somewhere underground,

its great fish holding themselves
head-on into the dark currents
mayflies, even, dancing upward

into the lusterless sky
of soil and stone and roots.

The Refusal

The big trout rose to your fly, and backed,
still uplifting, downstream, then turned
away, unfrightened. What

could he have seen
that told him
"This is not real!"

For after all, the light was right,
your body camouflaged,
the stream dappling your face

with sun and leaf-shadow,
and you stood quietly, the current
soft around you

the great sun swift all around you,
and your shadow drifted
soundless downstream,

and after all you must have seemed
only one particularity
among the gorgeous many.

Wading

Wading upstream, through Rainbow Rapids,
the river piling down
in a shudder of mists.
A couple of times I try to cross,

but the water's too high,
discolored, coldly
through waders and long johns
clasping my legs, boosting me off-

balance, downstream
toward half-submerged Sand Island, a bone
in its teeth. I wedge my foot
against a downstream rock

brace and lean
into the river, the roar
and scour of the river bed, through soles,
calves, thighs, explosions

of sands and gravels, boulders
trembling in their sockets. Two shuffling steps
toward the thread of the current,
and I hear the siren caterwaul

from Bolton Dam—no more
than ten minutes and the water's up,
twigs and leaves thick
in the drift lines,

so I give up, back off,
turn in time,
head shoreward borne
downstream, riding the current tip-

toe rock-
to-rock, barely
in control, crossing back
to the muddy flats on the longest

of the long diagonals.

Schoolies

They come into the cove on the tide
at the point, just in the rip
off the Yacht Club dock

a joyous fuss and flurry, sprinkle
of silver where the sand eels are trying
to skip away, and I cast

among them, and catch
nothing, and as fast as they come
they disappear. For an hour

I idle on the dock, hoping
for action, but I never ask myself
about this any more,

or pretend there's more to it
than there is. I think instead
of those times

when over on the ocean side
my arm could get the best
out of a big rod

straight on into a hard
onshore wind, the rocks
crowding me from behind,

and the big surf salting
my eyes, and every second
the white line of the beach

on the far point
delicately receding.

Coffin Flies

...the spinners
snowing down, making
against the alders that pale light,
and so I threw a Leadwing
Coachman—in those days

having sternly been instructed
to presentation, the color
thought no matter
for concern, the main thing being
to divert attention from the natural,

when the water was covered
with naturals, and nothing to choose
between them—therefore

the Coachman, opaque, brown-bearded,
iridescent green, dun-winged,
to the nearest riser, and it cocked

nicely, made a perfect float
along the feeding lane all the way
to the drag, trout
rising behind and before it,
to pluck down living flies.
But I thought I knew
that sooner or later they'd come to it

and though that afternoon
they did not, nor the next
and next, kept at it
each day for the hour

of spinner-fall from the first lightfall
to wholly dark—two hundred yards upstream
and down, rainbows

breaking,
a spangle of rainbows
wherever I'd happen to look, and the dusk
full of spinners, in the air their wings
an ashy blur, but in the hand transparent.

Advice Concerning the Salmon Fly

for Phil Castleman

Let us suppose
that for the one time in your entire life
it will ever be possible, you find yourself
on a great pool of the Restigouche,

and that there before you
because of a good light
and a pale streambed you see
nine, ten, a dozen

big, restless salmon which you feel,
in your heart you know,
to be in a taking mood,
and as in a terrible dream

open your fly book to discover
that by some crochet of chance
it is empty, and that you must leave
the stream to the fish and return

to your tying bench, where, owing
to press of time you may dress
only one black fly—Black
Rat, Black Dose, or Black Bear—all of them dark

to the utter resolutions of darkness. But then,
you come to yourself, and
for the moment at least, because
you honor proportion, and are much given

to an undeviating joy in display, you make
one bright fly—a hairwing Jock Scott, perhaps,
the tag a fine oval silver followed
by turns of lemon floss, tail a topping, butt

black ostrich herl, then back
to the lemon floss, nicely
tapered, and veiled
with yellow toucan, silver-

ribbed, amidships
an interruption of black ostrich
herl, then the body's
resumption, for credibility—

after all this ostentation of radiance—
a black floss palmered black,
the throat
of speckled guinea fowl, wing

a sparseness of scarlet
yellow and blue monga, and over all
a few strands
of cinnamon bear—

but it is imperative
that your pleasure in the making
be not diminished by what no doubt
will be error and mishandling enough.

Remember, always, that craft is improved
by exercise and discipline, in fact
the vision (I mean this fly, this little roar of light
as it will be in its grand sweep

across the salmon's lie,
an inch from the terrible toothed gasping
and ungasping of his kype) being part
of art's virtue, itself

improves. But please do not allow
such considerations
ever to override
the practical—for this is,

after all, a fishing fly,
and so you must, for a plain example,
take care to leave room
for the riffle knot at the head

(which will be of black silk,
smoothly wound and justly tapered,
then varnished to a black
and lustrous shine)—all this,

of course, no more
than the merest recipe—
for the same fly tied by another, and apparently
in detail of form and material utterly

the same, may occasion twice
the killing, or none
at all, and what's
to account for that?

Painting of an Angler, Fishing the Source

An angler slashed on in black
to crouch in a chaos
of daisies and mulleins, on a riverbank,
from beyond the high ridge of which blooms

an apple orchard that demonstrates
signs of human labor, a rake
against a tree, a basket. The picture employs
a sunny landscape, though its flowery background

is considerably faded, and because
of the thickness of paint and rapidity
of its application, his face
is badly cracked, as are his coat

and hands, though only the crazing
of the face at first concerns us (later
the rest). And—somehow
a continuity—the cypress

erupts, black against a landscape
in which all the light
is white, and each color
merely an exclusion

of white, orchard and cypress glowing
beneath a petrifact white body neither sun
nor moon—and beyond this
an extrusion of beech and sycamore,

and from that forest
issue the first rapids of the stream,
the angler, preparing,
in an exhilaration

of fear and foreknowledge
of consequence, to cast,
though discovering it difficult to see
through these shifting perspectives

of watery light in which the light
devours color
and shadow. The angler—
the focus of all this rather

than a subordinate element,
one who has come to know how it is done,
but not how it comes out—
crouches at the tail of the pool,

while above him from a black
discontinuity of the earth, the source
pours over the radiant first
of its chalky falls.

From HOUSE
AND GARDEN

(UNIVERSITY OF NOTRE DAME PRESS, 2001)

The Guardian of the Lakes at Notre Dame

I cannot any longer bring to mind
the name of the ancient, hated Brother
who patrolled the lakes at Notre Dame,
and ran us kids off, shouting in a voice
that from one hundred yards away
was dangerous as sword blades.

Retires to guard the lakes, the old man did;
and for him to wake up was most powerfully to insist
that turtles be troubled merely to feed,
herons to fly, snakes to dream of toads.
Himself the caring center of all careless
natural grace, at last he died;
the lakes were fished.

There is perhaps something to be said
in favor of old men who raise
the guardian arm and voice against
the hunting children, who but lately come
to Paradise, pursue
the precedent beast unto its dumb destruction,
and persist.

And surely the sky came more and more to seem
like a dark vault
of the dead box-turtle's shell. Perhaps he thought
to cry against the children was like love,
love being often in rebuke of innocence.
In all event they plundered the far shore,

and he waved his gun, and shouted out at them
Go home go home! in fierce stern order that
they might be made to see, how, in the end
the bellowing angel raises up his fist,
and how that is to be
forfeit of name in the memory of men.

Adam Looking Down

From the hilltop at the edge of the pine grove
I look down onto the blooming orchards.
I watch the slow emergence

of spring. I feel
obligation of retrieval.
The air carries with it

the taste of mushrooms, apples,
the smell of sour muds. Far below
the orchards blossom, the season

is gathering. I look down
on the resumptive body of the world,
on whatever I am obliged

to make of it to see or touch,
by which necessity
it will bear names, and be.

Adam Remembers Moving

One gets used to everything.
It's painful to recognize
the skill we have at it.

What we really desire
is to be alive in somebody's
eyes, we line up to be

remembered. In the bedroom
when the bed is taken out, there
is the floor showing

the honey-brown of the old pine boards
in the shape of the bed, painted around,
surrounded by a glossy field, a garden-plot

of green-going-to-black,
one of the spaces to be
dispensed with, disposed of utterly,

and helpless against being
returned to. To walk
through the dark doors

and find we are no longer in
has to be watched out for.
There are rules for this kind of thing,

severe penalties once
we exceed the boundaries
of the general unhappiness. Whatever

is lost or out of place
in the place we lived—I don't mean
the ordinary landscapes

of the house, lightfall
in a room, or the peculiar
echoes of closets, earth smell

of basements, water stains shaded
and contoured to the shapes
of a woman's face, a map,

I don't mean
these things, they
are recoverable, they insist

on their availability. I mean everything
closed off from view, and one day
released to the dumb lament. Make it

so that I can say it plainly, if not simply,
let these things go down with me.
Keep me faithful to loss.

Eve among the Willows

Among the yellow branches
a feathering of wind, dusts
of sun through the little holes
in the green shade. Our voices,

quiet enough from the very first,
have long ago been swallowed up
in the leafy whisperings of this place.
And where we cannot

and will never again see them,
the great flowers of the garden,
alive to the memory of light,
must still reach and blossom

and breathe their showy breaths. As for us,
oh, our hearts
beat so inexpertly when we looked
at one another! What he heard and saw

I was never able to tell, so that I
would never become
of like mind with him. Now I believe
we've always lived

as we were meant to live,
here in the middle of a world
that burgeons coldly around us,
in the yellow dust of a dry sun

and this green mottling of narrow leaves. Here
is where we've made our home.
I think our hearts
may well have outlived our voices.

These big willows seem borne down,
though in fact they strive equally
to sun as to earth. We walked
under the trees, heavy

on the world, in such a gravity
not even silence escaped us.

Adam Considers His Death

Please let it be
the work of an instant!
Do not require us to wake slowly
under a burden of earth

smothered in a web of roots. I wonder—
this morning in which I lie
awake, breathing freely, speaking
to you from the shadow of these willows

a lively sky sparking through
the moving leaves, as I will wonder
in that morning to come,
which I so fear: how

will we be different? Forgive us, allow us
this one peace, in which
if we must leave at all
the warm earth will stir

and fold softly back
and we'll fly from our graves
into a fine brightness,
our bodies new and shining,

the last grains of the planet
sifting through our fingers,
the petals of our hearts
trembling to life,

beginning to move again, let it be
that we will be no less at peace
than ever . . . but no more! It must have been
you loved us after all,

for having called on us to die,
you left us trapped in yearning.
Oh that was a gift! We would not otherwise
have reveled so in hope.

Adam among the Silences

I looked for the names
among those first silences,
thinking of them
as I thought of my hands

where they newly moved before me,
clasped and unclasped themselves,
stroked the sides of my face, shielded
my eyes from the sun

and every weather—I
had not commanded them,
they knew by themselves they had to come
to terms with my face, my eyes,

each other, they had
obligations—but always
they went about their business
without sound, wordless, foreknowing

they had to perish . . .
whereas beyond what I could see
the sky thinned
into utter colorlessness

though from somewhere
came light enough that through my hands
before my eyes I saw
thin blood-colored translucencies,

and heard a heart beat
brittle as the first crinkling skin
of the first ice. But my tongue
did not hurry to help me out.

I will never know what it was feeling then.
My tongue seemed willing to wait
for a long time, it was at least
faithful to the silences—

I am willing to confess that,
alone among much from which I turn away.
As for my hands, they stroke
the sides of my face, shield

my eyes from the sun
and every weather
every turn of the blood—and still
I do not command them

but have come too late and far too late
to this business
of putting names. What I heard and saw
I can never tell—but what I came to

were the silences.
What I entrusted myself to
was not then clear to me, nor now,
but what it came to

were the silences. For all
the labyrinthine babble, straight lines
on the page, the world's gone on
in its stillness without me.

Eve Measuring the Distances

We should have understood. Distance
measured itself from where
we lay or walked or slept.
Birds sang to be heard.

Light found us
so that it might be seen.
We were given to see
the clear orders of Paradise,

each morning the earth
came about us as an ocean
of flowers and leaves, then
fields, waves, oceans of color

that rushed on and away to break
in the distance on the icy
mountains where it must have been
nothing could live.

Adam in Late March

The season's a buffeting of desolation, nights
like breath stopping, days
the bore of the wilderness flooding
these dry lawns. And onto the lawn where I am standing,

by virtue of an afternoon's high wind, the elm,
of its green self almost wholly shed, scatters
most of its dying crown, and I snatch up and shatter
huge branches of deadwood against

the rotting bole, make piles of slash, set fires
all over the yard and garden, so that in the growthless afternoon
of this day in this late March, my hands
fiery with shock, everything around me ablaze as if

the muddy fires of the Torment have broken through,
it breaks through in me
how the season is neither generous nor kind,
and how we suffer the belief that we

will never be alone, that the still presence
of the beloved is more sure than that the absence
has been spoken, and long ago, and endures. In a rage
that lasts all afternoon, legs akimbo, body bent and braced,

I swing with all my strength at the beetle-ridden bark,
smash and splinter every branch I can lift, heave it
onto the fires, or stab with the jagged butt
into the soft lawn until it strikes and stops on ice, stab

and stab at the muddy earth in plain assault
on what does not love or has abandoned me, the season
straining to brighten itself, myself
straining to believe there is in fact everywhere about me

a loosening earth, a greening of lawns through the scurfs
of all the grassy years that have passed into the violence
of termination, this last ice-edge of season, the season's
most bitter concurrence in the stern orders of loss.

Adam and the Heron

Gathering marsh marigolds,
on the lookout for sundews, orchids,
pitcher plants, I come
on this flat clot of feathers

in the shape of a heron, head
caught back in the slow contraction,
and then a hundred yards out
a great blue heron takes flight

just as I begin plucking the long hackles
from the smelly flesh
to rib my spey flies,
and of course I have to stop

what I'm doing, and watch
his huge awkwardness
utterly transform itself, long legs
streaming out behind, the big wings

after the first few embarrassing flaps
strong and steady, neck
curved back a little, the marsh
still echoing some with the gross

croaking of his fear, but nothing
to pay attention to, he was flying,
and watching him I kept on trying to pull
dead feathers from the dead bird,

both of us earthbound and flightless,
both in our own ways gone heavy, tugged
at the beautiful gray-blueness of feathers
that even rooted in that week-old

stinking vulgarity
of movelessness, resisted,
seemed somehow to pull back.

Eve among the Trees at Night

Maples overhang the deck.
We live fully among trees.
It's different up here,
up here we recognize and speak to one another,
not at all the same as wandering in a grove,
leaning up against a rough trunk,

stumbling on a root—
no, the true life of trees is above us,
especially, I think, when the sun glints
through the interstices of moving leaves
and dapples earth and body
so that one seems

the other. During the day the trees
mediate between light and us
but at night up here among the leaves,
the pines sighing but ready to roar, the aspens
fluttering, the maples
ashuffle with rustlings,

the stars sparking a little
through the leaves,
below us the lightless garden
all day drowned in the shadows of trees
every night bone-still in the planet's shadow
below us in the still gardens,

sunflowers and roses,
primroses closed tight
on daylight, the light
of yards and houses

and of the flowers themselves
folding in on the planet's heart,
the day disappearing before
our astonished eyes—

and then the cyclonic ebbing of light
that froths and currents
about the big roots of the trees—
at such times

the trees are given to
speaking most clearly
and we most given
the grace to hear.

Adam in the Late Dusk of a Summer Night

In the late dusk of some summer night
when the garden has grown
to its fullness of blossoming and fragrance,

and she is standing at the window, half-
asleep, eyes half-closed, the stars
sharpening to brittle points, the night

on the other hand delicate
in its embraces, dawn
already impatient for its turn, I'll come,

because I'll know she is expecting me,
and arrive with my eyes fixed on her thoughts,
the night dense in my nostrils

as in hers, the stars
grown needle-keen. Because the place
is nothing, because it's unimportant,

we'll leave it behind; but as for time,
I suppose that must travel with us.

Eve Complaining of the Heat

All night it seemed a giving off of voices
from the garden, an occasional
soft fragrance of joy, malodor

of rage or desolation, often
long silences of the kind
that exist only before

what is about to be spoken
is spoken, then nothing
but the rise and fall of wind

which carried nothing
in it of discourse or cadence,
but was merely

the wind. Now, this morning, the flowers
are mute, their leaves droop
with an early heat, and the trees

look to be molting. A rankness of ivy
smothers the roadsides. All day I expect the gardens
will seethe without a word.

Adam in October

"Fall." That word. Our word.
A triumph, as triumphs go
these days, a little glimmer
in the moving shadows of memory—
as on the mountain this morning
with clouds rooted

in gray layers of undershadow
piling, billowing, even roaring up,
and wide blades of sunlight
slicing through, long slivers
of light slanting eastward
from peak to foothills, striping the mountain

with oranges and yellows
of the coloring maples, the mountain
igniting, a blaze
of moving lights trailed
by ashy shadow, until
at last rain comes and the sun

wholly fails. Mostly
we've lost the talent
for words. But now and then
something breaks through,
from back, far back, just enough
that our hearts leap, the word

forms itself, and for once, for a moment,
the earth comes alive,
and we take it back
into ourselves, and it lodges there,
begs our forgiveness
for what out of no will at all

it's spelled out
of all that's fallen away, of all
that's abandoned, unrecognizable.
Were we in love back then? We'll never know.

Time's silent on the matter. It's just
that now we're here, walking together
alone, under the lowering skies,
in the light of the unspoken world.

Adam Suffers Regrets in October

October evenings, in the face of the last
gatherings of light, more largely, even,
in the face of the last gatherings
of all the sweet bodies of the summers

to which in our uncommon time
the earth has given rise, it's come to seem
no more than ever much to ask
that nothing should be asked, that it is necessary

to be without need, that nothing
in the way of anger, bitterness, death or desire
is forgiven, or even unforgiven;
that what one desires of the other

is required to be taken, or gone without.
This is what comes of whatever may have been
in the beginning, by reason of which
each of us might have gone on

to love the other. This
is what comes of it, and it breaks through to me
how the season is neither generous nor kind,
and that we have seemed to affront it,

for having believed we might never die;
that the still presence of the voice within us,
in which we might have spoken to whom
we might have loved, is more certain

than its absence. Meantime
I breathe in these risings of night air.
Night lies at the edges of my pillow. October
is the first edge of the still season: that

is its consonance, and this thought
so intervenes to my special sorrow
this October evening, that therefore

is my heart more than ever
borne in upon by the heavy body
it has grown accustomed to sustain.

Adam and the Voice of the Wind

The wind sang about my house. The gardens
sang back. The weathers were difficult. The
voice
too was difficult, though it sang back

to the wind, knowing neither
its honor nor its place. Never doubting
its happiness, it sang *me! It's me!* It thought

it knew my name. Forever it chose me,
I never knew its mind. And now this voice
is trying to find a name

for itself, it's in a hurry, it's trying
to absolve me of my life, it's trying
to tell me if there's to be life,

then life is to be this way.

Eve at the Edge of Winter

What hierarchy of love and choice
shall have exacted it of us,
that to the shame of all our yearning
the body goes foul on its bones, beyond

its own or any pardon?
The sky already is quivering
with snow, and I think how it was
all summer the leaves of the McIntosh

were green as I have imagined ice
at the hearts of glaciers to be green,
while in July there were times
when, about to sleep, I might have sworn

that by morning the lawns would be stiff with frost,
the calendulas collapsed on their stems,
petals corollas of golden ice;
might equally have sworn

that in August one dawn I awakened
to a blizzard—though it was only
a swarming of white butterflies at a dead mole
in the grass. All summer

and well into the fall we worked
in the old orchard cutting apple wood,
three cords of it split and stacked
and just in time. Now, yet only October,

snow storms at the edges of the lawn.
I close the door,
light up the first fire of the year,
and outside the weathers are gathering.

Adam at Noon

By noon what's left
of the sky has faded
into the neighborhoods,
and the late roses
give off a cold smell.
The first souring

of wet leaves is likewise
cold, and the chill eye
of the October night
crowds up to the windows,
and stares in. Furniture

dims in the clouding rooms,
and in October I begin
to move carefully, take cover
in shadows, among the tall grasses
of the season become

especially vigilant,
looking around me, hoping
it is not for me as it is
for the trees, skies, roses.
But already the breath

has begun to sour
in my throat. Duration
draws a circle around me. I live
in conspiracies of furniture. Overhead

the sun shows no warmer
than the moon. The door of the sky
swings closed. The leaves
have begun their tiresome fall.

Adam Opening the Clam

I stand on the beach, the sea
washing the sand out from under
my feet, and hold the muddy stone
of the clam, pry with my knife
at the lip, and as the muscle tears
and gives, I notice a stirring

in the shallows, a small eddying
of bottom sand, a flurry
of sand eels, and then a calm
so absolute I'm startled, and look down

into the open shell onto a flesh
which must have just cried out
with a sound beyond my hearing, look down
onto a pearly flesh more like the sea

than any but the plasms
of my own sperm.

Adam and the Raccoon

I saw him a little before dawn
in the dense growth of the daylilies
and ferns at the far back of the garden
against the fence, creeping

along the fence, small shadow, stopping,
peering about, casting about, cautious for dog
or cat smell, and I kept too far away
for him to notice, and kept still, and strained

to keep him from getting lost
in the general shadow, to keep
from mistaking his shadow
for something else, not alive, or not as he

was alive . . . then heard him
at one of the apples I'd earlier thrown
out there against the fence hoping
just this . . . to have seen him there,

wild shadow near to being lost
in the shadows of the garden,
to have drawn him there, to have known
he would come, to have known

he could not help but come. Oh, that
undeviating determination
to hunger! He will die for it one of these days!

Eve and the Great Circle

The sky is beginning to tremble with rain again—
the puddles from the last storm
merely half-dried—but the gardens
are grateful, the weight of the winter

is lifted from them, and they open themselves
to any sky awash with rain or sun,
it doesn't matter to them, their roots
spread and tangle every which way

patternless, in dumb commotion, forcing themselves
up, until abrim with leaves, the gardens tuft, bud, climb
their trellises, in the gardens this endless
dim flowing of green shadow, and then the flowers

return—and standing here
in the middle of all this I catch myself
asking for life,—all around me
fleabane sprouting from the asphalt, the phlox

explosions of pink and blue, scarlet and claret,
climbing roses and clematis
shuddering with color, and the whole
bald dome of the sky awash

with rain and sun—it's purely
beautiful, I don't know why,
the flowers having come around again
in their great circling, I should be

so disheartened—maybe
it's too regular, too easy, the mind after all
rejoicing in disunities, most jubilant
in irresolution, and this resurgence of the gardens

is common, too easy, nothing in it
of the desirable silence, nothing
motionless, no hint
of the dead pole,

the leafless core of the world
about which we most naturally
in our steadfast immobility
of change (I mean

our happiness) dance awobble
on the great circle of the ecliptic.
This ascending and descending of saps and juices,
this huge formality of growth—it's

unnatural, it's not the work
I accomplish alone, or with anyone.

Adam Transplanting Perennials

An afternoon of spring light, the trees still waiting
for leaves and there arrives a power of rain,
which dwindles to something almost inexpressible
in the way of rain, a good day

to transplant azalea and rhododendron to fill in
the vacancies of winterkill, as well as the Purple Gem
mowed down by accident last fall. The first spadeful,
the first jab deep into the soil, and there wells up

a wild odor of earth, of severed maple roots,
bruised grass; another and the general air floods
the hole—nothing then but a moldiness
and souring of wet catkins, some faint inkling

of low tide, and even that dissolved
in the morning light . . . you'd think
from all I've said this must have been like opening
a grave—but I swear to you my youth shot up over me

with that first fragrance in that early morning
spring light like the light of almost-waking, this lightstream
I awakened merely by scooping out a hole, these recollections
all winter buried deep, rooted and stirring in me

like some disconcerting dream, subcorporeal
vegetation of anger, sorrow and regret—not that I slept
to this dream, far from it, only that it shadowed me
backward, its long emberous tail, dwindling fast

from one light to the next to the last incoherent luminosity of
the last hard kernel of fire long
beyond long in repose—but then
the slow outblooming of the fire's seed,
from the planet's fragrant centers.

Adam Fears Fire

But what is the man, otherwise courageous, to do
when his fears are of fire, of himself afire
and crying out, hair brittle

with fire, bones aglow . . . though it is the cold
that rightly should frighten him,
for everywhere he looks, in all the sleets

and rockscapes of the work, everywhere
the fragile spawns of the ice
flower and are heaving up

his lawns, everywhere they are springing up
and blossoming like trees.

Eve in the Garden at Night

When at last the shadow of the house
dissolved into the gardens
and the eyes still snowblind at least a little
thought *spring, spring!*

and when the night swept over
and we no longer could see
with any confidence, except once we thought
the neighbors embraced in their windows

and then looked about as if they thought
we might have been on the verge of noticing,
but we were on the verge
of sadness with unrest;

and when the night might have been ended
by merely a whisper from one of us
and we pretended to silence
and the night went on,

and we felt our hearts
beat angrily against one another:
when all of this became the one thing
that given a name remained nameless,

then we thought back to the time
we, with the night, the house, the gardens,
were together from nothing,
the hope of our time,

hearing the dry leaves of the garden
scraping together, that terrible racheting
of green life, and to the west the sky
torn with clouds, and to the east a ragged moon,

though color enough out there where we could not see,
and the next day moving over the garden—then
we thought back and the air
of the garden became

the cadences of heart and breath,
in the odd light of moonset
measured them out,
pretended to silence, dissolved ourselves

into the time allotted
—not that we slept,
far from it.

Eve in Sun and Shade

Having dreaded the night, and survived it,
I come to the window to watch the garden sleeping.
Nothing moves, nothing speaks, I have never known
such stillness,

though something deep in the patch of asters,
picks up a fiery point of dawn,
a cat's eyes, maybe, and then
birds start to awake in the trees,

and though nothing perceptibly stirs, the garden
begins to take notice, there commences
a difference to the stillness,
the ferns minutely shiver, the morning-glories

loosen, dew gathers and runnels and drips
from the great blossoms of white clematis,
and now this morning the white peonies,
so heavy with themselves and last night's rain

that they've doubled over, heads down,
stems ready to snapping;
and the reds are on the way, buds
barely opening, though still outshone

by the fuchsia bee-flowers,
and an abrupt burst of white iris.
Across the sidewalk bloom the last
of the rhododendron,

the exuberant, lavender, the white
having concluded last week, now
a snowbed of petals under the bush.
A single holdout buttercup, the rest

of last year's patch drowned out
by the crowding spread of lilies-of-the-valley
and evening primrose; and orange poppies
everywhere, all this

in the sunny garden at the front
of the house. The back garden
is another story: under the experienced
sun-stopping maples the clematis

seem not to mind the shade, and have opened
into huge white stars,
and the yellow marguerite
have made a patch of sun for themselves,

but most everything else holds back,
undecided. For another year
we've been put in position
of waiting, for another year

made to wonder if everything
will have its turn in the still shade, and wonder
at wondering for we know
and know we know

the answer: the back garden will be
the cautious yielding as always, the same
tentative, dispassionate opening
and narrowness of blossom. It's only

the habitual suspicion
that this hesitation, this holding back
and slowing is headed somewhere,
and that this may be the year.

Eve and the Peonies

The night has deceived itself
into the first quiver and shimmer
of morning, and still

stripped of everything the garden
shines as the sea shines
far out almost beyond

the power of the moon,
and abruptly this first light,
this first light bolts up

from among the strawy stems
of last year's blooming,
from the blind soils of the garden

just free of their snowbed
and the dense leaf light
of last October. I've never

slept a night through
to its end—early morning
and here I am to look out my window

over the garden, and the garden
shines like the sea,
for here have battered themselves through

the dusts and soils of the blind garden
the blunt fists of peonies,
first violence

of reds and scarlets. They
are of all that the garden
is determined to become,

the most ardent to bloom,
pure passion
of efflorescence, vision

without eyes
through the long cold on this earth
when the moon descends

onto the gardens and sinks
into their soils, then rebounds,
from the long cold.

Adam at Moonrise

The sea shines like a garden
through the sweet soils of which,
at the same time that it probes toward bedrock

with its tender root, the moon pushes up,
and the garden bulges with it, and soon
it will burst free in some sort of bizarre

blossoming—a dim circle of light,
widening in a bright ring,
then crumbling away to each side—and there

is the moon's bright crown,
then the great body of the thing itself
pulling free, the sands and gravels

of the under soils raining away,
until it tears free and rises
stemmed with a brilliant tendril

of root, rising and swelling,
grown round on itself
as a great peony in its slow way readying

to open itself out, to fill the sky,
burst out, and then unfold
in a huge flowering of light.

Eve Dancing among Moon Shadows

I doubted my eyes, my various shadows
sometimes twined and twisted like roots thrusting
from my feet, then again flung themselves away,

soft, without edges, diffuse from gold to green
to halos of rusty dun, pouring away over
the undulations of lawn, dying

into the ragged edges
of the fall garden.
I doubted my eyes, danced

and postured. But my shadows
refused me, they flew about
ragged and random as clouds.

They were nothing to do with me. The sky
veiled and unveiled itself.
The moon rode high.

The moon took on shapes
I had never imagined. Clouds overcame it.
Each time it emerged in a contrary light.

Eve and the Comet

for Jessica

It is not the final moon, or the last
vestige of sun, or the one dim light
of the last street of my concluding dream

that flickers silver-blue-and-yellow
over the exhausted houses,
the shadowed gardens, and I rejoice

for here is the comet, after years of wishing
and of failed light, here is the comet, about time
I knew it having waited this long time,

my eye wandering the skies,
desiring to rejoice, wishing my eyes
to be flung back by its light—motionless

cold dart of fire, great fiery tear,
as if the sun wept fiery tears,
casting the slight shadow I cast

so it seems slung counter-
sunwise, and flares back
into this lightlessness deeper than sleep.

Adam Pruning Lilacs

Spindly, leggy, sprouting fringes
of suckers, the lilacs have put their flowers
far out of reach, and I prepare
to cut them back for the sake

of next year's blooms—mount the ladder,
reach up pruning shears in one hand, one hand
for myself, and find myself
wobbly among the blooms, the air weighty

with their perfume—and remember a line
from a poem I can't otherwise
remember: *"Oh, he won't be hanged*
until it's lilac time!" the ladder

unsteady, the front legs in a loose
soil sunken in an inch or so. From here
I see the lake, and the mountains,
the woods gone a sweet green,

and I try to make a shape
of the lilac smell—oddly,
no freshness to it, nothing
warm about it, or breathed out, but somehow

an amplification of colors, the slow lavender
of the blossoms, likewise a cerulean
lightness such as you might expect
of a broken sky, this traced through

with infinitesimal threads of scarlet,
vermilion, blue—and, yes, a slight
chill of gray or white to it,
but all in all a powerful

suffusion of lights, intricate
embroidery of scents—it weighs me down,
and as I propose these futilities
the right leg of the ladder abruptly breaks through

the skin of the garden, and I plunge
through the lilac bush, whipped
by branches, shedding similes
all the way, to flat on my face

in the soft seedbed, warm dirt
in my mouth, nose,
eyes—blind with dirt and breathless—
then catch at my breath and sit up—

spitting, choking, clearing
my eyes—and by God here I am again,
back again to the original light,
from wherever it was

that for a second I was shocked to the notion
I'd started to take root, some flash
of a dream of blooming, some lengthening
upward into leaf-bearing branches—

but only for a instant, no
longer—and I have to get up
and back to the breath and eye
that are hard-bent on the cutting back,

that clamp down hard
on that determination,
though for no more
than a second I breathed in

the same air as the lilac,
in its manner of rooting
reached down.

Eve Overlooking the Garden

The garden has ignited.
It's feverish. Even the white clematis
flutters with sun,

and the red lilies and coral bells
burn back at it. Windblown petals
of cardinals flash

across the buttery primroses:
a good year for gardens.
Everything shines.

I write this standing at my window.
I don't go down into the garden.
From here I see everything

at once, all the flowers trapped
in color, in their showy, slow
ignition—petal, pistil, leaf and stamen

separating off. Perhaps
there is a way
out of such fiery

gorgeousness. It must
be wearing. Even at night
when I've gone blind

I hear a splendid confusion
of harmonics, what only can be
the sharp yellowing

of gloriosas, the speckle-
throated oranging
of the Canada lilies.

Adam among the Perennials

These perennials,
unweeded, unthinned,
and left to go wild,

have won out this year,
have strangled everything
that shouldn't be here.

The earth is choked with growth!
Long ago I had foreseen
this bright day, this empty place.

Well, all to the good. Let the houseplants
burst their pots, let them make it
or not. Let the garden grow

and seed and grow and seed,
dry up, collapse under the fall
leaves, let the composts

commence their rich
fever, let the dead leaves
of the geraniums go

unpicked, let pansies seed,
let leaves and petals blow
into the neighbor's yard

and make colorful drifts
at the roots of his fences.
Nor will I prune the grapevine:

but let it tangle and hood the little
wild apple at the end of the porch, let it
climb as high as it likes, and stop

where it likes. I've decided
the gardener's duty
is to wildness. I'm the only one

who knows how to follow the flagstones,
having placed them here
and for fifteen years,

watched them slowly overgrown
by their ravenous borders.

Adam Considering the Rugs

Sometimes you have to exalt
artifice, especially when
it's useful, as with

rugs, laid down to render
our passages inaudible, proposing us
to ourselves as in our process

weightless—sometimes
it's even good to abandon
reason and all reserve, as now I say

the meaning of this house lies
in its rugs: outflowering
its gardens, fierier, more verdant

than its gardens, efflorescences
of oranges, yellows,
carmines and scarlets beyond scarlet,

densities of root hues otherwise true
only beneath the surfaces
of gardens, symmetrical

false dazzlements
of gardens, overdone resiliencies
of bloom, but bearing

in outright color, light
and silence our whole
intolerable weight.

Eve at the Looking Glass

The house lives its life
without us. Sunlight wanders
its green walls, the mirrors

don't recognize us,
they are intent to reflect
the perspectives of room

on diminishing room,
that close on the vanishing point
of our dead silences,

where we conclude—
and then commence to open,
open and reopen, broaden, cascade

against the blind backs of mirrors
into which in passing
we must from time to time

incuriously have peered, our rooms
gone echoing before us
into the conjunct lightlessness.

Eve Considers the Possibility of Resurrection

I do not want to die,
to fall back, to see
the reverse of things, to decompose

to the source, that absolute
fierce bounty of Desire
from which I sprang.

I have never understood
how it can be the seasonal truths
are kept. I know

that spring is the literal, lemony shoot
of sourgrass in the gardens, then redbud, dogwood,
the air stained with scent and color

for yards around, then the blossoms of cherry,
apple, peach, in the pasture
the white, deadly buttons

of the amanita, on the hill
russula like small hemispheres of fire
in the pine duff. I fear such growing

beyond where it might be recalled
to have begun—now all this life has become
a considered dividing on itself,

flaming outward and back from the fat
sugary summer green, then folding back
onto the root, the horned sun

burgeoning inward
onto an utter density of lightlessness from which
the sky is desperate to rebound. I fear

what may be growing outward, ready
to distend and burst
the tender flesh of the planet, I fear

that at the end my mind will keep on,
will not finally sigh
onto the peaceful inmost seed of dream—all this

though I am made to think
that something will rise, all this
though I have felt

that in my body something
that does not appear within its outline, something
deep and materially hid

which does not advance upon the tomb,
itself suffers, thinks, works, and will be torn away
from the body, all this

seems somehow manifest
in the world's entire life, in each
massive rising of day and night, all this

crying out against the mortal fiction,
all this rising and crying out
in the glorious accents of the particular.

Eve Considers the Possibility of Pardon

In one dream I am made watchful.
In this dream the name we never clearly have heard
is spoken . . . which name, if we knew

and could speak it, would call back to us
those whom in time we will have come to love
and who will die; would bring them back to us

like us abandoned again
to his terrible consequence,
the silence between us

forever affirmed. And in whatever
might constitute the pardon
would come down in a fragile rain

the whole matter of all
we will ever love, the whole
fiery blade of space, ten billions of suns

suddenly blossoming small and cool
as snowdrops over the opening graves,
the world shimmering with the blue

delicate membrane of the fallen sky,
while above us the forsaken voice calls out
come back come back

as if calling the name
each of us had long forgotten
until that very instant not remembered

as proper to our hearts.

Eve Walking at Dawn

At the foot of the hill I came on a hollow
where a doe had been hamstrung and brought down
and fed upon, her violet guts

spilled out onto the pine duff,
and when I walked back to the house
and through the garden, the dawn light

fell all wrong,
my shadow leaped stumps and lay askew
on the lawn, lost itself

in a tumult of peonies, because
I had once more been made
to believe in the large, murderous heart

of the night, in the adversary
beasts of the night.

Adam in November

It was a long fall
after a dry summer, in which
the McIntosh bore for the first time.
Now, even in November,

I smell apples, there is some
virtue of breath at work,
something is moving, the names of things
branch up and there are dreams

in which nothing seems strange. I ought
to have trained myself better to waiting
and even better to silence,
but knowing that I cannot with anything

in the way of grace be properly silent,
cannot edify my image before others
or pretend to much of pride and balance, assume
credible lineaments of virtue, consult

with generosity, love or justice, I tend
to speak though lacking clarity,
not knowing the names, not having in need
the language, given to interminable

revision of the text. And this is where
the true anger locates itself,
that I have no ability or hope
that I may speak to the ordinary

with much in the way of truth or generosity.
And it must seem I make my rituals
to be the sole judge of the truth,
instead of what they are, mere sanctimonies

of procedure . . . and so
the names refuse themselves, and always it ends
in so unsatisfactory an obliquity as this.

The Neighborhood Prepares Itself for Melancholy

The garden's an untended
overgrowth of moonflowers, ragweed,
goldenrod, thickets

of witch grass—it's rusting,
it draws back and buries itself
in what's left of its fragrances.

Sometimes at dusk
I walk into the garden,
shuffle through leaves, pull

a weed or two, examine
the fragile stems of the clematis
for signs of rot or weakness,

pick a handful
of the last of the gloriosas
and cosmos, but in the last analysis

none of this matters, the air
is starting to squeeze
the breath from things,

the world's becoming
a mineral landscape,
it's getting away from me.

Eve Sleepless

Downstairs everything
is where it ought to be,
in place, a close serenity

of rugs and furniture,
though in the night
the storm door flung itself open

and three times banged hard shut.
Each time the hot night shimmered
and my head thudded

with possibilities. A long dreamlessness
stretched ahead. The cat cried,
water drizzled in the sink.

Outside the weathers gathered
snow to the south, up north
bloomed the brightest day

of the year, while here
is a steamy rain
and feverous wind from off

the lake, rain and wind,
and blood-surge in my ear.

Adam after the Ice Storm

The cedars lie uprooted
in the exuberant snow.
But I am unsentimental

about trees, I find it not difficult
to imagine this insult
means nothing to them. Soon enough

will arrive some formal
quickening, then what?
After all what can they know

about what they've become?
Or, for that matter, what
they've been—fine exhalations

swelling into a summer night, blind
windings of roots into the perennial beds,
dispassionate buddings

and unfurlings and spring
never more an observance
than winter? I fail to see

how I cannot be right in this, I think
it's as much for them to slow
into their green chill

as when something
warms in them, begins
to crowd up in them—though

if they are other
than I've made them out to be,
they might from the first

have shared with me
in this ardent confusion.

Eve at First Light

The gardens blur
in this cloud of early light,
the sun multiplies, clouds

like huge peonies explode
into luminous concentricities
of petals, bright rays

of leaves, everything
outlined in radiances
of its own shape.

And through this density
of light, faces
look back, so formed

and variously unformed
that what they might
have shaped themselves into

of love, anger, hatred,
seems unclear. Around me
the house of remembrance

goes still. I stand in my window
overlooking the garden,
it's midnight, and the moon

is creeping in and out
of clouds. I'm near
to dying here,

in this house
where the mirrors speak
only among themselves.

Adam and the Cardinal at the Window

The cardinal battering
his reflection in the window glass
falls dazed to the porch floor.

I tap the window,
but he just lies there, one wing
outspread. He's disheveled, hurt,

maybe dead, seen this way
less red than when
from the edge of my eye I catch him across the yard

flirting from twig to twig of the lilac
or in his long swoop
from fence to feeder. Suddenly

he twitches himself up
and into the air,
and the whole yard,

garden and all, for the instant
ignites, rises from its shadows—
everything notices, it's forever

in us, this hunger
for rush of color, this strong notion
of the blood.

Eve Overlooking the Lake

Outside is the dense quiet of an October rain
a cool rising of pines on the hill
and the lake bursting on its reefs
feathering there, wash of some passage,

night noise of water widening shoreward
meeting our house lights which spread
back into the lake in a thin wash
and diffusion of fire, and halfway

absorb themselves. What
will come of all this? I look back
through the thick drifts of time
and it seems always to have been gathering

and regathering to this: the one tree,
the one water, beneath it all a rising ice,
the world a fragrance of snow and apples—it seems
all about to be in the way of a naming, except

that what might be spoken outright
in such a place would be in the instant
unspoken. How everything goes still! How the roots
which do not speak grope at the ankle and coil

about the wrist, how the sky, clouds, grass
are preparing to lash themselves
into a million furies, this rain
of matter upon sense so deeply

flooding it that therefore
are the names not made or spoken,
not of any being at the poise of limit
and ready to spring back

onto the original impulse, nor
of any which may have hurled themselves
beyond limit, have gone flailing lightward
as the body, named or not,

for balance must. The lake
distantly whispers. I back away,
into the house, close doors and windows
on the night, on the world out there,

on all the cold blossomings of recognition.

Adam in the Graveyard

How cold it is,
that white sun smoking overhead,
powerful contours of snow

braiding, dividing
around the stones,
sheeting and rumpling as if

something were struggling
to break through.
In this place

memory's no salvation,
there's no cause to wake
or trouble us, in this place love

has dwindled to fatigue
like winter gardens
discarded to this

whirl of dirt,
to these heaviest
of days, to this most durable

of our inclinations.

The Orders

In this house
everything is where it ought to be.
The mirrors reflect
a perfect order. We cannot say

the same for what goes on
outside the doors and windows,
wilderness of up-
and-down, slantwise, crosswise,

to-and-from—earth-
eating roots gone
every which way purposeless,
rain, great jumbles of snow,

a cardinal dropping from the cedar
into the spreading of white alyssum—
all the processional put up against
the serenities of alignment

· for which we've worked: stillness
of knives, spoons, forks
in their drawers,
the calm reaches of carpets,

flat clasp of wallpapers,
and the forceless diagonals
of banisters, even
the unbreathing

stillness of the bouquets
of orange calendulas
in their shaggy symmetries arranged
to the precise centers

of tables. And here we are
standing here, looking on, trembling
with something more we knew,

for which we can invent no theory.

Adam Thinking Back

Here is the dry bed of the river,
and on both sides the tumble of rocks
of the old abutments. Now I walk across
dry shod. And here is the road we followed

as it formed, unrolling itself before us
to lead us . . . where? Neither of us knew
but hoped the other did. We never asked
but each secretly followed the other

as if each led. Oh, it was another world
that sprang up to each side, trees and flowers,
meadows, rivers. Out there in the farthest distance
loom the mountains that on that day

stirred on the horizon, shifted, upthrust,
then arranged themselves
like clouds, then gave themselves
shape. We never looked behind us. Behind us

the wind exploded like laughter. Ahead was nothing,
if silence is nothing. And to each side
the world kept pace, rooting, blooming,
twisting in the new wind. When we came

to where we are, it was as if
we had always known this place. And here
our hearts came to rest in the great mercy
(though how slowly

I reentered that knowledge!) that I could still
make names, name and in turn be named
as what I entitled changed before
my eyes, so on and on, so that

forever therefore these inhabitable silences
by the awkward act of my regard flash and blaze
into these so gorgeous variegations! We've lost
the kingdom, but borne away

this greatest of its treasures. So here
in the dry streambed I name
love and *bravery, honor, joy,*
I call out *orange* and *maple tree,*

and when I sleep dream *night,* and waking
whisper, *daylight, day, morning,* think ahead
to that moment when I'll turn to her,
to where she lies asleep,

under the blazing trees beside the dry stream,
the mountains clouding the horizon,
the new word at my lips.

Adam Signing

There in the cool birdlit realms,
my breath drawn out into the sky
which more than myself
had come to wish to breathe, I stood

at the verge of the cliff, far short
of where the impulse to go on
had much lessened; and I stared
down on the Garden's silences

not seeing her, who, in that instant
risen from the light of the yellow
seedling grasses, looked up at me
and could not catch my eye or call out,

somehow signal me, finding herself
to be still faint and tremulous of voice,
the soft flesh of her hands
still taking place; and saw me make

suddenly, without warning, into the milky air,
the difficult signs for *flight,* for
danger, as well as the simpler one
for *love,* not thinking to be seen

or answered, and therefore
gesturing so swift, so gorgeously complex
into the calyx of the sky
that she—looking into the rushed dance

of my hands—in that first
most urgent measure of these silences
could not well follow me.

Adam Awakening & Thinking of the Garden

1

This is the kind of night
on which Yuan Chen will cry out
to his dead wife, when one
dreams of another, are both
aware of it? the moonlight
blackening his bed, the ice roaring
in the great rivers. From such a night

I myself awoke, knowing none of this
had ever been, opened my eyes
onto the glorious mess of the contingent,
propped myself on one elbow,
and without astonishment gave names
to the bee-orchid, the giraffe.

2

If, when I awaken,
I am lying beside you,
I reach out to touch
the warm ridge of your spine.
It is how I try to tell you
there are imbalances, the end,
the ineloquent function,
begins to demonstrate itself.

It is finished, the silence between us,
the frightening stars, the Great Bear
riding the horizon, even
the darks of the farther lawn
are nothing: I wish to tell you

it is finished,
knowing fully the lie, knowing
if there is this silence,
it is measurable,
nor does the need lessen.
For now I touch you with my hands
that are hands. Later
the dust will not forget
what it has loved.

Eve in the Garden at First Light

I visit the garden in the early morning
before anything is fully awake, the white peonies
too heavy for their stems droop
with dew, and the scarlet poppies

have just begun to open. I trail
a heavy shadow. It's done. Everything is named
that I could name, that I saw
to name. I'm not a fool, much

was beyond me. Too much
was beyond me, much reserved, and now
it's becoming hard to breathe, hard
as at the very first when I required

instruction, those first
gasping breaths and I knew
how easily I might drown in that sweet air,
by virtue of that sweet air,

those first tentative
inspirations on which I hawked and choked—
and then by God it grew easier and evened
and sight cleared and there before me, there they lay

before me, the great meadows and mountains of the world,
the morning rising, and the waters
bursting and flooding up from the deepest centers
of the earth, gathering, currenting, rushing down

to pool in the low voids which filled and overflowed
as I stood still close to breathless watching, all the while
light exploding upward from beyond what I had not yet known
to name as light, whereby I saw, I saw, and saw . . .

Now from beyond the pines at the far edge of the garden
crows call, take fright, flare up in hard black shapes
against the sky, wheel, funnel back, then resettle
into the trees and the business of their voices.

Under the branches, in the green shadows of pines,
the golden duff of pine needles softly
thickens and the morning that enters the grove to drift
among the scaling boles seems the remains of light—something,

a further morning, a sea of light
with no opposing shore,
withdrawing.

Adam Recounting the Seasons

Spring evenings near the house
sitting together among
the fiddleheads, trillium, May-apple,
at the foot of the hill, the peepers

whistling and groaning
from the coppery bog,
we would repeat it all,
the whole story, from the beginning.

It was our passion
to have forgotten nothing.
The evenings would go shadowy
with owls and whippoorwills,

and of course we tried to sleep
but our thoughts multiplied
and rounded on themselves,
and we were abandoned to their treachery.

This was in the spring.
In the fall at times we felt otherwise.
In the fall we might well have been
of some more proper order, we called each other

by each other's names, there might well have been
something more between us, and between us
and the clamorous leaves
and the yellowing grass, and the emptying blossoms

of the gardens. In the flowerless winters,
watching the sad gestures
of the falling snow, we considered
what we had become, that we shared

the false brightness snow gave off at night.
In the strong light of winter days
there grew a blueness in the ice
that later would spend itself, give itself up,

to the clear, imperative skies
of earliest summer. In summer
breathing the blind light of the blind sun
we were most capable. By then

everything had rearranged itself.
We tended to blame no one,
not even ourselves, for the warm silences
in which we sometimes thought

we heard our names spoken aloud
from among the arrogant blossomings
of the woods—though not
as if we had been spoken to,

but as if the names were being tested
for the sake of the tongue,
their truth—and we'd fall silent,
we'd sit stock-still, listening. Such evenings

were sadnesses. Such evenings
we were never quite sure
what to do with ourselves, fearful
to sleep, the voice of our dreams

advancing on us
whispering our names, the woods around us,
fruitful with shadow, dark crimsons
and violets of apples and plums.

UNCOLLECTED
POEMS

————————————————

Poem on My Birthday

Sitting here with me
in this room at this very
moment, you look up

and ask *"Remember
the time . . . ?"* I tell you it takes
my attention, for

I've been presented
evidence of breath,
I mean

that after all I
had truly been there as I
am here, then as now

fixed on retrieval,
on all the days in the long
intervals of their

neon brightenings
and darkenings around—for
the moment—us.

Yesterday I Sat in a Room at the Met

*" . . . I think about Molly as a toddler putting her hand against the wood
stove at my parents' house, and her expression which it was my privilege to
witness exactly when she realized how much hurt had just entered her body . . ."*
—David Huddle

Yesterday I sat in a room at the Met
crumbling a stale biscotti
into a paper cup, Ugolino and his sons
monumentally starving to my right, while at left

the Burghers of Calais milled about
not yet having brought themselves
to the grand gesture, just beginning to wonder
if it's likely to be worth it—or so I chose

to have it seem, sitting there
in a pretty bad mood, stiff in my chair,
my leg gone numb, my back
slowly gnawing away at my hip, definitely

not ambulatory, definitely
in practice for something more difficult
to come. But now, today, I've arrived back
to Vermont to a heavy storm

and rain coming through the living room ceiling,
as well as to your letter, and I was glad for it,
for it was in all respects more plain
than that huge suffering

I'd viewed with such impatience . . . *impatience!*
At the Met! with hundreds, maybe thousands
of Crucifixions and Piétas overhead,
an Expulsion around every corner,

every Greek penis in Classical Statuary
hacked away, the eyes of Sveti Jovan
and his brethren in Slavic sanctity
gouged out by the Ottomans . . . and all I could think

was suffering's a bore the instant
it's decided to take up residence,
and invent its rights . . . thus
my bad mood then, and now, at 3:40 a.m.,

as, having set out pans, tarps and buckets
against the heavy leaking of my house,
groaning to go to sleep, I take time
to write to you instead.

Advice and a Rant

Set aside anger
and contempt, or be condemned
to live in a house loud
with groanings from

its attic, or the horrors
a night wind can enact
with loose doors, roof
tiles, windows—or awaken

to watch a crack begin
from nowhere,
race across
an unscarred ceiling,

run part way down
a wall—be spared
such discordance
when you choose to reside

in forgiveness . . . *but oh!*
the exuberance, the grand
domesticities of rage!

Cain to Himself

What could we
have wanted to know?
The world burgeoned

about us, we were never
more than silent, we sat
together but never spoke

throughout the cold nights
under the polished moons
that night upon night

rose, blossomed and thinned,
the darknesses declining
into chilly mornings, daylight

striking deep into us.
I can't remember . . . how
were we then, did we

think of them or they,
for that matter,
of us? But we were nothing

made to last, neither
of us, though one of us
far less than the other.

Family Portrait

It is eighty years ago
my mother sits
at one end of a bench
on which beside her in a row
arrange themselves

to look to where the lens
looks back Euphrasia
my father's mother Bill
her husband the tailor
and Marguerite fat

daughter of that household
which includes back row right
to left the one who will be
my father together with
his three brothers Vincent

Bill and Jimmy all intent
on keeping still. My mother
on the other hand stares
away smiling some
at a blank fence

and dull shrubberies
but this was
eighty years ago
the picture is in black
and white the sky

grayed out
the lawns bleached featureless
and they are all and every one of them
dead and I
am left to no more

than guess the times
of day the weathers
of that place and what likely
might have been
the colors of things.

The Dead

My grandmother was 85 when she fell and broke her hip
and lay another two years the rest of her life
in a hospital bed. They came to her
all of them: Leon, her husband, dead

ten years by then, Etta
and Ella, the sisters, Lloyd,
fast-talking huckster for whatever
needed selling (TV antennas, aluminum

siding, brooms and brushes)
but who failed in his last pitch
and ended up in a thicket of blackberry bushes
along the back road to Bawbeese Lake. And Eleanore,

my mother, dead young and early
out of some bitter justice—and there they were,
no question, she followed them
with her eyes, turned her head on the pillow

to this corner and that, to the chair
beside her bed, to the doorway, greeted
them when they arrived, and said goodbye,
held their hands, chatted happily

about this pattern of chintz, a recipe
for molasses cookies, the leak
no one could fix in the old rowboat,
made plans and appointments . . . she was happy

those last days when they came to her
or rather must have seemed
never to have left. Only we were not
happy, and our selfsame dead

hadn't the time of day to spare for us
who kept them far away, beyond
any least danger of retrieval, we
who wept at loss and memory,

and for her old dear body
helpless in the bed, but most of all from fear
they might after all take notice, turn
and speak to us, require regeneration

of that difficult love we gave them once
that from the very beginning
imperceptibly altered itself
into the final language, that passionate strange discourse

of fear and mourning.

My Mother's Heritage

I have this from you: a dislike
of severity: you gave me over
helpless to motley and gorgeous
scatterings of stuffs, our house
folds and drapings of old brocades
cut velvet throws, light

unfocused and flowering back
in warm petals of brightness from lustre cups
and pitchers, bowls and plates,
potpourri everywhere (pine cones,
rose petals, lavender and cinnamon)
French needlepoint and porcelains, mercury
and Bristol glass in all
the cupboards. And Chinese lacquer, brasses
everywhere: Belgian

bedwarmers, candlesticks
platters and sconces . . . I dazzled
and staggered through your rooms
then out, and far away, gathered
and took them with me. And here
I am today, primed for the joyous confusion

I hope for: dusty light, and every corner
forever beautifully unsquare.

Family Photographs

Who are these quaint people
who do not feel themselves perceived
and are therefore needless of glance
or touch or love, and stand

motionless, wholly contained,
behind them perhaps a fine shrubbery
or fading distances of field or lawn,
all of this under skies aglare with light

that blinded the cheap lens
in that instant of an instant which belonged
to us, to us, to us, to those among us
who opened the shutter to them

and they entered so that now they appear
to need neither to eat nor breathe air nor sleep
nor to be concerned for pain
or death or love or whatever changes

in whatever may be the world
and in utter innocence stare back
at the vacant eye of the lens
from the blind, absolute assurance of being.

Outelot Creek in Flood

This river which crested in April,
then receded, bled away and hardened
almost to the rubbles of its bed,

is up and about again, and the rainbows
are excited, they've begun to move, to feed,
they're lashing around and around

the pool, a few of the big ones
hurl themselves at the falls and are flung back—
there's heavy rain somewhere upstream,

and though it's dry enough here,
the sky an experienced blue, and plenty of sun,
still in only an hour the water's come

over the ledges, overpoured
the old chutes and spillways, begun coiling
and eddying into big pillows of foam

along the oxbow of the close bank.
From up on the wall, even at the darkest crest
of tonight, there'll be an excited braiding

of light from below—Oh, this
is a proper, indisputable river, a rumble
and bellow of water so thick with upstream soils

that it's become a glassy, glistening cliff,
at the falls, sheeting down, bearing down with it
more of the solid earth

than it can hold and still run clear.

Rising Stream

At first only a scattered drift of twigs and leaves
in the main thread of the current, then
little rafts of yellow foam, and something angular

and unnatural in the downstream sweep
and belly of the line. But I was intent
on the rise against the far bank

just under the overdroop
of a black willow, a big rainbow
rising to ants, and I narrowed

and worried myself to the angles,
light, shadows, fly and drag, until
it caught me that the lower branches of the tree

had begun to trail in the current
and that I was bracing myself
against the river, and that suddenly

the stream was wider, higher
on the banks, and I started
to get out of there, and made it,

and stood for awhile on the bank
watching that wild growth, watching the river
thicken with its old muds

and swirl and bubble and foam with vapor,
deeper than I was tall where I had stood—
and here I stand, telling you

about it—how that gradual power of river
built and bore down on me
and might have drowned me.

I tell you, over the years
out of obscure purpose I've made it to seem
it came up on me with purpose,

had me marked down
for the big eddy of driftwood
just ought of sight around the bend.

The cold smell of that water comes to me
over and over in a dream, sometimes,
especially, these days, when I'm otherwise

wide awake, the smell of that day
chill and sour, and oddly
flavored, like fresh earth.

Killing Ants

A black sky trailing dangerous talons of clouds
(exactly like the ones that used to get me,
out of the general terror, to crying and running
the eight blocks home from Cub Scout meetings)

bores in from the west. Tonight, a maker of low orders,
I wait on the University's cold steps
for someone or something, three stories down
from the dark-windowed Department of English,

and transform ants with the black rubber tip of my cane,
five of them so far and plenty more
where they came from, heading them off
from their nest, corralling them,

herding them left and right, back and forth,
and finally resolving them into little
brown smears on the pavement. Why?
Damned if I know. I have nothing

against ants, probably I do this
just for the hell of it. But push me,
and to shut you up I might say
that I relish confusion,

it animates purpose, and besides
all I ever wanted was safely to come home.

Poem for Your Birthday

for Jessica

Time is so ceremonious, stately
in greeting, full of congratulation,
exquisite in manner, insistent
on protocol (place settings

just so, right down
to fish knives, asparagus forks,
the crispest of linens, every candle
perfectly upright and burning

at precisely the same rate). And above all Time
is orderly, never mind
the coil and swirl of counter currents
in the sullen pantries, the mutterings

of servants . . . these he ignores. But now
here you are at last, once more as every year
arrived at this party, at this door,
outside in the soft night watching

the windows brighten and darken
with the shadows of the other guests
who've come on time, watching his windows
flicker with candles; and you hear

their polite murmurings, their small
swellings of applause, and then
silence as the cake enters
grand in the coronal aura of its light.

Though you are very late,
you halt at the door. You can choose, if you like,
to not go in at all. But after all
you suffer obligation, you've been invited,

found yourself unable to refuse. Still
you hesitate, though you know
he knows you're there, your hand
hesitant on the bell. Yet, forever tactful,

he waits for you to ring, he understands
the embarrassment you'd feel
should the door open on you
in your reluctance. You must

make up your mind. Fear fidgets
in your breast, but then goes stolid
and assured. Nevertheless you must
make up your mind. Everyone's

been waiting, the food is gone,
and the cake is ready
to be cut. You must decide, must do your best
to require of your heart

that just for the moment
it overwhelm doubt, and seem joyous. Try
to look forward to Time's greeting: knock
and be admitted. After all, what is the worst

that can happen? He will do no more
than open the door to you, and stand there,
slim, elegant, eyes hooded and welcoming,
forever courteous. He will not

reproach you. Rest assured
your comfort and enjoyment
will be everything to him.

Onlooker

At last, because it was the last day of the season,
my father rowed me out to his secret fishing hole
the one he'd been keeping for his own
the whole summer, putting me off

every time I asked to come along. But now,
with him a little more drunk than usual
that time of morning, nevertheless I was there,
and it looked good, and, apart

from everything I understood, I was ready
to believe . . . for after all that whole summer
there'd been prophecy, the promise of provision,
and now this plenitude!—the mysterious water

gloriously deep, glassy green
the bottom ridges of bony sand, pickerel weed
shivering in the small current, and a school of big perch
black-and-gold striped, ready to be taken. So I baited up,

tossed my hook in and the bobber cocked,
and I commenced to watch and wait . . . upon which he,
against every rule he'd ever made for me, stood
staggered, tipped and fell and vanished into a huge

convulsion of bubbles and green water,
and I looked down on him threshing at the bottom,
in clouds of mud and shredded weed, goggling
up at me, eyes wide, mouth wide, and just there

among the lily pads, his calm hat
rocking a little in the settling wash—then nothing,
because I looked away. Crows were calling from the birches
on the far shore, among the cattails redwings screamed,

and a scarlet dragonfly lighted on my rod tip. Then he
surfaced, grabbed at the gunwale, hauled himself
into the boat, lay gasping and dripping
and yes, yes, o yes, I'd had it in me

all along to leave him there, to let him drown,
row myself home, tie up the boat
tidy things away, reel in,
unjoint my rod, free

the leftover night crawlers to the wet soil
at the swamp's edge, go on up
to the cottage, have myself a snack, and wait—
just wait.

Until one day abruptly I'm caught and plunged
into the horrible dry vortices of dust and fire
Channel 3's become, for days struggle
near to drowning, the whole time gaping up into the cold

terror of my own onlooking—
finally somewhat come to, somewhat
catch at thin air again, find the room
as it has always been, daylight calm

along the floors . . . and no,
it hadn't ended there, for nothing truly
submits itself to being named—fifty years ago
I'd rowed him home, helped him

up the path, into the cottage
into a chair, then fled
to sit beside the lake and wait . . . for what? I suppose
a serenity of stars, sleep, a still

morning. But in the morning
he was there. What words unmake
our difference from the dead? It's been
a long pretense. I've always known.

1945

In Mr. Pitkin's Civics class—
beautifully removed from things,
given wholly over to the practice
of my being, and having just lost my way

in the desolate still landscapes
of recollection, *i.e.,* my lapse
in understanding just what it was
Joyce Summersgill the night before

so obscurely had desired of me,
so that she'd flung hay at my face
then sulked and burrowed
beyond reach—abruptly

I was resurrected by Pitkin shouting *Engels!*
You Are What Is Wrong With
American Education! And I have to tell you
I took that as OK, seeing it was

Distinction, however it had come: *Me!* template
for my generation, *Me!* mapped out
by Pitkin furious at the consoling
inattentiveness I'd brought to bear

against that first discernment
of the boundaries of shame,
regret and disillusion—*Me! Me!*
who had against all reason of hope

and hopeful expectation plotted
and plotted out of love and the deepest
reaches of desire, and got her,
Joyce Summersgill,

into the hay of the Freshman Hayride,
and then . . . love, it turned out,
would deride me, and ignorance
win the moment, and desire

run bleating somewhere deep into
the greater and more changeful dream
which was to be my life, and where
never did I wholly find him out.

Pump

I'd take hold of the cold iron handle
of the old Federal water pump, and pull down

and it would slam hard, echoing
all the way down to the dark

reservoir, need priming, and I'd give it
a dribble of rusty water from the #10

Tommy's Constant Quality Coffee can
into the slotted top, and give it another try,

and there'd come clank and rattle
of linkage, and then from deep, deep, utterly deep

the slow rumble of ascending water—at least that's
what I've chosen to recall. There was more,

I'm certain, but it was long ago and those days
I took that water-errand for a chore . . .

no pleasure to the long walk
through the sweet-scented pine grove up the hill,

the bucket clattering at my knee, then down again
the blind weight of the bucket hauling back.

But I'm getting deaf to that particular
landscape. What I remember best

is the dull resistance of water to my hand,
the long hiss of air from around

the leather gasket, a faint effluvium of iron,
and then that the water on my tongue

declared itself the cold taste of the planet.

Memento Mori

Came close to killing Philip Baxter with an axe,
whacked him on the head who stole my sparrow
I'd trapped in our garage behind a broom rake, and then erred
in showing to him . . . this when we were six,

I think, or seven. I don't know. What I recall
is the lovely rage, the ache of joy that shivered in me when
he bled all down himself, bawled and howled—though soon
myself I'd caught it in the head, hand-smacked

by my gentle mother, who, were she not dead,
would on this day—as on that one she'd despaired—
despair to think me agent of all that blood, me, John,
her peaceful boy! Well, thoroughly I hid myself

those days . . . though when that axe
flew unbidden to my hand, and I'd cracked
the flat down on his crooked head,
and the blood leaped so and I stood joyous—oh

but it came together in me then, surged and largely fed
and comforted and brothered me for sixty years
and more. Now mostly it's shadowed, next to dead.
Whole armies of thieves could bluster at my door,

rampage through my house, looting, mocking, and
no matter in what degree provoked
I'd just look on, not very interested, raising
neither voice nor hand . . . and yet, and yet

I'm sad at how it's staled, slips and staggers out of
breath, broken, ghostly, bent, this remnant joke
of outrage, and do lament its passing, having grown
sick of everything used up, failed, going

and gone dead in and around me, everywhere,
and when. *But God, by God, that once by God!*
I'd truly had it lively in me then.

Good Breakfast

For me, it's fake eggs
so that the blood runs clean
and unimpeded, some toast
with Lemon Curd

or, as my old man would have said,
to keep the pipes clean,
oatmeal or grits at least
once a week, but that's enough

of that. And coffee,
of course, two pots of it,
from 6 a.m. till I've begun to sweat
and go lightheaded and dizzy

. . . then I quit (though true enough
I don't skip lunch
or supper or a little something
before bed). And here I am

hungry to share this news
of my but slightly
blemished virtue, how
for seventy-four years

I've taken the trouble
to keep myself going from one
breakfast to the next without
a hitch (except an occasional

farty night, courtesy
of the fibres). It's my happy moment,
breathing, fingers wiggling, toes
alive, the stove singing out

from the corner, glasses
crowded brilliant on the sunlit counter
and the breakfast table
swaying joyous on its legs.

To a Student

you have a little time yet . . .
meantime *world* still

is only a word
even though it bears with it

in its wild swing
through the unspeakable calmness

of the void seas
and gardens, all the enormities

of light, everything
that daily comforts you,

tree, cloud, hand, lip . . .
somehow, rightly,

all this has been willed . . .
somehow in justice

it has been made
to be so . . .

as likewise that today
it is not your turn.

This Afternoon at Dusk

This afternoon at dusk
the sun bled slowly from the clouds
onto the sky which just as slowly
returned it. Thus it went
for an hour until
abruptly it was night,

though this did not mean
an end to shadows—
for they were everywhere
casting about, blind, uncertain
where to attach themselves . . . thus
a tree-shape sprang

from my feet to race across the lawn,
while the tree itself sheltered
and made darker the dark
neighborhood with something
like a hood of spread wings.

We slept. By morning
everything had cleared.
and the day spread pale
around its hollow star.

Angina

All week it's rained, this has been the first day
work might have been done,

and I've been tilling the back garden
turning under the leftovers

of last fall—some leaf
skeletons, sunflower stems, a rotted

dahlia I missed in October
and the frost heaved up—the soil

loose, and ready. But when it hits
I'm unready . . . nowhere is safe. I sit down

breathless, my head on my knees, the dirt
fragrant and breathing back. There's a fine view

to be had here if I open my eyes, but
I keep them closed. After awhile

everything calms itself, and I can stand
and walk away. And beginning right now

down will come the suns one after another.
What sends me this comfort? What

is this brightness, precisely not the light of glory,
by which I consider the garden, and it stares coldly back?

The Treachery of Expectation

I hadn't known it snowed
in Virginia, because Virginia was
South . . . so I was surprised
when what had been near Lynchburg the random
fluttering flake and by Roanoke
a sort of pretty flowering of the air
by Blacksburg had turned purely mean and at Ivanhoe
was by anybody's standard a wholehearted
blizzard. By then

you seemed to have forgotten
everything Vermont had taught you about winter driving
and decided to take that weather head-on,
and as if it had been all along our destination
ploughed over the cattle guard,
charged into the dead chill middle of that field

on top of the hill above Ivanhoe
with everything the old Chevy Celebrity
could muster and buried her
clean up to her windows in a drift so that the doors
were cramped tight shut and we had

to crawl over the seats and out the tailgate
into a white frenzy of ten below, then wade
thigh-deep a freezing half mile to your house—
the snow and wind by then so wild

we had to feel our way along a fence
and over the ridge, me with my cane,
bad back and half-dead leg,
until at last we made it to your house, and safe,
and your family took us in. And there we were

both grateful we hadn't died but pretty embarrassed
by it all . . . especially you next morning when to top it off
Arnold came to drag the car out and you put it
into Drive and he ripped the rear bumper clean away. That

was 30 years ago, in 1976, and here I am
writing this poem about the treachery of expectation
instead of wearing that snow like an eternal shirt.
This happened in what I'd thought to be
the warm birdsong-ridden South gorgeously abloom

with huge American flowers, gloriously throbbing
with melodramas of American light
over a green triumph of fields. In the truth
of that place I find myself stuck in a cliché
of terror the wind blowing through my skull
on a day so cold that to look ahead
is to see the world something like a drowned face
under the uncut ice of a river. This is one of the landscapes
one of the strong times
I need not even step outside
my house to enter.

That Day

Through the shimmering fluids of memory
the Norfolk & Southern locomotive shrieks
and my voices complain that outside
is an autumn light encrusting strange trees
with unfamiliar colors. The train shrieks

not fifty feet from where I'm dozing in a warm bath
in a borrowed house. Not fifty feet away
a boy I will never see walks on the tracks
wearing headphones, reading a letter
the locomotive hammering through

the closing transparencies of silence
between them—that is the first thing.
And then the phone calls out,
and your mother, in her first terror of disremembering,
cries that we are expected, we are late,

we have not arrived as we promised we would . . .
and at the house the table is laid, bread curling
on the plates, the crystal dulled
by a fine rain of shadow, and voices whisper
window to window. Outside

roots work loose from their soils,
and we hear the hard breathing
of shrubs and flowers. Later that day
as we leave her bedside, your mother calls out
that she loves me. That day

the land behind the house had sloped
away to the town, the tracks beyond, and yellow fields.
The oaks and gums were made luminous by the sun
of a late afternoon that flowed
over my face and arms like a wind

on the cooling verges of sleep.
We've abandoned ourselves
to the cold waters of memory.
May the spaces we've occupied
beneath these unmoving skies
bear witness.

INDEX OF TITLES

JOHN ENGELS

is the author of eleven volumes of poetry and is professor of English at St. Michael's College in Vermont. A graduate of the Iowa Writer's Workshop, he has garnered numerous awards for his poetry, including National Endowment for the Arts, Guggenheim, Fulbright, and Rockefeller fellowships. His work has appeared in *The Nation, The New Yorker, Harper's,* and many other publications.